Cultural Change and Urban Identity in Southeast Asia

CULTURAL CHANGE AND URBAN IDENTITY IN SOUTHEAST ASIA

B Kumar

MD PUBLICATIONS PVT LTD
NEW DELHI
www.mdppl.com

Published by :

MD Publications Pvt Ltd
"MD House", 11, Darya Ganj,
New Delhi - 110 002
Phone : +91-11- 45355555
E-mail : contact@mdppl.com
Website: www.mdppl.com

ISBN : 978-81-7533-346-8

Published and Printed by Mr. Pranav Gupta on behalf of **MD Publications Pvt Ltd** at Repro India Limited.

PREFACE

Wedged between South and East Asia, the Indian and the Chinese worlds, the Pacific and the Indian oceans, projecting Asia far into the Tropics, spanning the Equator and pointing towards Australasia, Southeast Asia is largely influenced by its nodal position while, at the same time, it constitutes a world of its own. Southeast Asia consists of eleven countries that reach from eastern India to China, and is generally divided into "mainland" and "island" zones. The mainland (Burma, Thailand, Laos, Cambodia, and Vietnam) is actually an extension of the Asian continent. Muslims can be found in all mainland countries, but the most significant populations are in southern Thailand and western Burma (Arakan). The Cham people of central Vietnam and Cambodia are also Muslim.

A distinctive feature of Southeast Asia is its cultural diversity. Of the six thousand languages spoken in the world today, an estimated thousand are found in Southeast Asia. Archeological evidence dates human habitation of Southeast Asia to around a million years ago, but migration into the region also has a long history. In early times tribal groups from southern China moved into the interior areas of the mainland via the long river systems. Linguistically, the mainland is divided into three important families, the Austro-Asiatic (like Cambodian and Vietnamese), Tai (like Thai and Lao), and the Tibeto-Burmese (including highland languages as well as Burmese). Languages belonging to these families can also be found in northeastern India and southwestern China.

Cultural changes began to affect Southeast Asia around

two thousand years ago with influences coming from two directions. Chinese expansion south of the Yangtze River eventually led to the colonization of Vietnam. Chinese control was permanently ended in 1427, but Confucian philosophy had a lasting influence when Vietnam became independent. Buddhism and Taoism also reached Vietnam via China. In the rest of mainland Southeast Asia, and in the western areas of the Malay-Indonesian archipelago, expanding trade across the Bay of Bengal meant Indian influences were more pronounced. These influences were most obvious when large sedentary populations were engaged in growing irrigated rice, like northern Vietnam, Cambodia, Thailand, Burma, Java, and Bali. Rulers and courts in these areas who adopted Hinduism or forms of Buddhism promoted a culture which combined imported ideas with aspects of local society.

Urbanization is a significant trend in cities of the developing world. About 120 million people across the globe have moved to the cities, mainly for economic gains, and a similar pattern has been observed in the industrializing countries of Southeast Asia. Greater urbanization demands high investments in urban infrastructure including housing, transportation, and water and sewerage services. National authorities are also faced with challenges in environmental protection to ensure the provision of good air and water quality, as well as overall quality of life.

I am very grateful to Mr. Pranav Gupta, Director of MD Publications Pvt Ltd, New Delhi, for his kind cooperation and support for this book.

B Kumar

Contents

1

Historical Origins of Southeast Asia

Though this large region encompasses many different situations, much communal management of forest and forest land historically developed around swidden agriculture in order to control use of land or soil, and around rights to use of natural vegetation that was subject to group control. Village or clan households typically had the right to cultivate specific plots and to claim exclusive collection rights from useful tree species. People from outside had to ask permission and sometimes pay rent or a fee for collection rights. In many cases, the institutional coordination of land use practices of swidden cultivators was relatively weak, based on public discussion and without strong community sanctions.

The strongest group action often was directed at preventing outsiders from monopolizi ng specific resources. Many of these traditional management systems have weakened and broken down as colonial regimes and national governments have progressively introduced legislation to restrict local land rights to lands actually being cultivated, and as the introduction of new land use practices involving commercial cropping lessened local interest in forest products. Communal ownership and management of swidden areas have consequently diminished. In many areas, land is now typically owned by individual households and worked by individual household labour forces or reciprocal, but not communal, work groups. During recent decades there has been a huge expansion in the areas designated as state forests in some of the main countries of the region.

Reasons for this include government interests in tapping valuable forest resources, increasing pressures to exercise physical control over upland areas for strategic reasons or because of their importance as a land bank for surplus lowland populations, and growing concerns about preventing downstream damage resulting from overuse of upland areas. As the extent of state control has increased, its focus has tended to shift from control over population, labour or particular species to territorial control. Though agrarian legislation in support of development of rural populations usually exists, it often has been overridden by forestry legislation that severely restricts local people's activities in areas designated as forests. Although the combination of government restrictions, logging activities and other commercial enterprises, and impacts of demographic and local economic changes have generally combined to discourage and undermine local forest management, some common property systems have survived, and in some situations new ones have emerged.

This is particularly the case in hill areas, which have only come under pressure relatively recently, but common property systems also can be found in the remaining forested areas in the more intensively settled lowlands. For example, in north and northeast Thailand, the most resilient forms of common property usually have been traditional sacred forest protection systems. In addition, some communities protect watershed forests and areas of communal woodland set aside for fuel and other needs. Many of these local forest regimes began to emerge about 30 years ago in response to growing shortages of water and forest products. Increasing local protection and management also reflect a more intensive utilization of their resources by communities, in response to growing pressures from the state, loggers and other outsiders. Increasingly, communities are concerned with giving more formal institutional form to their forest protection initiatives, e.g. by having them endorsed by village councils, recording them as written rules and organizing patrols to monitor adherence to the rules.

At present, such communal forest areas have no legal basis because forest land is considered state property, though it is widely exploited by commercial users and settlers on a *de facto* open access basis. Legislation is being drafted, but the government's priority is to regularize the position of squatters on alienable forest land by granting them individual rights, though this focus could undermine collective management. A draft Community Forest Act will give more tenurial security, but is designed more to support new programmes than to empower existing indigenous group systems, and would not cover common property systems in the conservation areas where many of the indigenous regimes are located. Sometimes forest departments are willing and able to mitigate the impacts of legislation vesting control of forest areas in the central state by working out arrangements with local people that enable the latter to maintain at least a measure of control over management of a local forest resource. Examples of this have been reported in northern Thailand and parts of Indonesia.

Collective control can also be found where it proves to be consistent with modernization of local livelihood systems. In parts of West Kalimantan, Indonesia, for instance, people have adapted their resource use and management practices in response to reduction in the land area to which they have access and to greater exposure to markets as the rural road infrastructure has been extended. A feature of this adaptation has been the incorporation and intensification of cultivation within the forest of tree crops with economic value, such as rubber, rattan and durian. This has been achieved within local control systems that introduce greater individual control over the production and marketing of products, alongside elements of the earlier collective systems for managing the resource. Southeast Asia or Southeastern Asia is a sub region of Asia, consisting of the countries that are geographically south of China, east of India and north of Australia.

The region lies on the intersection of geological plates, with heavy seismic and volcanic activity. Southeast Asia consists of two geographic regions: the Asian mainland, and island arcs and archipelagoes to the east and southeast. The mainland section consists of Burma (Myanmar), Cambodia, Laos, Thailand, Vietnam and Malaysia (or to be more precise, Peninsular Malaysia). The maritime section consists of Brunei, East Timor, Indonesia, Malaysia, the Philippines, and Singapore. Some definitions include Taiwan at the north. Austronesian peoples predominate in this region. The major religions are Buddhism and Islam, followed by Christianity. However, a wide variety of religions are found throughout the region, including many Hindu and animist-influenced practices.

DIVISIONS

POLITICAL

Definitions of 'Southeast Asia' vary, but most definitions include the area represented by the countries:

- Brunei
- Burma (Myanmar)
- Cambodia
- Indonesia
- Laos
- Malaysia
- Philippines
- Singapore
- Thailand
- Vietnam
- East Timor

All of the above excluding East Timor are members of the Association of Southeast Asian Nations. The area, together with part of South Asia, was widely known as the East Indies or simply the Indies until the twentieth century. Christmas Island and the Cocos (Keeling) Islands are considered part of Southeast Asia though they are governed by Australia. Taiwan is sometimes considered part of Southeast Asia as well as East Asia but it is not a member of ASEAN. Sovereignty issues exist over some islands in the South China Sea. Papua is politically part of Southeast Asia through Indonesia, although geographically it is often considered as part of Oceania. Southeast Asia is geographically divided into two sub regions, namely Mainland Southeast Asia (or Indochina) and the Maritime Southeast Asia (or the Malay Archipelago) (Indonesian language: *Nusantara).*

Mainland Southeast Asia includes:

- Burma (Myanmar)
- Cambodia
- Laos
- Thailand
- Vietnam

Maritime Southeast Asia includes:

- Brunei
- East Timor
- Indonesia
- Malaysia
- Philippines
- Singapore

The eastern parts of Indonesia and East Timor (east of Wallace Line) are considered to be geographically parts of Oceania. The Andaman and Nicobar Islands of India are geographically considered part of Southeast Asia. Bangladesh and the Seven Sisters in India is culturally Southeast Asia and sometimes considered both South Asian and Southeast Asian. Hainan Island and several other southern Chinese regions such as Yunnan, Guizhou, Fujian, Guangxi and Guangdong, as well as Hong Kong and Macau are considered both East Asian and Southeast Asian. Taiwan, which sits on the Tropic of Cancer and borders the South China Sea, is likewise often included in definitions of Southeast Asia as well as East Asia. The rest of New Guinea is sometimes included so are the Federated States of Micronesia, Palau, Guam, and the Northern Mariana Islands, which were all part of the Spanish East Indies.

Solheim and others have shown evidence for a *Nusantao* (*Nusantara*) maritime trading network ranging from Vietnam to the rest of the archipelago as early as 5000 BCE to 1 CE. The peoples of Southeast Asia, especially those of Austronesian descent, have been seafarers for thousands of years, some reaching the island of Madagascar. Their vessels, such as the vinta, were ocean-worthy. Magellan's voyage records how much more maneuverable their vessels were, as compared to the European ships. Passage through the Indian Ocean aided the colonization of Madagascar by the Austronesian people, as well as commerce between West Asia and Southeast Asia. Gold from Sumatra is thought to have reached as far west as Rome.

Originally most people were animist. This was later replaced by Brahmanic Hinduism. Theravada Buddhism soon followed in 525. In 1400s, Islamic influences began to enter. This forced the last Hindu court in Indonesia to retreat to Bali. In Mainland Southeast Asia, Myanmar, Cambodia and Thailand retained the Theravada form of Buddhism, brought to them from Sri Lanka. This type of Buddhism was fused with the Hindu-influenced Khmer culture. The history of Southeast Asia has been characterized as interaction between regional players and foreign powers. Though 59 countries currently make up the region, the history of each country is intertwined with all the others. For instance, the Malay empires of Srivijaya and Malacca covered modern day Indonesia, Malaysia, and Singapore while the Burmese, Thai, and Khmer peoples governed much of Indochina.

At the same time, opportunities and threats from the east and the west shaped the direction of Southeast Asia. The history of the countries within the region only started to develop independently of each other after European colonialization was at full steam between the 17th and the 20th century. Evidences suggest that the earliest non-aboriginal Southeast Asians came from southern China and were Austronesian speakers. Contemporary research by anthropologists, linguists, and archaeologists (Bellwood) suggests that the inhabitants of the Malay Archipelago migrated from southern China to islands of the Philippines around 2,500 BCE and later spread to modern day Malaysia and Indonesia. The earliest population of Southeast Asia was animist before Hinduism and Buddhism were exported from the Indian subcontinent. Islam arrived mostly through Indian Muslims and later dominated much of the archipelago around the 13th century while Christianity came along when European colonization started around the 16th century.

During the classical age, the existence of Southeast Asia had been known to the Greeks. The Greek astronomer Ptolemy in his *Geographia* named the Malay Peninsula as *Aurea Chersonesus* (Golden Peninsula) while Java was called *Labadius*. Labadius was probably a corruption of Sanskrit *Yavadvipa* which refers to the same island. An ancient Hindu text may have earlier referred to Southeast Asia as *Suvarnabhumi* which means land of gold. The region has been an important source of spices and this was one of the reasons European explorers were attracted to the Far East. During the colonization period, states of the region became important assets to the British, the Dutch and the French. British Malaya for instance was the world's largest producer of tin and rubber while the Dutch East Indies was the source of Dutch's wealth.

During the 1990s, Southeast Asia emerged as the fastest growing economy in the world. Its successes have caused some to call Southeast Asia an economic miracle and Singapore one of the "Four Asian Tigers". Though the Asian Financial Crisis struck in the late 1990s and left many crippled, the economy of the region has started to pick up again at a more sustainable rate as demand from the United States and People's Republic of China soar. Archaeologists have found stone tools in Malaysia which have been dated to be 1.83 million years old. Before the latest ice period, much of the archipelago was not under water. Sometime around the Pleistocene period, the Sunda Shelf was flooded as thawing occurred and thus revealing current geographical features. The area's first known human-like inhabitant some 500,000 years ago was "Java Man" (first classified as Pithecanthropus erectus, then subsequently named a part of the species Homo erectus).

Recently discovered was a species of human, dubbed "Flores Man" (Homo floresiensis), a miniature hominid that grew only three feet tall. Flores Man seems to have shared some islands with Java man until only 10,000 years ago, when they became extinct. The oldest human settlement in Malaysia has been discovered in Niah Caves. The human remains found there have been dated back to 40,000 BC. Another remains dated back to 9,000 BC dubbed the "Perak Man" and tools as old as 75,000 years have been discovered in Lenggong, Malaysia. Agriculture was a natural development based on necessity. Before agriculture, hunting and gathering sufficed to provide food. The chicken and pig were domesticated here, millennia ago. So much food was available that people could gain status by giving food away in feasts and festivals, where all could eat their fill.

These *big men* (Malay: *orang kaya*) would work for years, accumulating the food (wealth) needed for the festivals provided by the *orang kaya*. These individual acts of generosity or kindness are remembered by the people in their oral histories, which serve to provide *credit* in more dire times. These customs ranged throughout Southeast Asia, stretching, for example, to the island of New Guinea. The agricultural technology was exploited after population pressures increased to the point that systematic intensive farming was required for mere survival, say of yams (in Papua) or rice (in Indonesia). Rice paddies are well-suited for the monsoons of Southeast Asia. The rice paddies of Southeast Asia have existed for millennia, with evidence for their existence coeval with the rise of agriculture in other parts of the globe. Yam cultivation in Papua, for example, consists of placing the tubers in prepared ground, heaping vegetation on them, waiting for them to propagate, and harvesting them.

This work sequence is still performed by the women in the traditional societies of Southeast Asia; the men might perform the heavier duties of preparing the ground or of fencing the area to prevent predation by pigs. From Burma around 1,500 BC, the Mon and ancestors of the Khmer people started to move in while the Tai people later came from southern China to reside in the mainland in the first millennium AD. It was around 2,500 BC that the Austronesian people started to populate the archipelago and introduced primitive ironworks technology that they had mastered to the region. By around the 5th century BC, people of the Dong Son culture, who lived in what is now Vietnam, had mastered basic metal working. Their works are the earliest known metal object to be found by archeologists in Southeast Asia.

Southeast Asia has been inhabited since prehistoric times. The communities in the region evolved to form complex cultures with varying degrees of influence from India and China. The ancient kingdoms can be grouped into two distinct categories. The first is agrarian kingdoms. Agrarian kingdoms had agriculture as the main economic activity. Most agrarian states were located in mainland Southeast Asia. Examples are the Ayutthaya Kingdom, based on the Chao Phraya River delta and the Khmer Empire on the Tonle Sap. The second type is maritime states. Maritime states were dependent on sea trade. Malacca and Srivijaya were maritime states. A succession of trading systems dominated the trade between China and India. First, goods were shipped through Funan to the Isthmus of Kra, portaged across the narrow, and then transshipped for India and points west.

Around the sixth century, CE merchants began sailing to Srivijaya where goods were transshipped directly. The limits of technology and contrary winds during parts of the year made it difficult for the ships of the time to proceed directly from the Indian Ocean to the South China Sea. The third system involved direct trade between the Indian and Chinese coasts. Very little is known about Southeast Asian religious beliefs and practices before the advent of Indian merchants and religious influences from the second century BCE onwards. Prior to the 13th century, Buddhism and Hinduism were the main religions in Southeast Asia. The first dominant power to arise in the archipelago was Srivijaya in Sumatra. From the fifth century CE, the capital, Palembang, became a major seaport and functioned as an entrepot on the Spice Route between India and China. Srivijaya was also a notable center of Vajrayana Buddhist learning and influence.

Srivijaya's wealth and influence faded when changes in nautical technology in the tenth century CE enabled Chinese and Indian merchants to ship cargo directly between their countries and also enabled the Chola state in southern India to carry out a series of destructive attacks on Srivijaya's possessions, ending Palembang's entrepot function. In the Philippines, the Laguna Copperplate Inscription dating from 900 CE relates a granted debt from a *Maharlika* caste nobleman named *Namwaran* who lived in the Manila area. This document shows strong Srivijayan influence, and mentions a leader of Medan, Sumatra. Java was dominated by a kaleidoscope of competing agrarian kingdoms including the Sailendras, Mataram, Singosari, and finally Majapahit.

Europeans first came to Southeast Asia in the sixteenth century. It was the lure of trade that brought Europeans to Southeast Asia while missionaries also tagged along the ships as they hoped to spread Christianity into the region. Portugal was the first European power to establish a bridgehead into the lucrative Southeast Asia trade route with the conquest of the Sultanate of Malacca in 1511. The Netherlands and Spain followed and soon superseded Portugal as the main European powers in the region. The Dutch took over Malacca from the Portuguese in 1641 while Spain began to colonize the Philippines (named after Phillip II of Spain) from 1560s. Acting through the Dutch East India Company, the Dutch established the city of Batavia (now Jakarta) as a base for trading and expansion into the other parts of Java and the surrounding territory.

Britain, in the form of the British East India Company, came relatively late onto the scene. Starting with Penang, the British began to expand their Southeast Asian empire. They also temporarily possessed Dutch territories during the Napoleonic Wars. In 1819 Stamford Raffles established Singapore as a key trading post for Britain in their rivalry with the Dutch. However, their rivalry cooled in 1824 when an Anglo-Dutch treaty demarcated their respective interests in Southeast Asia. From the 1850s onwards, the pace of colonization shifted to a significantly higher gear. This phenomenon, denoted New Imperialism, saw the conquest of nearly all Southeast Asian territories by the colonial powers. The Dutch East India Company and British East India Company were dissolved by their respective governments, who took over the direct administration of the colonies.

Only Thailand was spared the experience of foreign rule, although, Thailand itself was also greatly affected by the power politics of the Western powers. By 1913, the British occupied Burma, Malaya and the Borneo territories, the French controlled Indochina, the Dutch ruled the Netherlands East Indies while Portugal managed to hold on to Portuguese Timor. In the Philippines, Filipino revolutionaries declared independence from Spain in 1898 but was handed over to the United States despite protests as a result of the Spanish-American War. Colonial rule had a profound effect on Southeast Asia. While the colonial powers profited much from the region's vast resources and large market, colonial rule did develop the region to a varying extent. Commercial agriculture, mining and an export based economy developed rapidly during this period. Increased labor demand resulted in mass immigration, especially from British India and China, which brought about massive demographic change.

The institutions for a modern nation state like a state bureaucracy, courts of law, and print media and to a smaller extent, modern education, sowed the seeds of the fledgling nationalist movements in the colonial territories. In the inter-war years, these nationalist movements grew and often clashed with the colonial authorities when they demanded self-determination. During World War II, the region was invaded by the Japanese Imperial Army and included in the Greater East Asia Co-Prosperity Sphere. Thailand was the only country to maintain a nominal independence by making a political and military alliance with the Empire of Japan. With the rejuvenated nationalist movements in wait, the Europeans returned to a very different Southeast Asia after World War II. Indonesia declared independence in 17 August 1945 and subsequently fought a bitter war against the returning Dutch; the Philippines were granted independence in 1946 after a bloody war with the United States; Burma secured their independence from Britain in 1948, and the French were driven from Indochina in 1954 after a bitterly fought war against the Vietnamese nationalists.

The newly-established United Nations provided a forum both for nationalist demands and for the newly demanded independent nations. During the Cold War, countering the threat of communism was a major theme in the decolonization process. After suppressing the communist insurrection during the Malayan Emergency from 1948 to 1960, Britain granted independence to Malaya and later, Singapore, Sabah and Sarawak in 1957 and 1963 respectively within the framework of the Federation of Malaysia. In one of the most bloody single incidents of violence in Cold War Southeast Asia, General Suharto seized power in Indonesia in 1965 and initiated a massacre of approximately 500,000 alleged members of the Indonesian Communist Party (PKI). Recent evidence from the US National Security Archive published by George Washington University suggests this massacre was carried out with the support of the United States embassy in Jakarta, which supplied lists of names of suspected PKI members to Suharto.

The United States intervention against communist forces in Indochina during a conflict commonly referred to in the United States as the Vietnam War meant that Vietnam, Laos and Cambodia had to go through a prolonged and protracted war in their route to independence. In 1975, Portuguese rule ended in East Timor. However, independence was short-lived as Indonesia annexed the territory soon after. Finally, Britain ended its protectorate of the Sultanate of Brunei in 1984, marking the end of European rule in Southeast Asia. Modern Southeast Asia has been characterized by high economic growth by most countries and closer regional integration. Indonesia, Malaysia, the Philippines, Singapore and Thailand have traditionally experienced high growth and are commonly recognized as the more developed countries of the region.

As of late, Vietnam too had been experiencing an economic boom. However, Myanmar, Cambodia, Laos and the newly independent East Timor are still lagging economically. On

August 8, 1967, Association of Southeast Asian Nations (ASEAN) was founded by Thailand, Indonesia, Malaysia, Singapore, and the Philippines. Since Cambodian admission into the union in 1999, East Timor is the only Southeast Asian country that is not part of ASEAN, although plans are under way for eventual membership. The association aims to enhance cooperation among Southeast Asian community. ASEAN Free Trade Area has been established to encourage greater trade among ASEAN members. ASEAN has also been a front runner in greater integration of Asia-Pacific region through East Asia Summits.

INDIANIZED KINGDOMS

Very little is known about Southeast Asian religious beliefs and practices before the advent of Indian merchants and religious influences from the second century BCE onwards. Prior to the 13th century, Buddhism and Hinduism were the main religions in Southeast Asia. The Jawa Dwipa Hindu kingdom in Java and Sumatra emerged around 200 BCE. The history of the Malay-speaking world begins with the advent of Indian influence, which dates back to at least the 3rd century BC. Indian traders came to the archipelago both for its abundant forest and maritime products and to trade with merchants from China, who also discovered the Malay world at an early date. Both Hinduism and Buddhism were well established in the Malay Peninsula by the beginning of the 1st century CE, and from there spread across the archipelago.

Cambodia was first influenced by Hinduism during the beginning of the Funan kingdom. Hinduism was one of the Khmer Empire's official religions. Cambodia is the home to one of the only two temples dedicated to Brahma in the world. Angkor Wat is also a famous Hindu temple of Cambodia. The Majapahit Empire was an Indianized kingdom based in eastern Java from 1293 to around 1500. Its greatest ruler was Hayam Wuruk, whose reign from 1350 to 1389 marked the empire's peak when it dominated other kingdoms in the southern Malay Peninsula, Borneo, Sumatra, Bali and the Philippines. The rest of the Philippines also provided tributes to the empire. The Cholas excelled in maritime activity in both military and the mercantile fields. Their raids of Kedah and the Srivijaya, and their continued commercial contacts with the Chinese Empire, enabled them to influence the local cultures. Many of the surviving examples of the Hindu cultural influence found today throughout the Southeast Asia are the result of the Chola expeditions.

TRADE AND COLONIZATION

CHINA

Chinese merchants have traded with the region for a long time as evidence of Magellan's voyage records that Brunei possessed more cannon than the European ships so it appears that the Chinese fortified them. Malaysian legend has it that a Chinese Ming emperor sent a princess, Han Li Po to Malacca, with a retinue of 500, to marry Sultan Mansur Shah after the emperor was impressed by the wisdom of the sultan. Han Li Po's well (constructed 1459) is now a tourist attraction there, as is Bukit Cina, where her retinue settled. The strategic value of the Strait of Malacca which was controlled by Sultanate of Malacca in the 15th and early 16th Century did not go unnoticed by Portuguese writer Duarte Barbosa, who in 1500 wrote "He who is lord of Malacca has his hand on the throat of Venice".

EUROPE

Western influence started to enter in the 1500s, with the arrival of the Portuguese and Spanish in Moluccas and the Philippines. Later the Dutch established the Dutch East Indies; the French Indochina; and the British Strait Settlements. All of Southeast Asian countries were colonized except for Thailand. European explorers were reaching Southeast Asia from the west and from the east. Regular trade between the ships sailing east from the Indian Ocean and south from mainland Asia provided goods in return for natural products, such as honey and hornbill beaks from the islands of the archipelago. Europeans brought Christianity allowing Christian missionaries to become widespread. Siam also allowed Western science and technology to enter their country.

JAPAN

During World War II, the Imperial Japan invaded most of the former occidental colonies. The Shôwa occupation regime committed violent actions against indigenous civilians such as the Manila Massacre and the implementation of a system of forced labour, such as the one involving 4 to 10 millions romusha in Indonesia.

PRESENT

Most countries in the region enjoy national autonomy. Democratic forms of government and the recognition of human rights are taking root. ASEAN provides a framework for the integration of commerce. Conflicting territorial and maritime claims continue to exist, including the conflicting claims by Taiwan and China over the Spratly Islands.

GEOGRAPHY

Geologically, the Indonesian archipelago is one of the most active vulcanological regions in the world. Geological uplifts in the region have also produced some impressive mountains, culminating in Mount Kinabalu in Sabah, Malaysia on the island of Borneo with a height of 4,101 metres (13,455 ft) and also Puncak Jaya in Papua, Indonesia at 4,884 meters (16,024 ft), on the island of New Guinea.

BOUNDARIES

The Australasian continental plate defines a region adjacent to Southeast Asia, which is also politically separated from the countries of Southeast Asia. But a cultural touch point lies between Papua New Guinea and the Indonesian region of Papua and West Papua, which shares the island of New Guinea with Papua New Guinea.

CLIMATE

The climate in Southeast Asia is mainly tropical-hot and humid all year round. There is a lot of rainfall. Southeast Asia has a wet and dry season caused by seasonal shift in winds or monsoon. The tropical rain belt causes additional rainfall during the monsoon season. The rain forest is the second largest on earth (with the Amazon being the largest). Exception to this type of climate and vegetation is the mountain areas in the northern region, where high altitudes lead to milder temperatures and drier landscape. Other parts fall out of this climate because they are desert like.

ENVIRONMENT

All of Southeast Asia falls within the warm, humid tropics, and its climate generally can be characterized as monsoonal. The animals of Southeast Asia are diverse; on the islands of Borneo and Sumatra, the Orangutan (man of the forest), the Asian Elephant, the Malayan tapir, the Sumatran Rhinoceros and the Bornean Clouded Leopard can be also found. Six subspecies of the Binturong or *bearcat* exist in the region, though the one endemic to the island of Palawan is now classed as vulnerable.

The Wild Asian Water Buffalo, and on various islands related dwarf species of Bubalus such as Anoa were once widespread in Southeast Asia, nowadays the Domestic Asian Water buffalo is common across the region, but its remaining relatives are rare and endangered. The mouse deer, a small tusked deer as large as a toy dog or cat, can be found on Sumatra, Borneo and Palawan Islands. The gaur, a gigantic wild ox larger than even wild Water buffalo, is found mainly in Indochina.

Birds such as the peafowl and drongo live in this sub region as far east as Indonesia. The babirusa, a four-tusked pig, can be found in Indonesia as well. The hornbill was prized for its beak and used in trade with China. The horn of the rhinoceros, not part of its skull, was prized in China as well. The Indonesian Archipelago is split by the Wallace Line. This line runs along what is now known to be a tectonic plate boundary, and separates Asian (Western) species from Australasian (Eastern) species. The islands between Java/ Borneo and Papua form a mixed zone, where both types occur, known as Wallacea.

As the pace of development accelerates and populations continue to expand in Southeast Asia, concern has increased regarding the impact of human activity on the region's environment. A significant portion of Southeast Asia, however, has not changed greatly and remains an unaltered home to wildlife. The nations of the region, with only few exceptions, have become aware of the need to maintain forest cover not only to prevent soil erosion but to preserve the diversity of flora and fauna. Indonesia, for example, has created an extensive system of national parks and preserves for this purpose. Even so, such species as the Javan rhinoceros face extinction, with only a handful of the animals remaining in western Java.

The shallow waters of the Southeast Asian coral reefs have the highest levels of biodiversity for the world's marine ecosystems, where coral, fish and mollusks abound. The whale shark can be found in the South China Sea. The trees and other plants of the region are tropical; in some countries where the mountains are tall enough, temperate-climate vegetation can be found. These rainforest areas are currently being logged-over, especially in Borneo. While Southeast Asia is rich in flora and fauna, Southeast Asia is facing severe deforestation which causes habitat loss for various endangered species such as orangutan and the Sumatran tiger. Predictions have been made that more than 40% of the animal and plant species in Southeast Asia could be wiped out in the 21st century. At the same time, haze has been a regular occurrence. The worst regional haze occurred in 1998 in which multiple countries were covered with thick haze. In reaction, several countries in Southeast Asia signed the ASEAN Agreement on Transboundary Haze Pollution in order to combat haze pollution.

ECONOMY

Even prior to the penetration of European interests, Southeast Asia was a critical part of the world trading system. The Ryukyu Kingdom often participated in maritime trade in Southeast Asia. A wide range of commodities originated in the region, but especially important were such spices as pepper, ginger, cloves, and nutmeg. The spice trade initially was developed by Indian and Arab merchants, but it also brought Europeans to the region. First the Portuguese, then the Dutch, and finally the British and French became involved in this enterprise in various countries. The penetration of European commercial interests gradually evolved into annexation of territories, as traders lobbied for an extension of control to protect and expand their activities. As a result, the Dutch moved into Indonesia, the British into Malaya, and the French into Indochina.

While the region's economy greatly depends on agriculture, manufacturing and services are becoming more important. Newly industrialized countries include the Philippines, Indonesia, Malaysia, and Thailand, while Singapore and Brunei are well-established developed countries. The rest of Southeast Asia is still heavily dependent on agriculture, but Vietnam is notably making steady progress in developing their industrial sectors. The region notably manufactures microprocessors. Reserves of oil are also present in the region. Seventeen telecommunications companies have contracted to build a new submarine cable to connect Southeast Asia to the U.S. This is to avoid disruption of the kind recently caused by the cutting of the undersea cable from Taiwan to the U.S. in a recent earthquake.

DEMOGRAPHICS

Southeast Asia has an area of approx. 4,000,000 km^2 (1.6 million square miles). As of 2004, more than 593 million people lived in the region, more than a fifth of them (125 million) on the Indonesian island of Java, the most densely populated large island in the world. The distribution of the religions and people is diverse in Southeast Asia and varies by country. Some 30 million overseas Chinese also live in Southeast Asia, most prominently in Christmas Island, Malaysia, the Philippines, Singapore, Indonesia and Thailand, and also, as the Hoa, in Vietnam.

ETHNIC GROUPS

According to a recent Stanford genetic study, the Southeast Asian population is far from being homogeneous. Although primarily descendants of Austronesian, Tai, and Mon-Khmer-speaking immigrants who migrated from Southern China during the Bronze Age and Iron Age, there are overlays of Arab, Chinese, Indian, Polynesian and Melanesian genes. There are also large pockets of intermarriage between indigenous Southeast Asians and those of Chinese descent. They form a substantial part of everyday life in countries such as Vietnam, Singapore, Thailand and the Philippines. Indonesia and Malaysia also has a few mixed Southeast Asian-Chinese populations.

On the mainland the Khmer peoples of Cambodia remain as ancestors of earlier Pareoean peoples. Similarly, remnants of the Mon group are found in parts of Myanmar and Thailand; the ethnic mixture there has been produced by overlaying Tibeto-Burman and Tai, Lao, and Shan peoples. The contemporary Vietnamese population originated from the Red River area in the north and may be a mixture of Tai and Malay peoples. Added to these major ethnic groups are such less numerous peoples as the Karens, Chins, and Nagas in Myanmar, who have affinities with other Asiatic peoples. Insular Southeast Asia contains a mixture of descendants of Proto-Malay (Nesiot) and Pareoean peoples who were influenced by Malayo-Polynesian and other groups. In addition, Arabic, Indian, and Chinese influences have affected the ethnic pattern of the islands.

In modern times the Burmese account for more than two-thirds of the ethnic stock of Myanmar, while ethnic Thais and Vietnamese account for about four-fifths of the respective populations of those countries. Indonesia is clearly dominated by the Javanese and Sundanese ethnic groups, while Malaysia is more evenly split between the Malays and the Chinese. Within the Philippines, the Tagalog, Cebuano, Ilocano, and Bicol groups are significant.

RELIGIONS

Countries in Southeast Asia practice many different religions. *Mainland* SEA countries, which are, Thailand, Cambodia, Laos, Myanmar, and Vietnam practice predominantly Buddhism. Singapore is also predominantly Buddhist. Ancestor worship and Confucianism is also widely practiced in Vietnam and Singapore. In Maritime Southeast Asia, people living in Malaysia, western Indonesia and Brunei practice mainly Islam. Christianity is predominant in the Philippines, eastern Indonesia and East Timor. The Philippines has the largest Roman Catholic population followed very distantly by Vietnam. East Timor is also predominantly Roman Catholic due to a history of Portuguese rule.

Religions and peoples are diverse in Southeast Asia and not one country is homogeneous. In the world's most populous Muslim nation, Indonesia, Hinduism is dominant on islands such as Bali. Christianity also predominates in Philippines, New Guinea and Timor. Pockets of Hindu population can also be found around Southeast Asia in Singapore, Malaysia etc. Garuda (Sanskrit: Garuda), the phoenix who is the mount (*vahanam*) of Vishnu, is a national symbol in both Thailand and Indonesia; in the Philippines, gold images of Garuda have been found on Palawan; gold images of other Hindu gods and goddesses have also been found on Mindanao. Balinese Hinduism is somewhat different from Hinduism practiced elsewhere, as Animism and local culture is incorporated into it.

Christians can also be found throughout Southeast Asia; they are in the majority in East Timor and the Philippines, Asia's largest Christian nation. In addition, there are also older tribal religious practices in remote areas of Sarawak in East Malaysia and Papua in eastern Indonesia. In Myanmar, Sakka (Indra) is revered as a *nat*. In Vietnam, Mahayana Buddhism is practiced, which is influenced by native animism but with strong emphasis on Ancestor Worship.

LANGUAGES

Each of the languages has been influenced by cultural pressures due to trade and historical colonization as well. Thus, for example, a Filipino, educated in English and Filipino, as well as in his native tongue (e.g., Visayan), might well speak another language, such as Spanish for historical reasons, or Chinese, Korean or Japanese for economic reasons; a Malaysian might well speak Malay, Chinese, Tamil as well as English as a second language. The language composition for each country is as follows: (official languages are in bold.)

Andaman and Nicobar Islands	Nicobarese, Bengali, English, Hindi, Malayalam, Punjabi, Tamil, Telugu, Shompen, Andamanese languages, others
Brunei	Malay, English, Chinese, indigenous Borneian dialects
Burma (Myanmar)	Burmese, Shan, Karen, Rakhine, Kachin, Chin, Mon, Chinese dialects, Indian languages, others
Cambodia	Khmer, English, French, Vietnamese, Thai, Chamic dialects, Chinese dialects, others
Christmas Island	English, Chinese, Malay
Cocos (Keeling) Islands	English, Cocos Malay
East Timor	Tetum, Portuguese, Indonesian, English, Mambae, Makasae, Tukudede, Bunak, Galoli, Kemak, Fataluku, Baikeno, others
Indonesia	Indonesian, Acehnese, Batak, Minang, Sundanese, Javanese, Sasak, Tetum, Dayak, Minahasa, Toraja, Buginese, Halmahera, Ambonese, Ceramese; English, Dutch, Papuan languages, Chinese, and so much others
Laos	Lao, Thai, Vietnamese, Hmong, Miao, Mien, Dao, Shan; French, English others
Malaysia	Malay, English, Chinese dialects, Indian languages, Sarawakian and Sabahan languages, others
Philippines	Filipino/Tagalog, English, Cebuano, Ilocano, Hiligaynon or Ilonggo, Bicol, Waray, Pampango, and Pangasinan
Singapore	English, Mandarin (Chinese), Malay, Tamil, other Chinese dialects, other Indian languages, Arabic dialects, others
South China Sea Islands	English, Filipino, Malay, Mandarin (Chinese), Vietnamese
Thailand	Thai, English, Chinese dialects, Malay, Lao, Khmer, Isaan, Shan, Lue, Phutai, Mon, Mein, Hmong, Karen, others
Vietnam	Vietnamese, English, Chinese dialects, French, Khmer, mountain area languages (Mon-Khmer and Malayo-Polynesian)

CULTURE

Rice paddy agriculture has existed in Southeast Asia for thousands of years, ranging across the sub region. Some dramatic examples of these rice paddies populate the Banaue Rice Terraces in the mountains of Luzon in the Philippines. Maintenance of these paddies is very labor-intensive.

The rice paddies are well-suited to the monsoon climate of the region. Stilt houses can be found all over Southeast Asia, from Thailand and Laos, to Borneo, to Luzon in the Philippines, to Papua New Guinea. The region has diverse metalworking, especially in Indonesia. This includes weaponry, such as the distinctive Kris, and musical instruments, such as the Gamelan.

INFLUENCES

The region's chief cultural influences have been from either China or India or both, with Vietnam considered by far the most Chinese-influenced. As a rule, the peoples who ate with their fingers were more likely influenced by the culture of India, for example, than the culture of China, where the peoples first ate with chopsticks; tea, as a beverage, can be found across the region. The fish sauces distinctive to the region tend to vary.

THE ARTS

The arts of Southeast Asia have no affinity with the arts of other areas, except India. Dance in much of Southeast Asia also includes movement of the hands, as well as the feet. Puppetry and shadow plays were also a favoured form of entertainment in past centuries. The Arts and Literature in some of Southeast Asia is quite influenced by Hinduism brought to them centuries ago.

The Tai, coming late into Southeast Asia, brought with them some Chinese artistic traditions, but they soon shed them in favour of the Khmer and Mon traditions, and the only indications of their earlier contact with Chinese arts were in the style of their temples, especially the tapering roof, and in their lacquer ware.

In Indonesia, though they converted to Islam, they retained many forms of Hindu influenced practices, cultures, arts and literatures. An example will be the Wayang Kulit (Shadow Puppet) and literatures like the Ramayana. This is also true for mainland Southeast Asia (excluding Vietnam). Dance movements, Hindu gods, Arts were also fused into Thai, Khmer, Lao and Burmese cultures.

It has been pointed out that Khmer and Indonesian classical arts were concerned with depicting the life of the gods, but to the Southeast Asian mind the life of the gods was the life of the peoples themselves-joyous, earthy, yet divine. In Vietnam, the Vietnamese share many cultural similarities with the Chinese.

MUSIC

Traditional music in Southeast Asia is as varied as its many ethnic and cultural divisions. Main styles of traditional music can be seen: Court music, folk music, music styles of smaller ethnic groups, and music influenced by genres outside the geographic region.

Of the court and folk genres, Gong-chime ensembles and orchestras make up the majority (the exception being lowland areas of Vietnam). *Gamelan* orchestras from Indonesia, *Piphat / Pinpeat* ensembles of Thailand & Cambodia and the *Kulintang* ensembles of the southern Philippines, Borneo, Sulawesi and Timor are the three main distinct styles of musical genres that have influenced other traditional musical styles in the region. String instruments also are popular in the region.

WRITING

The history of Southeast Asia has led to a wealth of different authors, from both within and without writing about the region. Originally, Indians were the ones who taught the native inhabitants about writing. This is shown through Brahmic forms of writing present in the region such as the Balinese script shown on split palm leaf called *lontar*, right:

The antiquity of this form of writing extends before the invention of paper around the year 100 in China. Note each palm leaf section was only several lines, written longitudinally across the leaf, and bound by twine to the other sections.

The outer portion was decorated. The alphabets of Southeast Asia tended to be abugidas, until the arrival of the Europeans, who used words that also ended in consonants, not just vowels. Other forms of official documents, which did not use paper, included Javanese copperplate scrolls. This would have been more durable in the tropical climate of Southeast Asia.

2

Youth Cultures and Aspirations

Southeast Asia is a region of immense richness and diversity. Scholars say man may have lived here as early as half a million years ago, at a time when much of the world lay covered with ice and island Southeast Asia was connected by land bridges to the Asian mainland. Several centuries of human migration, the influence of the great religions and civilizations of the East, and the coming of Western rule followed by independence have resulted in multiethnic, multireligious and multilingual societies. The diversity of the countries of ASEAN is reflected in their widely divergent sizes, the heterogeneity of their populations, the many religions practiced, the number of languages used and their different historical experiences.

And yet amid the diversity common threads weave them together-their habitation of a common geographic area, the interlacing of their histories, the growing integration of their economies, and the unifying influences of knowledge and information in contemporary times. In 33 years of regional cooperation under the aegis of ASEAN, Southeast Asia has evolved from a region of isolated states and cultures into "a concert of nations."

THE CULTURAL MIX

All the countries of Southeast Asia, except for a small part of Myanmar, are within the tropical zone, with the equator cutting through some of them. Southeast Asia stretches across three time zones so that it is about as wide as Europe. The countries in the region share a monsoon climate. The monsoon winds created by rising warm air from the landmass and sinking cold air from the expanses of ocean, have given the region a climate conducive to trade by seafaring vessels, to the growth of forests and the flow of rivers, and to systems of agriculture that can feed large populations. These elements have therefore a tremendous influence in the shaping of Southeast Asian culture.

Even during prehistoric times, long before they felt Indian and Chinese influences, South-east Asians already had their own culture. They had their own unique ways of interpreting and dealing with their unique environment, which were transmitted from one generation to the next. This culture had many variations but the variations bore many common characteristics, being part of a network of animist cultures, including those of the Melanesian, Micronesian and Polynesian cousins of the Southeast Asians. The mythology of ancient Southeast Asians was oriented to the seasons of the movement of the sun, moon, stars and planets, being the product of a monsoon climate and an irrigated system of agriculture.

Many settlements were along riverbanks, and houses were built to cope with floods as the rivers swelled under steady rains. Many communities were organised around the cycle of rice cultivation. Rituals, arts, the shapes of houses and communal structures were designed to celebrate the life-giving qualities of rice. Marriages, migrations, homecomings and rites of passage were timed to the planting, harvesting, transport, storage and consumption of rice. The peoples who came in contact with Southeast Asians brought various cultural influences, including the great religions. Thus, Malaysia, Indonesia (except Bali which is Hindu), Brunei and the southern Philippines are a realm of Sunni Islam; Myanmar, Laos, Thailand and Cambodia, all extensively Indianized, adhere to Theravada Buddhism; while Vietnam, much influenced by Chinese culture, professes Mahayana Buddhism. Hinduism remains widespread in the region. The Indian epics, the Ramayana and the Mahabharata, in many versions, have been indelibly etched on the Southeast Asian soul. The Philippines, except for the southernmost part, is predominantly Roman Catholic.

Underneath all the layers of religious and cultural influences, a common Southeast Asian culture survives to this day, unobtrusive but real. There are some 1,000 languages, which scholars have classified into Sinitic, the languages of the Chinese communities of the region; Tibeto-Burman; Karen; Miao-Yao; Tai, which includes the national languages of Thailand and Laos; Malayo-Polynesian, the largest and most widely distributed group of languages from the region, ranging from Madagascar to the South Pacific; Mon-Khmer, Viet-Muong; and Papuan, which is spoken in eastern Indonesia. The colonial languages have persisted: French is still spoken in Indochina but is losing ground. Some Indonesians still speak Dutch. Spanish is no longer widely spoken in the Philippines, but a large Spanish vocabulary has become embedded in the various Philippine languages. A large body of Portuguese words has been similarly absorbed into the Indonesian language. The emerging lingua franca of the region, which is also that of the world, is English.

Today the signs of the encroachments of Western pop culture may seem pervasive all over Southeast Asia, as they are all over the world. But what looks like cultural imperialism is really an interpenetration that enriches both sides. A popular brand of hamburger may retain its American packaging, but its taste has been altered to suit the local passion for spices. A teenager may wear blue jeans, but she tops it with a sarong or kebaya. But in an increasingly interdependent global economic system, the process of urbanisation and modernisation and other global influences have affected many of the region's traditional societies. ASEAN's concern is how to fulfil its aspirations to progress and prosperity and at the same time preserve its cultural heritage. Against this background, cooperation on culture and information lies at the heart of the ASEAN agenda.

The ASEAN leaders believe that:

- There is a need to enhance mutual understanding and respect of one another's cultures, value systems, nuances and sensitivities;
- There is a need to promote the richness of Southeast Asia's culture to its peoples and to others outside the region and to raise its profile in the international community;
- It is important to preserve and protect the region's rich cultural heritage from the vagaries of nature and modernisation; and
- Southeast Asian peoples need to foster a sense of regional identity and a spirit of regionalism that is supportive of its aspirations.

KEY DECLARATIONS AND POLICIES

In its history ASEAN recognised culture and information as key areas for cooperation. One of the association's earliest agreements was the promotion of the regional mass media and cultural activities. These early projects included film festivals, the exchange of radio and television materials and artists, and exhibitions and performances on each other's arts and culture. The First ASEAN Summit in Bali in February 1976 provided the framework for cooperation on culture and information. One of its key documents, the Bali Declaration of ASEAN Concord, promised that "member states shall vigorously develop an awareness of regional identity and exert all efforts to create a strong ASEAN community." It declared support for "ASEAN scholars, writers, artistes and mass-media representatives to enable them to play an active role in fostering a sense of regional identity and fellowship."

The ASEAN Committee on Culture and Information (COCI) was formed and held its first meeting in 1978. Based on the Bali Concord, COCI's mandate is to promote "effective cooperation on culture and information to enhance mutual understanding and solidarity among the peoples of ASEAN as well as to further regional development." To finance the association's cultural programme, the ASEAN Foreign

Ministers in 1978 established the ASEAN Cultural Fund, to which Japan initially contributed five billion yen. The Fund is open to contributions from member countries, other dialogue partners of ASEAN and international organisations. The ASEAN Secretariat serves as custodian of the Fund and has engaged the professional services of fund managers to handle its investment. Only 80% of the Fund's annual earnings go towards financing cultural and information projects recommended by COCI. The rest is ploughed back into the Fund.

Since its establishment in 1978, COCI has carried out an average of 15 projects every year in culture and information. These projects have seen the active involvement of artists, children and youth delegates, writers and mass-media practitioners, and experts from institutions like ministries of culture and information, national radio and television networks, film institutes, news agencies, cultural commissions, heritage boards, museums, archives and libraries. Universities, art institutes and similar institutions have also taken part in COCI activities. As ASEAN brought all ten Southeast Asian countries under its roof and spurred them towards the common goal of regional cooperation and integration, it has increasingly turned its sights towards extending and deepening the sense of community within the region.

At their Second Informal Summit in Kuala Lumpur in December 1997, the ASEAN leaders laid out their vision for ASEAN in the 21st century as a "community conscious of its ties of history, aware of its cultural heritage and bound by a common regional identity." To realise this vision, the ASEAN leaders adopted the Ha Noi Plan of Action of 1998, which called on the culture and information sector to provide more intensified promotion of ASEAN awareness and improvement of its standing in the international community. This mandate governs current ASEAN cooperation on culture and information.

THE WINDOW OF CULTURE

Until recently, cultural projects of ASEAN were categorised under three areas: literary works and ASEAN studies, visual arts and the performing arts. Since 1978 cultural activities undertaken have ranged from publications on literature and cultural studies to performances, exhibitions, festivals, workshops, fellowship grants and academic researches. The literary and ASEAN studies programme has produced several materials on Southeast Asian cultures. It has also organised forums and workshops and trained scholars and cultural specialists on specialised fields such as archaeology, museology and conservation. A series of monographs on music, dance, theatre, traditional and modern literature, the mass media and other topics is being completed.

A multi-volume anthology of ASEAN literatures has been completed containing important short stories, essays, poetry and other literary works, both modern and traditional. Among ASEAN's invaluable collections is an anthology of folk literature, which brings together the riddles, proverbs, myths, legends and folk tales of the region. A two-volume research study on traditional festivals-intended as reference material for students, researchers and academicians-is being printed. The first volume covers the mainland Southeast Asian states and the second deals with the island-countries. The region's librarians have also done their bit for regional cooperation. In the mid-nineties they organised a series of seminars on ways to improve reading habits and library services in ASEAN. Recent exchange visits between ASEAN and Korean senior librarians enabled them to observe the application of information technology to library management.

Archaeologists and anthropologists, archivists and other conservators of heritage have also been organising their own projects. Among the more notable projects have been the joint field excavation works and seminars done by ASEAN anthropologists in select sites around the region. In the visual arts, ASEAN has organised art competitions, workshops and exhibitions among children, youth and noted masters of member countries. One of its more acclaimed projects was the installation of ASEAN sculptures in the parks or squares of member countries. Some of the symposiums and workshops have produced a number of excellent publications on ASEAN art and aesthetics. These have been distributed to art organisations and schools in member countries. ASEAN's activities in the performing arts are perhaps the most colourful and enjoyable, for they have brought together young artists, performers and cultural experts to do joint productions. These productions have covered dance, theatre and the musical arts. Workshops and forums on traditional music have resulted in the production of compact discs featuring originally recorded authentic traditional sounds. The holding of children's choir and youth music festivals is among the favourite projects of ASEAN organisers.

In building closer relations with its dialogue partners, ASEAN has undertaken joint cooperative projects with them on culture and information. With Australia, ASEAN has undertaken workshops for the development of strategies in managing cultural heritage. A number of activities are being drawn up to help heritage institutions in the region improve their skills in collections management. In 1998 and 1999 ASEAN and Japan organised a joint "Multinational Cultural Mission" to deepen intellectual and cultural discourse between ASEAN members and Japan. The mission visited all ASEAN countries and Japan and enabled leading scholars to exchange views with their counterparts. In Thailand a special discourse was arranged between the scholars and rural folk.

CURRENT CULTURAL PROGRAMME

One of ASEAN's first acts as it entered the 21st century was to sign a Declaration on Cultural Heritage. Promoting a sense of regional identity, ASEAN feels, requires an awareness of the cultural heritage of Southeast Asia and appreciation by the member countries of one another's cultures. Three broad strategies guide the Committee on Culture and Information (COCI) in this current programme: cultural heritage and preservation, cultural promotion and appreciation, and the production of cultural showcases. ASEAN has pledged to document, preserve and safeguard national treasures and cultural properties, antiquities and works of historic, archaeological, anthropological or scientific significance throughout the region. Guided by the Declaration, COCI has drawn up an integrated work programme to eliminate duplication of activities and set aside ad hoc proposals low in regional priority.

A vital part of this work programme is the establishment of an on-line cultural heritage information network that will link up all the cultural heritage institutions of the region and organise regional databases on a Web site. Cultural promotion and appreciation activities today are aimed at the younger generation. In spite of more than three decades of ASEAN cooperation, Southeast Asian peoples still have a long way to go in understanding and appreciating one another's cultures, and in grasping what ASEAN is and how it is relevant to their lives. ASEAN seeks to overcome this challenge by developing and producing source materials and teaching aids on ASEAN cultures and history. More activities that promote "people-to-people" contacts will also be undertaken. A continuing project along this line is the ASEAN Youth Camp, where youth leaders of member countries interact and where they are exposed to ASEAN issues and the history and cultures of member countries.

Two such camps have been held: one in the Philippines in 1998, which focused on arts and the environment; and the other in Thailand in 1999, which concentrated on cultural heritage. Being completed is a compilation of children's songs, dances, games and stories that will be made available to schools and other institutions in all member countries. To continue stimulating creativity and enhancing the artistic and professional talents of ASEAN artists and writers, COCI will continue to organise arts and cultural showcases. Since the early eighties, these festivals, performances and exhibitions have enthralled audiences both within and outside the region. At present COCI is carrying out a number of exciting projects in this area. The first is Realizing Rama, a modern dance production of the Indian epic. In its many variations, the Ramayana theme is discernible in all traditional Southeast Asian cultures. Realizing Rama fuses traditional and contemporary musical and dance forms. The theme has been updated and deals with the struggle of modern-day ASEAN leaders to overcome temptation. The work, premiered in Ha Noi during the 1998 ASEAN Summit, has completed its tour of ASEAN capitals. Arrangements are now being made to stage the production in key capitals in Europe in 2001.

Another outward-bound project is the ASEAN Exhibition on Contemporary Art, a travelling show that will visit Europe this year. The project is being coordinated by the Singapore Art Museum in collaboration with the curators of national galleries of other member countries. The exhibition will consist of 60 to 70 contemporary works by the finest artists of the region. COCI is also producing a series of documentaries in the form of coffee-table books and videos. The first is a book featuring the cultural heritage sites and landmarks of Southeast Asia. It is scheduled for launching in Nov-ember 2000. Another showcase of ASEAN literary works being planned is a book compiling award-winning short stories by writers of the region in the last three decades.

INFORMATION AS BRIDGE

Cooperation on mass-media activities helped ASEAN greatly in its early years, when member countries were still groping to understand each other's ways. The news media circulated news of ASEAN decisions and projects around the region. The holding of film festivals involving the region's favourite movie stars and singers brought life and colour to ASEAN activities. These were complemented by the exchange of television and radio programmes among the broadcasting organisations of member countries and the production of a number of documentary films on ASEAN. Until recently, activities in information were grouped into print and interpersonal media and broadcast media involving radio, television and film. In the print media, most of the activities have been directed at the region's media practitioners to improve their coverage and understanding of regional events and issues.

The ASEAN News Exchange programme links the news agencies of member countries in a news network that carries the leading news stories of the day. The programme has organised training sessions, study tours, workshops and seminars for journalists. It has also brought together in several conferences editors of national newspapers, including news directors and producers from the electronic media, and their counterparts from the ASEAN news agencies. In broadcasting, besides festivals and exchanges of audio and video materials, workshops have been organised for producers and scriptwriters to help improve their professional skills.

A notable project is the radio programme called ASEAN in Action, produced in the national languages of member countries and aired on national networks at least once a week. The project, now in its seventh year, covers a variety of topics ranging from public affairs to "infotainment"-to help promote ASEAN awareness. In 1989 the ASEAN Ministers Responsible for Information organised themselves to enhance cooperation on information and mass-media activities. Among the activities they have promoted is the expansion of the ASEAN Web site to include national Web sites on culture and information. Through a regular forum on the Internet, they also share and exchange information on developments in this new technology.

AWARENESS AND IMAGE

In line with the Ha Noi Plan of Action, COCI has reoriented its efforts towards raising public awareness of ASEAN's work, building up its image internationally, and conducting a more coherent cultural cooperation programme. COCI and the ASEAN Secretariat are carrying out a communications programme aimed at developing an awareness of ASEAN and transforming this awareness into support for ASEAN and its work. The broadening agenda of ASEAN, from political and security cooperation to economic integration and functional cooperation, needs to be conveyed to many publics. At their Sixth Conference held in Ha Noi in October 2000, the ASEAN Ministers Responsible for Information promised to promote ASEAN awareness as a regular function of their information agencies.

In this spirit, each member country has drawn up a National

Communication Plan that delivers the following messages:

- ASEAN is the family of all Southeast Asian nations working to win the future for the region's 500 million people. As described in Vision 2020, that future has three basic components: peace, prosperity and fulfilment of the human potential.
- ASEAN is already bringing concrete benefits to the peoples of the region.
- ASEAN's work contributes to the making of a more peaceful, more just and more prosperous world.
- ASEAN deserves the support and help of its publics, and it is in the interest of these publics to support and help ASEAN.

The ASEAN information ministers also recommended that, in view of current perceptions about ASEAN and their effects on its image, work and economy, ASEAN should formulate strategies to harness in a coordinated way available resources to advance and reinforce a positive international profile of ASEAN. The ASEAN Secretariat and COCI are doing much of the work of developing the content of communication materials. Leading this campaign, the Secretary-General of ASEAN has been speaking at international forums.

The Secretariat has been strengthening its contacts with the mass media by providing them news, features and other materials. It also maintains the ASEANWEB, which carries not only official ASEAN documents but also current news and developments within the association. Besides the linkages and exchanges among the news and information networks of member countries, COCI is launching an ASEAN quiz competition, a photo competition and other activities intended to bring the ASEAN message to the Southeast Asian grassroots.

OUTLOOK

Cooperation efforts on culture and information are guided by the conviction that through pride in their rich cultural heritage and extensive contact through the information media, the peoples of Southeast Asia will experience a sense of community that matches the close cooperation of their governments. As culture celebrates the diversity of the region and what is special about each ASEAN country, information turns its people into a constituency for ASEAN regions.

The process is well under way. From their isolation back in 1967, the peoples and countries of Southeast Asia are being integrated in ever widening circles of involvement-in politics and economics, in science and technology, in health and education, in agriculture and industry, in the environment, in social development, and in culture and communications. At the start of the 21st century, global influences are driving ASEAN to tighten those bonds even more. An increasingly interdependent global economic system, the emergence of new regional security threats and the dangers posed by transnational problems have made it imperative for ASEAN countries and peoples to work even more closely together. All these underscore the role of culture and information on the ASEAN agenda.

CHILD BEGGARS IN ASIA

WORLD OF WORK, NO. 26, 1998

Until recently, the incidence of child beggars was overshadowed by the more visible and voluminous trade in women and children being trafficked for prostitution. But experts see begging as the newest trend in child trafficking throughout the Mekong region. Poipet, Cambodia: The children had been caught begging illegally in Bangkok and deported by Thai immigration authorities. Now, they sat quietly in single file on the dusty ground, sweating under the high sun, tired from their bumpy four-hour ride to the Cambodian border and awaiting an uncertain future. Some will be claimed by their parents, others handed over to charities or officials, and a few will slip through the net altogether, cajoled or coerced by agents into returning to Thailand.

The youngest was a four-year-old named Bon. His dirty

condition, club foot, and twisted legs were a contrast to the wide grin on his face. The child traffickers loitering at the border kept a sharp eye on him; a handicapped child brings in more money. A few days before, compassionate and unsuspecting foreigners had been dropping coins into outstretched tin cups, confident that their donation to a scarred street child would buy food for him. Not so. The money will end up in an agent's pocket, confirming the equation that wealthy tourists plus needy child equals money. Until recently, the number of child beggars was dwarfed by trade in some 80,000 women and children being trafficked since 1980 for prostitution. But experts are seeing a rising number of trafficked children used for begging throughout the Mekong region. Since 1997 the number of children caught begging illegally in Bangkok - 95% of them Cambodian - has more than doubled to 1,060.

A SYMPTOM OF CAMBODIA'S PAIN

That they are Cambodian should come as no surprise. Neither should the fact that they ended up in Thailand, still the region's economic hub despite Asia's ongoing economic crisis. Cambodia is limping into recovery from a long period of civil war and many Cambodians face malnutrition, poor health, and excessive poverty, with little hope for the future. Life expectancy is 53 years; literacy is 35%, and nine-tenths of the population lives in the countryside, still littered with land mines. Cambodia ranks 153rd out of 175 countries on the Human Development Index of the United Nations Development Programme (UNDP), which rates living standards. Previously a few individuals would come but now it is becoming a business, said Claudia Coenjaerts, Subregional Programme Coordinator for the International Labour Organisation (ILO)' International Programme on the Elimination of Child Labour (IPEC) in the ILO Regional Office for Asia.

It is an earning opportunity for more and more criminals, and law enforcers really don't care. It is an easy way to make money, so people at the border wait for the children, to take them away. It is one of the most horrendous forms of forced labour. However, abhorrent any trafficking in children, the trade in beggars may be even more sinister than initially thought. Dr Dominica Garcia of the Jesuit Refugee Service works with children at Bangkok' immigration centre. Recently she treated two little boys aged four and eight who had unnatural deformities. I hoped I was mistaken, she said, but these children looked as though they had been mutilated on purpose. Their feet were swollen, some of their fingers appeared as though they might have been hacked off, and there was a clear dent on their skin which could have been the mark of a tightly tied piece of string.

As border officials patrol the rows of silent children, Veng, a strong-looking youth of 15, looks around warily. He is an old Thailand hand, 10 years old the first time he left Cambodia. I was swimming in the river and a Vietnamese man came into the water and pulled me out, Veng said. He put something on my face and made me sick, and put me into a taxi and brought me to Bangkok. He taught me how to beg, where to put my cup, how to ask for money. I was afraid but he beat me if I didn't make money. He took it all and kept it and gave me some food but never enough. I was always hungry. These days Veng crosses the border willingly. Free from his agent, he prefers begging in Bangkok to starving in Phnom Penh.

Veng is a trafficked child. According to a just-released ILO report, a trafficked child is one who is recruited and transported from one place to another across a national border, legally or illegally, with or without the child' consent, usually but not always organised by an intermediary: parents, family member, teacher, procurer, or local authority. At the destination, the child is coerced or semi-forced (by deceptive information) to engage in activities under exploitative and abusive conditions.

Held captive, the children might receive as little as US$0.25 a day in pocket money. But they may hand their agent US$20 or more every day. Some like Veng, become experienced and escape, striking out on their own. They learn how to avoid the police and may even become traffickers themselves, shuttling between Bangkok and the border, and earning money from the trade. They sleep under bridges, in parks or along highways, with other marginal dwellers. As illegals, they shift around more and may end up in the drug trade or prostitution.

EXPLOITATIVE CHILD LABOUR

According to the ILO report, trafficked migrant children are among the most severely affected victims of exploitative child labour. The report, commissioned by ILO-IPEC from the Institute of Population and Social Research of Mahidol University in Thailand, says children living in a foreign country with foreign customs and language are easily deceived and often treated like slaves. In their isolation, they don't know where to turn for help. They can't use normal channels, and often face discrimination and harassment. Some are victims of kidnapping or coercion but most trafficked children are sold or given up by relatives. Don, 14, and his 10-year-old sister were asked to go to Bangkok by their mother.

School was finished and my neighbour saw me and wanted to take me, he said. My parents said I should go because they needed money. Don was spotted begging by Thai police and couldn't escape without leaving his little sister behind. So they both got caught. To help stop this trafficking, ILO-IPEC recently brought together experts from throughout the Mekong region to draft a framework for cooperation and action.

ILO-IPEC ACTION

We will have to see what works and what doesn't, says Ms Coenjaerts of ILO-IPEC. Part of the difficulty is that these children are hidden and invisible, which makes them very difficult to identify. Interventions will be needed both at the national level and the sub regional level, aiming to prevent the problem, harmonize legislation, coordinate information and establish bilateral agreements. One way is to prevent child labour at the community level by showing children and their parents the real problems they will face if they go to the city, and by organising community-based surveillance.

Families are often lied to by agents and promises of jobs and money are rarely kept.

The other approach is through rehabilitation and re-integration once the children return home. Since many children have been forced to lead a criminal existence, reintegrating them into everyday life is not easy. Given the illegal and fluid nature of the trade, tackling child trafficking has to be a joint effort across borders by governments and non-governmental organisations. But experience on the ground is limited and few organisations work with child beggars, though this may change as the problem grows. Child labour is at the top of the international agenda.

Delegates to the International Labour Conference in June 1998 called for a new Convention which would immediately penalize the worst forms of child labour, the scope of which includes, among others, slavery and practices similar to slavery, such as the sale and trafficking in children, forced or compulsory labour, debt bondage or serfdom. It would reinforce the ultimate goal of the ILO Minimum Age Convention, 1973 (No. 138), to abolish child labour. By concentrating on its most extreme forms, the new Convention would provide immediate protection, paving the way for the longer-term and broader effects of Convention No. 138. - Third World Network Features.

CHILD LABOR NEWS SERVICE, 15 NOVEMBER 2000

Thailand and Cambodia have agreed to sign their first bilateral memorandum to combat trafficking in women and children, a measure expected to help protect those targeted by human smuggling syndicates. The basics for a draft memorandum of understanding were discussed at a two-day workshop on ending trafficking in women and children organised by the Mekong Region Law Centre, the National Youth of Thailand and the Coalition to Fight against Child Exploitation. The sketch draft requires both governments to provide education and vocational training along with job opportunities to protect women and children vulnerable to trafficking; provide better social welfare services for the underprivileged; exchange information and develop a legal framework for prosecution of traffickers; treat people being trafficked as victims and repatriate them safely through diplomatic channels and facilitate the recovery and reintegration of victims into their communities.

Saisuree Chutikul, Chairperson of the Sub-committee on the Elimination of Trafficking in Women and Children, National Youth Bureau, said the memorandum was inspired by the increasing number of children and women from Cambodia who have been lured into working illegally in Thailand. The Cambodians are lured and forced into work as prostitutes and beggars in Thailand. Some are beaten and abused when they refuse to work. The draft will be a mechanism and channel to facilitate the suppression of syndicates, to prevent them from continuing their work, Saisuree said. According to the draft, the trafficking category would include those people smuggled into the country for purposes of prostitution, forced domestic labour, servile marriage, false adoption, sex tourism and entertainment, pornography and forced begging.

Saisuree stressed that women and children who are found to have been trafficked into Thailand tend to be deported at the earliest opportunity, thus preventing police from obtaining key information and evidence directly from the victims. Those victims are excellent sources for police and the concerned authorities. So they should stay in shelters in Thailand to provide information about the syndicates before being sent back, Saisuree said. It is not certain when the memorandum would be completed or when it would become effective. It is up to both countries to decide. Once the memorandum goes into force, it could be a model for further agreements Thailand could have with other countries.

YOUTH IN POLITICS

The role of youth in the region has taken a high profile following the Asian economic crisis. In Indonesia, they were instrumental in calling for the resignation of former president Suharto. Housed in universities and well organised, they were the core of the Reformasi movement in the archipelago. Similarly, in Malaysia, much of Anwar's supporters are youth. They are the ones behind Reformasi and show up in large numbers at talks and demonstrations. This is not surprising, since Anwar was previously a youth leader himself. It establishes clearly the connection between youth and politics and the attraction youths have for others in the past who have been student leaders.

In the not too distant periphery, there are the Burmese university students in exile in Thailand. They have been championing the cause of Burma for quite a while now and are well known for their activism. Youths in the Philippines have been traditionally active domestically, regionally and internationally. Theirs is a comparatively well developed youth political structure vis-à-vis rest of Southeast Asia. Thai youths are also active in political NGOs and as members of political parties. Following democratization in Thailand their participation has increased. Most often, these youth are prominent only within their respective countries. Networking among youths of different Asian nations is minimal. There has been an attempt through the Asian Youth Council (a grouping of progressive youths) to bring regional youth together. This group exists through the loose participation of the Philippines, Thailand, Indonesia, Malaysia and Taiwan.

Another recent example would be a Youth Camp on human rights in Thailand taking place in October, where Korean and Thai youth are working together to establish regional co-operation. In most regional meetings such as the ones above, you will find that Singaporean youths are often under-represented. Most often they are unaware of such meetings and collaborative opportunities, or there is not an alternative/ independent youth organisation through which to connect Singapore to these events and activities. Singaporean youth participation at present is only limited participation in some Japanese-sponsored exchange programs or at government-to-government contacts, facilitated through the Singapore

International Foundation, the National Youth Council and youth representation from the People's Association.

There is also some contact through the youth arms of the Rotary and Lion Clubs. However, most contacts of this nature are not political but educational and cultural. The absence of youth in regional and Singapore politics is of historical nature, stemming from the participation in the Hock Lee bus riots, where the Chinese middle schools were very active, as were the highly-political Nanyang University students. There were also the very politically aware students of the University of Malaya. Students took political sides with political parties and issues. Political awareness was so great that it resulted in the government issuing suitability certificates in order to screen and prevent political types from studying at the University. Further, the University statutes were linked to enactments in Parliament in order to hinder chances for University and student union constitutions to be amended and to structurally divide students at the Universities.

Even the physical landscape of tertiary institutions was designed in a manner as to prevent quick large scale mobilisations. Thus, crippled domestically, they were also crippled regionally. As a result, youth in politics in present-day Singapore is limited. The most developed of participation can be mainly found in the Young PAP. Again, this can be divided into two broad categories: At one level, some youths join the Young PAP because they share the party's policies and aspire for a career within it. On the other level, it is made up of youth who have no other outlet for political expression, who join the Young PAP for purposes of exploration, and when they find that it is not in sync with their own political philosophy, they leave. In opposition parties, the youth wings are hardly developed. In fact, there are very few youth that it does not make opposition parties a significant conduit for youth political expression.

At the National University of Singapore (NUS), there is the Political Association and the Democratic Socialist Club. There is also a current affairs club at NTU, although the polytechnics do not have any explicitly political clubs. Most of these youth organisations at the universities are all currently dormant as much of the sting has been taken out of them during the 1988 alleged Marxist conspiracy, where some students were found to be politically active on and off campus. It followed a spate of more careful attention and scrutiny over students' political explorations. At the junior college level, again, there is no form of political education, only perhaps in discussions within the context of the General Paper, and now recently some talks on national education, which is primarily the passing of information on Singapore's history, rather than a critical political education.

Other conduits such as the SIF, NYC and PA Youth do not have explicit political programmes but are active on the educational and cultural fronts. On the average political awareness, actions and education is very much on the low side for most young people. This explains while youth are not active politically in regional and international meetings, as the culture at the domestic level is weak. In my personal experience at NUS from 1988-1992, the general impression I gathered was that no relationship was encouraged or tolerated by either, university administrative staff, lecturers or even the students themselves when it came to students and politics. This made commentators reduce NUS students to nothing more than distributors of condoms, quibblers over the cost of building floats during the Rag-n-Flag week or just a pathetic lot. To add to this discourse, PAP politicians, like clock-work, would issue their timely warnings that students should not involve themselves in politics or they would risk having their student grants cut off.

Student liaison officers at the University would vet all magazines or plans to organise even vaguely political activities. The principle reason they would offer is that they were doing it for the student's own good. More telling was the political culture: lecturers and fellow students did not approve of alternative political expressions. Any attempt to do so would be seen as suspect, and even illegal. This resulted in its own in-built checking where EOGMs were often used by students themselves to remove other politically progressive counterparts from occupying positions of leadership in student organisations. With launching of the Singapore 21 university students as citizens can take up the S21 banner for active citizenship. It is desirable that youths should take the opportunity to be more politically active.

However it is interesting to note that, even when PM Goh Chok Tong asked students to affiliate themselves to political parties, there were no takers, most preferring to take up the usual card of non-partisanship. But nevertheless there is room for students and youth to contribute to politics. And the students need to decide for themselves how they would like to pursue these ideas. This forum "From Student Politics to Real Politics" offers in a small way and opportunity for more young people to be politically aware. Hopefully as more people take part in future forums and join in the endeavour to be more politically aware, it will contribute to the country's overall development. I personally feel that a good dose of activism can only lead to a better rounded education.

With the majority of the world's population now living in cities, the 21st century is undoubtedly an urban century. Mega-cities add millions of new residents each year and many small- and medium-sized cities are growing at unprecedented rates. Such rapid urbanization poses serious challenges to local governments and urban managers in the developing world, as they confront crowded slums, congested streets, poor environmental conditions, and stark social inequalities. That urban conditions are harsh in the developing world is not a new phenomenon, but some have suggested that a new urgency exists. As many of these countries go through demographic transitions, the potential for increasing youth cohorts to create conflict in cities seems, to some researchers, to be reaching acute proportions. On April 8-9, 2003 the Comparative Urban Studies Project joined with the Urban Management Centre of the Asian Institute of Technology in Bangkok to examine the linkages between urbanization, youth populations, poverty, and conflict, with particular emphasis on Thailand, the Philippines, and Indonesia.

Dr. Peter Xenos, of the East-West Center, began the conference by analyzing current demographic trends in Southeast Asia. Indeed, Dr. Xenos noted rising numbers of youth, especially in urban areas. Youth increasingly make up a larger share of the national population, he said, and growth rates for youth populations seem to be significantly higher than growth rates for populations as a whole. Dr. Xenos maintained that the importance of growing youth cohorts nationally is made all the more important when combined with current social trends: the urban ward movement of youth, later marriage, rising school enrollment, and declining proportions of youth in the workforce. However, the implications for levels of conflict remain unclear.

Throughout the conference, participants expressed concern about linking demographic trends to a somewhat hazy notion of conflict. In the first panel, Dr. Yap Kioe Sheng, of UNESCAP, cited three dictionary definitions of conflict: "fight, struggle," "sharp disagreement" and "emotional disturbance from clash of opposing impulses or from inability to reconcile differences." Dr. Yap argued that the concept of conflict was sufficiently vague to promote misconceptions about inevitable causal linkages between large youth populations and violence. Both Dr. Yap and Dr. Xenos highlighted the need to pursue further research, disaggregating youth populations within cities to further determine the conditions that lead to social instability and more importantly, to devise development strategies appropriate for urban populations.

During the remainder of the conference, participants examined the particular situations of youth in Thailand, the Philippines, and Indonesia. Panelists emphasized the roles of civil society and government in devising strategies for improving the lives of youth in Southeast Asia, but noted that the inclusion of youth themselves in the process was of the utmost importance. In the case of Thailand, participants agreed that the theoretical framework for improving the lives of youth already exists. Dr. Vitit Muntarbhorn, of Chulalongkorn University, and Senator Prateep Ungsongtham Hata both noted that the Thai constitution contains provisions guaranteeing the right to education until 12 years of age, banning forced labor, and obligating the state to protect children against violence.

Senator Unsongtham Hata also noted that the National Council for Child and Youth Development was established in 1985, linking government to nongovernmental organizations to better coordinate policies of youth organizations. And yet, Dr. Vitit argued that the recent implementation of violent methods of drug enforcement laws as well as the persistence of human trafficking, sexual abuse, and domestic violence has made conflict all too common. In combating such conflict, Dr. Vitit underscored the importance of after school activities and educational curricula that focus on tolerance.

Father Joseph Maier, of the Human Development Foundation in Bangkok, explained that one of the principal problems for youth is the negative impact of adults on many of their lives. In the eyes of many children living in slums, adults are the root of their problems. Additionally, many children view education not as a gateway to a better life but instead as an additional means of adult control. Improving intergenerational trust and combating sexual and physical abuse are vital to improving the lives of these youth, Father Maier maintained. Additionally, providing decent compensation to educators, and formulating curricula that correspond to youth needs are vital to their success, noted Dr. Bhichit Rattakul, former governor of Bangkok. Dr. Rattakul also emphasized the need to provide avenues for recreation through the construction of sports facilities and the establishment of better after-school programs.

Amina Rasul-Bernardo, of the Magbassa Kita Foundation, argued that the Philippines have been headlined in the media as a hostile environment for youth. She noted that majority Muslim metropolitan areas are growing faster than metro

Manila and that poverty rates in Muslim communities are significantly higher than in non-Muslim communities. In many areas, then, youth have the choice between becoming engines of progress or joining insurgency groups. The challenge is not only to alleviate poverty for youth but to ensure that they feel included in community development and feel a sense of commitment to their communities. The greatest challenge, not surprisingly, is to reach those sections of the population who live outside of formal social structures, including victims of sexual and physical abuse, street children, and out of school youth.

Felicitas Rixhon, of the Consuelo Foundation, emphasized integrated basic and technical education as a means for improving the life chances of youth. By providing livelihoods for youth, such education programs can greatly reduce the risk of conflict among out of school youth. Angela Desiree Aguirre, of the Ateneo de Manila University, confirmed that according to a series of youth surveys, education, protection, and livelihood were top concerns among youth populations.

In Indonesia, unclear mandates relating to youth at different levels of government remain an obstacle to effective youth programming, according to Dr. Bakti Setiawan of Gadjah Mada University. Dr. Setiawan argued that unless agencies and nongovernmental organizations coordinate better and emphasize capacity building for local institutions, they would be hard-pressed to improve youth programming.

Particularly, he noted that food insecurity, child abuse, human trafficking, high dropout rates, and high rates of child labor remain serious areas of concern in Indonesia. Linking youth to their communities is indeed vital to preventing conflict. In a case study of Jatinangor, a region to which the government relocated a number of educational institutions, Dr. Teti Armiati Argo, of the Bandung Institute of Technology, noted the power of youth to improve a city's environment. In Jatinangor, youth see themselves as true agents of change. The emergence of youth organizations, she argued, was an attempt by students to improve relations between the intellectual communities of the universities in Jatinangor and the local community. These youth serve as a symbol of the potential for youth involvement to improve community relations.

Throughout the two-day conference, participants contended that youth they need to be involved much more in the development process. By working with youth to enable them to articulate their needs more effectively, development practitioners can improve the quality of services for youth. This requires establishing intergenerational trust, improving adult-child relations, and providing youth with education that includes a "skills for life" curriculum.

3

Singapore in Southeast Asia

Singapore officially the Republic of Singapore, is an island city-state located at the southern tip of the Malay Peninsula, lying 137 kilometres (85 mi) north of the equator, south of the Malaysian state of Johor and north of Indonesia's Riau Islands. At 710.2 km (274.2 sq mi), Singapore, a microstate and the smallest nation in Southeast Asia, is by orders of magnitude larger than Monaco, San Marino, Andorra and Vatican City, the only other surviving sovereign city-states. Before European settlement, the island now known as Singapore was the site of a Malay fishing village at the mouth of the Singapore River. Several hundred indigenous Orang Laut people also lived along the nearby coast, rivers and on smaller islands.

In 1819, the British East India Company, led by Sir Stamford Raffles, established a trading post on the island, which was used as a port along the spice route. Singapore became one of the most important commercial and military centers of the British Empire, and the hub of British power in Southeast Asia. During the Second World War, the British colony was occupied by the Japanese after the Battle of Singapore, which Winston Churchill called "Britain's greatest defeat". Singapore reverted to British rule in 1945, immediately after the war. Eighteen years later in 1963, the city, having achieved independence from Britain, merged with Malaya, Sabah, and Sarawak to form Malaysia.

However, the merger proved unsuccessful, and, less than two years later, it seceded from the federation and became an independent republic within the Commonwealth of Nations on August 9, 1965. Singapore was admitted to the United Nations on September 21 of that year. Since independence, Singapore's standard of living has risen dramatically. Foreign direct investment and a state-led drive to industrialization based on plans drawn up by the Dutch economist Albert Winsemius have created a modern economy focused on industry, education and urban planning. Singapore is the 5th wealthiest country in the world in terms of GDP (PPP) per capita. In December 2008, the foreign exchange reserves of this small island nation stood at around US$174.2billion. The Singapore government had for the first time in history tapped into her official reserves and withdrew some S$4.9 billion with the approval of the President.

The funds were then used as part of the S$20.5 billion resilience package unveiled by Finance Minister Tharman Shanmugaratnam on 5 February 2009. As of January 2009, Singapore's official reserves stand at US$170.3 billion. In 2009, the Economist Intelligence Unit ranked Singapore the tenth most expensive city in the world in which to live-the third in Asia, after Tokyo and Osaka. The population of Singapore is approximately 4.86 million. Singapore is highly cosmopolitan and diverse with Chinese people forming an ethnic majority with large populations of Malay, Indian and other people. English, Malay, Tamil, and Chinese are the official languages.

Singapore is a parliamentary republic, and the Constitution of Singapore establishes representative democracy as the nation's political system. The People's Action Party (PAP) dominates the political process and has won control of Parliament in every election since self-government in 1959. At different times in its history, Singapore has been a hub for the region. From the 7th to the 10th century, Temasek, as Singapore was then known, was a prosperous trading outpost of the Buddhist Srivijaya kingdom in Sumatra, welcoming traders from as far afield as India and China. Then, in the 11th century, the Hindu Majapahit Empire, centered in Java, supplanted Srivijaya. But Temasek continued in its role as an emporium for the region.

However, from the 13th century, Singapore was overshadowed by the rise of the Malacca Sultanate, and then lapsed into obscurity after the Portuguese defeated the Malacca Sultanate. It became what many writers have described as a "sleepy fishing village". Singapore's fortunes revived with its founding in 1819 by Stamford Raffles of the East India Company. It grew into an entrêpot and a centre, not just for the vast India-China trade, but also for trade within Southeast Asia. This upward trajectory, only interrupted by the Second World War, has continued to this day. What does Singapore's history tell us? Is it our destiny to be a trading hub? Indeed, in its long transition from a trading outpost of Srivijaya, to the modern metropolis of today, Singapore has been most successful when it made its living by connecting businessmen and traders, countries and regions.

But I would not be too quick to conclude that it is Singapore's *raison d'etre* to be a hub. It is not hard to imagine Singapore before Raffles, a lazy tropical island, where there was nothing much to do except to find enough food for the family. Meanwhile, the greater drama surged around. The British and the Dutch jostled for control of the trade routes that lapped past the shores of Singapore, trade that made the wealth of nations, and upon which empires were built.

That Singapore today is a vital modern metropolis and a vibrant hub is neither fated, nor pre-ordained. I would argue that if not for a bit of luck, and an act of political will, we would have remained a "sleepy fishing village", an obscure island at the tip of the Malayan peninsula. It was a stroke of luck that Raffles saw a potential in the "sleepy fishing village" of Singapore that others had overlooked. It was the political will of the first generation of leaders that wrested Singapore from an uncertain future at independence and transformed it into the success story of today.

BEING A HUB

Singapore as a hub in today's globalised world is much more than just a trading outpost or an entrêpot.

AIR HUB

Singapore is one of the three most important centers of global air travel today. Five of the world's ten fastest growing long-haul routes go through Singapore. Singapore is second only to London, which accounts for six of the top ten routes, while Dubai is number three, with two routes. For Singapore, this meant that at the end of last year (2005), 83 airlines operated more than 3,950 weekly scheduled flights, connecting Singapore to 179 cities in 57 countries around the world. In 2004, over 30 million passengers passed through Changi Airport. In 2004, Changi Airport handled 1.78 million tonnes of air cargo, retaining its pole position in Southeast Asia. But this is achieved not only because of Singapore's excellent air connectivity. It also depends on the presence of world-class specialist logistics providers in Singapore. This has led to success in most unexpected areas.

Singapore is one of the world's largest exporters of cut orchids. It is an irony, because we do not grow orchids in any quantity in Singapore. But we have the scientific know-how to develop attractive hybrids here. The hybrids are grown in Pulau Bulan to the south, and then brought back to Singapore, cut and packaged to be flown fresh to destinations around the world. We overcame our physical limitations by leveraging on both our connectivity as well as on other parts of the value chain, including our knowledge of the business of growing orchids and the market for cut orchids.

Similarly, Singapore is also the largest exporter of live tropical fish in the world, more than twice that of Malaysia, and more than three times our third closest competitor, Japan. We pack the fish into plastic bags, load them on aircraft, and fly them out fast enough so that they reach their destinations in Europe and the United States, perhaps a bit groggy, but still alive. Being connected is a necessary - but not sufficient - condition to be a hub. In the two examples of orchids and tropical fish, without efficient logistics operations here, it would not be possible to deliver orchids fresh, and tropical fish live.

SEA HUB

Let us now look at the Port of Singapore, which traces its pedigree to Raffle's East India Company. Today, PSA operates the world's largest transshipment hub. In 2005, its terminals in Singapore handled a record 23 million TEUs, overtaking Hong Kong as the busiest container port in the world. Singapore also continues as the world's busiest port in terms of shipping tonnage. It is connected to 600 ports in 123 countries. 200 shipping lines operate out of Singapore. This high level of connectivity means that it is more economical to transship through Singapore than to ship direct to India. So containers from Europe bound for India are first shipped to Singapore, and then transshipped back to India, retracing their path through the Malacca Straits.

How did Singapore grow from a hub for the India-China trade in the 19th century to become the world's busiest container port? Some would say it was serendipity, because someone - Mr Howe Yoon Chong, then chairman of PSA - was prepared to make a strategic bet, against the advice of the professionals, to build Singapore's first container terminal, at a time when containers had yet to establish a dominant position in shipping. His strategic bet gave Singapore first mover advantage. With the first container terminal in the region, the main lines began to ship containers to and from Singapore. New regional container lines emerged to connect Singapore to smaller ports in the region. A whole new business in port and container operations was built in the region, centered on Singapore. But as containers transformed the global maritime trade, our neighbours began to catch up.

They developed their own container ports. However, PSA continued to enjoy significant advantages over other ports in the region. It could turn around a large container ship within twenty four hours. Indeed, many ships came to Singapore to make up for time lost in delays in other ports. Singapore's connections were unmatched anywhere else in the region. So PSA reasoned that it would be hard to dislodge Singapore from its dominant position in the container shipping business.

Port of Tanjong Pelepas, a "green field" project built at the south-western tip of Johor, launched a plan to take on PSA.

The drama that would be played out between PSA and PTP hinged on competition between PSA's established and entrenched business model of common-user terminals versus PTP's new insurgent business model of dedicated terminals. Very briefly, any shipping line can use a common-user terminal, with the terminal operator guaranteeing berths on demand and turn-around time. In contrast, a dedicated terminal would be for the sole use of one shipping line and its associates, and would be operated by the shipping line itself.

PSA felt that its connectivity, efficiency and productivity were enough to keep the main lines anchored in Singapore. But Maersk, the largest container line in the world, pulled out from Singapore in 2000 and shifted to PTP to operate its own dedicated terminals. In 2002, Evergreen, the world's fourth largest container line, followed suit. Thereafter, PSA did the right thing. It took a hard look at the assumptions underpinning its business model, re-structured and re-organised, and Singapore is today the busiest container port in the world – at least for now.

A HYPERCOMPETITIVE WORLD

What does this episode tell us? Our competition is fast catching up. Each year, it gets more difficult for Changi Airport to stay number one, and for Singapore to remain the busiest port. There are many lessons to be learnt, but the most important one is that we cannot assume that our position at the top is unassailable. That Singapore once was a hub, that it is a hub, guarantees us nothing in the long term. We must always look over our shoulder. We must always assume that the competition will find ways to overtake us. So we must always look for new ways of doing things, and of doing things better, in order to stay ahead of the competition. As Andy Grove, one of the founders of Intel wrote, "Only the paranoid survive."

Many ask why we should worry if we are not number one. Why not be satisfied with being number two or number three? I believe that if we accept being second best, then we would have lost the will to be the best that we can be. It is our collective will as a nation to excel that has given us a large competitive advantage. But it is more than that. To stay ahead of the competition, it is not enough to just be excellent in what we do, or to work hard, or to be more efficient. These are important. But it is just as important that we are able and willing to think boldly and imaginatively. That is how Singapore became the dominant container port in the region, because Mr Howe was prepared to think out of the box, and to even go against the advice of his professionals.

If we continue to do the same things we are doing today, we risk getting stuck in a rut. Plans and policies that have worked well for us in the past will not guarantee success in a fast-changing and uncertain future. As China, India, Vietnam and others in Asia boom, our relevance as a transshipment hub could diminish as shipping lines find it more attractive to ship containers direct to their ultimate destinations. It is no longer a question of whether the ports of Shanghai or Shenzhen will overtake our port as the world's busiest. It is a question of when. And this may happen sooner than we think. This is what almost happened to PSA when it failed to imagine that a different business model by an untested challenger could succeed.

As Asian economies grow, so too will the competition for scarce resources, foreign investments and global talent. This has profound implications for Singapore. Our economy has relied heavily on trade and foreign direct investments (FDI). Indeed we are critically dependent on trade. Singapore has the world's highest trade dependency ratio in the world today, with the value of trade almost four times our GDP. In the growing competition for FDI, it is not just China and India that are opening up their economies and attracting foreign investors. Small economies with low corporate tax rates, from Ireland to Slovakia, have boomed in recent years thanks to large inflows of FDI. In such an environment, the economic formula that has brought us success for the last forty years will not be enough going forward.

What worked well for us in the past – open markets, external orientation, low taxes, attracting FDI, good infrastructure, trained workforce – are still necessary. But they are no longer as compelling and distinctive value propositions as before, because others are replicating these strategies. This is not to say that we should do not do everything in our power to maintain FDI inflows. Or that we give up our status as a transshipment hub without a fight. But we must also be prepared for a world in which these are no longer adequate to generate enough jobs and to raise living standards for Singaporeans. We have to make a far more purposeful effort in finding other sources of growth for Singapore.

A GLOBAL SHIFT IN POWER

History does not move along a straight line, but often in a series of rapid, discontinuous changes. Globalisation and technological change, the conservative reactions against these forces, and the conflicts they generate - all these are producing a more complex, uncertain and volatile world than ever before. What has worked well in the past - in the world of business or in the art of government -- are no longer an adequate guide for the future. They may even be obstacles to continued success, especially if they blind us to new possibilities, or lock us into fixed mental models and ways of doing things. Certainly, the world in ten to fifteen years from now will be radically different from today. The parallel rise of two ancient civilisations - of China and India - is unprecedented in history. Their simultaneous rise will herald a global shift in political and economic power.

By 2025, China will be the second largest economy in the world. India's economy will rival that of Germany's. Will we be able to position Singapore at the centre of tomorrow's China-India trade, just as Raffles did two centuries ago, or will that trade bypass us, as it did before Singapore's founding by Raffles? This shift in economic power will be accompanied by shifts in cultural influence. The world will no longer see things solely through Western or American lenses. Much of the Middle East already get its news from al-Jazeera (based in Qatar) and al-Arabiyya (based in Dubai), not CNN or BBC. Indians around the world are entertained by Bollywood, not Hollywood. Indeed Bollywood produces more films each year than Hollywood. In China, the Internet flourishes in Chinese. Even Google plays by the rules of the Chinese government. These trends reflect huge shifts. How do we tap into them, and what is the price that we will pay if we fail to do so?

Another issue that has assumed greater importance is energy. The era of cheap oil at US$25 per barrel is over. Today, oil at US$75 per barrel is the new reality. Some even predict that oil prices may shoot up to US$100 per barrel. A confluence of factors have led to this situation, namely, rising demand for energy, particularly from developing economies in Asia, especially China and India; the lack of spare capacity to meet this growing demand; and a spate of natural disasters and political instability in oil producing countries. Any further instability in the Middle East, such as Iraq and Iran, will further roil already volatile energy markets. Countries like China, India and Japan are already searching for alternative supplies of oil in places like Central Asia, Latin America and Africa, as well as alternative fuels like natural gas in Southeast Asia.

The fear that the "winner takes all" has prompted a new scramble for energy. The quest for energy has become enmeshed in the foreign policy goals of many countries. It has also given rise to greater interest in renewable energy, such as bio-fuels like ethanol and bio-diesel, as well as nuclear energy. What are the implications for Singapore, which imports all its energy needs? How will this affect Singapore's position as the third largest oil refining centre in the world?

OUR STRATEGIC RESPONSE

We are standing at an inflexion point, beyond which the changes I speak about will accelerate and transform the geo-strategic landscape in unrecognisable ways that we cannot fully predict. While we may not have formulated a complete set of strategies to replace the existing ones, that is no reason for inaction. Rather than planning exhaustively for every contingency before we move, we should adopt a "search and discover" approach: to act now before the window closes and to act boldly in areas where we sense opportunities. We must be prepared to experiment, even if we cannot be entirely certain of the outcome.

In the complex, even chaotic, space, the approach is to probe, sense patterns, and to act, even in the absence of complete information. The biggest failure will be the failure to act, because we fear to fail. We must learn not to operate in a "fail-safe" mode, but instead to operate in a "safe-fail" mode. This is the objective of World Singapore - a strategic response by the Public Service to a rapidly changing environment, and an uncertain world. Many of you would already have heard about World Singapore, or are participating in the 19 cross-agency action teams that have been set up. But first let me first explain why we chose World Singapore as the umbrella tagline for this strategic response. I started off my remarks by discussing Singapore's position as a regional and global hub.

While I argued that it is not Singapore's destiny to be a hub, I also argued that Singapore's success has depended critically on being connected to the rest of the world. If anything at all, it is Singapore's destiny to be the eponymous little red dot that former Indonesian President Habibie once described us as. Our strategic response to the limitations of our physical size can be either resignation, in which case we will revert to being a "sleepy fishing village", or to develop approaches that can create space for us in the strategic, political and economic domains. This means connecting Singapore to the rest of the world. Hence, there are rich meanings that we can associate with World Singapore, which include:

- The World in Singapore
- The World for Singapore
- The World with Singapore
- The World hubbed in Singapore
- The World trusts Singapore
- The World connected through Singapore

- The World finds opportunity in Singapore
- The World innovates in Singapore

And conversely:

- Singapore in the world
- Singapore networked with the world
- Singapore as a key node in the world
- Singapore leads the world
- Singapore finds opportunity in the world
- Singapore innovates for the world
- Singapore benchmarks for the world

These meanings reflect the key ideas in World Singapore that I will discuss further: trust, knowledge, connected. Finally, although we do not speak the little red dot that connects the World and Singapore, it is a subliminal reminder that we are indeed a little dot in a much larger region and an even larger world. That we operate in a much larger strategic, political and economic space than our physical size reminds us that it is going to be a constant struggle to maintain our position and to stay ahead. If we accept that geography is fate, then we will in the long term revert to a "sleepy fishing village".

The World Singapore strategy is based on three key ideas - Trust, Knowledge and Connected. These are the "horizontals" or cross-sector attributes from which we seek to derive new competitive advantages. Collectively, they constitute a "blue ocean" strategy to propel Singapore into uncontested market space. I will speak briefly on each of them.

TRUST

First, Trust. Singapore has established itself as trusted reference for many. The competition for the Next Generation Fighter for the RSAF was bitter, not because we were buying hundreds of aircraft, but because MINDEF has established a strong international reputation for its objective and professional procurement decisions. The French describe Singapore as "the customer of reference". Our decision would be the blue ribbon, the seal of approval, which the winning company could use to market their aircraft to other governments. Similarly in the civil sector, companies like Boeing and Airbus vie for Singapore Airlines' business because they know that a purchase by the SIA will be seen as an endorsement of quality. So when SIA bought the Boeing 787 Dream liners, Boeing stock rose.

Then SIA threw a lifeline to Airbus when it selected the A350 as well. Our trustworthiness, reliability and credibility can create real economic value for other companies. The question is how we can leverage on our reputation to create value for Singapore? For example, we are a trusted location for Business Process Outsourcing (BPO) because, even though we cost 30% more, our laws offer good protection to these MNCs. In the public sector, our agencies receive numerous requests from foreign governments keen to tap into our skills. In the last three years, we received more than 100 enquiries.

These were just not for training or consultancy. The Qatari government wanted our entire corps of water engineers from PUB to work on its water infrastructure. To capitalise on these opportunities, we will need to re-orientate our public service to find a balance between our domestic missions and the external opportunities that come our way. We will also have to make some trade-offs if we want to make a name for Singapore in high-quality and high-trust services and products. We may need for instance to moderate our traditional focus on keeping costs low and emphasise instead the quality and value-add of our services.

KNOWLEDGE

The second element is knowledge. Over the years, Singapore has built up stores of capabilities in both the private sector as well as in the public sector. We are now channelling more resources into R&D to generate new, commercially valuable intellectual property. We will need to be adept at transforming our knowledge into services and products that are commercially valuable and exportable. To attract talent and facilitate innovation, we will also need to increase our connectivity to other knowledge networks and enhance intellectual diversity in Singapore. This requires us to be ready to accept greater diversity of views, and manage the tensions that would inevitably arise. Increasingly, it will not be realistic to ask people to be innovative only in the "economic arena" and ask them not to apply the same sensibilities to social and political issues.

CONNECTED

The last element - "Connected" - may present the greatest challenge to the pragmatic and hard-headed civil servant in all of us. Connected is not just about connectivity. While Trust is why people will consider Singapore and Knowledge the reason why they will do business with us, we also need people who will walk with us. We need to build up a base of fans and friends worldwide that will be advocates for us and support us. This way, we have not just 4 million citizens but 20 million citizens, fans and friends. Do not misunderstand me. I am not saying that we will have 20 million citizens, fans and friends of Singapore. What I am saying is that Singapore can amplify its voice, its influence, and grow its space, if we can leverage on people and organisations around the world that are friends and fans of Singapore.

To achieve this, we have to move beyond the functional and utilitarian, into the emotive and cultural. We need to take a more coherent and deliberate effort to manage our national brand. But more than branding, we must be prepared to seek real changes in strategy and policy. This means making a sustained effort to build and maintain links with people who have studied, worked or lived here. It also means changes in our education system to develop a more international and cosmopolitan outlook among our young. It may even mean playing a more active role towards humanitarian causes in the region.

AN EXPERIMENT IN GOVERNMENT STRUCTURE

World Singapore is a strategic public service initiative of great significance for Singapore's future. At the same time, it is an experiment in networked government. As the action areas under World Singapore generally do not fall neatly within single ministries or agencies, most of you will know that 19 cross-agency action teams have been formed to develop strategies, and drive implementation. The teams will be able to apply for their own funding since some of their work will cut across different agencies.

Officers in these teams will be appraised and recognized for their contributions to this inter-agency work. They will continue to be involved even if they are posted to other public agencies. To me, these teams represent a new way to pursue national priorities that cut across multiple agencies. Executed well, they help break down organisational boundaries and give us the flexibility and agility that few governments can achieve, in effect creating a new comparative advantage for Singapore.

BEHAVIOURAL CHANGE AND MINDSET CHANGE

Beyond new strategies and structures, World Singapore will demand new ways of thinking and operating on the part of public servants. Going forward, the PS21 movement will be re-oriented to bring about the mindset shifts and develop the organisational capacities in our public service to support World Singapore. First, the public service will need to go beyond our traditional focus on problem-solving to adopt a mindset of identifying and seizing opportunities that create new value for Singapore.

Second, we will have to look beyond the domestic arena and think globally. Our officers need to anticipate change from a global perspective. Our systems and processes must allow us to seize global opportunities. We need to create services that look to the world as our customers. But it is not enough just to think globally.

We must also add a global dimension to our work. Some agencies have always had such a global dimension, for example, IES and EDB. However, in this new connected world of World Singapore, we need to act to get a place in the global space. Although operating domestically, there are many agencies that have put us on the global map. They should think and act globally to extend that reputation earned locally.

PSA as a good example of an organisation that now has extensive overseas operations which they did not have in the past by leveraging on its strong domestic position. Other agencies can follow this path. If we build a great global garden city, we can also market both this brand and expertise overseas. Third, we also need to move beyond being efficient in implementation towards being more flexible, more nimble, with a strong bias for action. The key to seizing new opportunities and first mover advantage hinges on whether we as a public service have the capacity and flexibility to change, re-organize and move quickly from ideas to action.

And lastly, we must move beyond the effectiveness of individual agencies to develop the ability to operate in an integrated manner. World Singapore as a strategy is only possible if all agencies act in concert. These new thrusts for PS21 are foundational to the success of the 19 action areas. Just as we are formulating new growth strategies for Singapore, we must in tandem develop the capacity for change and transform ourselves into a leading Public Service, one that pro-actively drives the success of World Singapore.

World Singapore is a call to action. In his play, Julius Caesar, Shakespeare penned these famous lines that could be a rallying cry for World Singapore:

"There is a tide in the affairs of men

Which, taken at the flood, leads on to fortune;

Omitted, all the voyage of their life

Is bound in shallows and in miseries.

On such a full sea are we now afloat,

And we must take the current when it serves

Or lose our ventures."

Strong backing from you and your colleagues will be critical to the success of World Singapore. On 29 January 1819,

Sir Thomas Stamford Raffles landed on the main island. Spotting its potential as a strategic geographical trading post in Southeast Asia, Raffles signed a treaty with Sultan Hussein Shah on behalf of the British East India Company on 6 February 1819 to develop the southern part of Singapore as a British trading post and settlement. Until August 1824, Singapore was still a territory controlled by a Malay Sultan. Singapore only officially became a British colony in August 1824 when the British extended control over the whole island.

John Crawfurd, the second resident of Singapore, was the one who officially made Singapore a British possession. He signed a treaty with Sultan Hussein Shah on 2 August 1824 in which the Sultan and the Temmenggong handed over the whole island to the British East India Company thus marking the start of the island's modern era. Raffles's deputy, William Farquhar, oversaw a period of growth and ethnic migration, which was largely spurred by a no-restriction immigration policy. The British India office governed the island from 1858, but Singapore was made a British crown colony in 1867, answerable directly to the Crown. By 1869, 100,000 lived on the island.

The early onset of town planning in colonial Singapore came largely through a "divide and rule" framework where the different ethnic groups were settled in different parts of the South of the island. The Singapore River was largely a commercial area that was dominated by traders and bankers of various ethnic groups with mostly Chinese and Indian coolies working to load and unload goods from barge boats known locally as "bumboats". The Malays, consisting of the local "Orang Lauts" who worked mostly as fishermen and seafarers, and Arab traders and scholars were mostly found in the South-east part of the river mouth, where Kampong Glam stands today.

The European settlers, who were few then, settled around Fort Canning Hill and further upstream from the Singapore River. Like the Europeans, the early Indian migrants also settled more inland of the Singapore River, where Little India stands today. Very little is known about the rural private settlements in those times (known as *kampongs*) other than the major move by the post-independent Singapore government to re-settle these residents in the late 1960s.

WORLD WAR II

Years before the rise of the Japanese, the British noted that Japan was building its forces rapidly. Wanting to protect its assets in Southeast Asia, the British decided to build a naval base on the Northern end of Singapore. However, due to the war with Germany, all warships and war equipment were brought over to Europe. During World War II, the Imperial Japanese Army invaded Malaya, culminating in the Battle of Singapore. The ill-prepared British, with most of their forces in Europe, were defeated in six days, and surrendered the supposedly impregnable fortress to General Tomoyuki Yamashita on 15 February 1942.

The surrender was described by British Prime Minister Sir Winston Churchill as "the worst disaster and largest capitulation in British history." The British naval base was destroyed before the Japanese could take over the base and make use of it. Widespread indiscriminate killing of the Chinese population occurred. The Japanese renamed Singapore *Shônantô*, from Japanese "Shôwa no jidai ni eta minami no shima", or "southern island obtained in the age of Shôwa", and occupied it until the British repossessed the island on 12 September 1945, a month after the Japanese surrender. The name Shônantô was, at the time, romanised as "Syonan-to" or "Syonan", which means "Light of the South".

INDEPENDENCE

Following the war, the British government allowed Singapore to hold its first general election, in 1955, which was won by a pro-independence candidate, David Marshall. Singapore soon became a self-governing state within the British Empire in 1959 with Yusof bin Ishak as its first *Yang di-Pertuan Negara* or president, and Lee Kuan Yew as its first Prime Minister. It declared independence from Britain unilaterally in August 1963, before joining the Federation of Malaysia in

September along with Malaya, Sabah and Sarawak as the result of the 1962 Merger Referendum of Singapore. Singapore left the federation two years after heated ideological conflict between the state's PAP government and the federal Kuala Lumpur government. Singapore officially gained sovereignty on 9 August 1965. Yusof bin Ishak was sworn in as the first President of Singapore and Lee Kuan Yew remained prime minister.

While trying to be self-sufficient, the fledging nation faced problems like mass unemployment, housing shortages, and a dearth of land and natural resources. During Lee Kuan Yew's term as prime minister from 1959 to 1990, his administration tackled the problem of widespread unemployment, raised the standard of living, and implemented a large-scale public housing programme. It was during this time that the foundation of the country's economic infrastructure was developed; the threat of racial tension was curbed; and an independent national defence system centering on compulsory male military service was created. In 1990, Goh Chok Tong succeeded Lee as Prime Minister. During his tenure, the country faced the 1997 Asian Financial Crisis, the 2003 SARS outbreak, and terrorist threats posed by Jemaah Islamiyah after the September 11 attacks in the United States. In 2004, Lee Hsien Loong, the eldest son of Lee Kuan Yew, became the third prime minister. Amongst his more notable decisions is the plan to open casinos to attract tourism.

GOVERNMENT AND POLITICS

Singapore is a parliamentary democracy with a Westminster system of unicameral parliamentary government representing different constituencies. The bulk of the executive powers rest with the Cabinet, headed by the Prime Minister, currently Mr Lee Hsien Loong. The office of President of Singapore, historically a ceremonial one, was granted some veto powers as of 1991 for a few key decisions such as the use of the national reserves and the appointment of judiciary positions. Although the position is to be elected by popular vote, only the 1993 election has been contested to date. The legislative branch of government is the Parliament.

Parliamentary elections in Singapore are plurality-based for group representation constituencies since the Parliamentary Elections Act was modified in 1991.

The Members of Parliament (MPs) consist of either elected, non-constituency or nominated Members. The majority of the Members of Parliament is elected into Parliament at a General Election on a first-past-the-post basis and represents either Single Member or Group Representation Constituencies (GRCs). The elected Members of Parliament act as a bridge between the community and the Government by ensuring that the concerns of their constituents are heard in the Parliament. The present Parliament has 94 Members of Parliament consisting of 84 elected Members of Parliament, one NCMP and nine Nominated members of Parliament.

The People's Action Party (PAP) has been the ruling party in Singapore since self-government was attained. There are several opposition parties in Singapore, the most notable being the Workers' Party of Singapore, the Singapore Democratic Party (SDP) and the Singapore Democratic Alliance (SDA). The Economist Intelligence Unit describes Singapore as a "hybrid regime" of democratic and authoritarian elements. Freedom House ranks the country as "partly free". Although general elections are free from irregularities and vote rigging, the PAP has been criticized by some for manipulating the political system through its use of censorship, gerrymandering, and civil libel suits against opposition politicians. Singapore has a successful and transparent market economy. Government-linked companies are dominant in various sectors of the local economy, such as media, utilities, and public transport. Singapore has consistently been rated as the least corrupt country in Asia and among the world's ten most free from corruption by Transparency International.

Although Singapore's laws are inherited from English and British Indian laws, and includes many elements of English common law, the government has also chosen not to follow some elements of liberal democratic values. There are no jury trials and there are laws restricting the freedom of speech that may breed ill will or cause disharmony within Singapore's multiracial, multi-religious society. Criminal activity is often punished with heavy penalties including heavy fines or caning and there are laws which allow capital punishment in Singapore for first-degree murder and drug trafficking. The Singapore government argues that Singapore has the sovereign right to determine its own judicial system and impose what it sees as an appropriate punishment, including capital punishment for the most serious crimes.

GEOGRAPHY AND CLIMATE

Singapore consists of 63 islands, including mainland Singapore. There are two man-made connections to Johor, Malaysia - Johor-Singapore Causeway in the north, and Tuas Second Link in the west. Jurong Island, Pulau Tekong, Pulau Ubin and Sentosa are the largest of Singapore's many smaller islands. The highest natural point of Singapore is Bukit Timah Hill at 166 m (545 ft). The south of Singapore, around the mouth of the Singapore River and what is now the Downtown Core, used to be the only concentrated urban area, while the rest of the land was either undeveloped tropical rainforest or used for agriculture. Since the 1960s, the government has constructed new residential towns in outlying areas, resulting in an entirely built-up urban landscape. The Urban Redevelopment Authority was established on 1 April 1974, responsible for urban planning.

Singapore has on-going land reclamation projects with earth obtained from its own hills, the seabed, and neighbouring countries. As a result, Singapore's land area grew from 581.5 km (224.5 sq mi) in the 1960s to 704 km (271.8 sq mi) today, and may grow by another 100 km^2 (38.6 sq mi) by 2030. The projects sometimes involve some of the smaller islands being merged together through land reclamation in order to form larger, more functional islands, such as in the case of Jurong Island. Under the Köppen climate classification system, Singapore has a tropical rainforest climate with no distinctive seasons. Its climate is characterized by uniform temperature and pressure, high humidity, and abundant rainfall.

Temperatures range from 22 °C to 34 °C (72° to 93 °F). On average, the relative humidity is around 90% in the morning and 60% in the afternoon. During prolonged heavy rain, relative humidity often reaches 100%. The lowest and highest temperatures recorded in its maritime history are 19.4 °C (66.9 °F) and 35.8 °C (96.4 °F) respectively. June and July are the hottest months, while November and December make up the wetter monsoon season. From August to October, there is often haze, sometimes severe enough to prompt public health warnings, due to bushfires in neighbouring Indonesia. Singapore does not observe daylight saving time or a summer time zone change.

The length of the day is nearly constant year round due to the country's location near the equator. About 23% of Singapore's land area consists of forest and nature reserves. Urbanisation has eliminated many areas of former primary rainforest, with the only remaining area of primary rainforest being Bukit Timah Nature Reserve. A variety of parks are maintained with human intervention, such as the Singapore Botanic Gardens.

ECONOMY

Singapore has a highly developed market-based economy, which has historically revolved around extended entrepôt trade, in other words an export driven economy hugely dependant on export of goods to other countries. Along with Hong Kong, South Korea and Taiwan, Singapore is one of the Four Asian Tigers. The economy depends heavily on exports and refining imported goods, especially in manufacturing. This explains why the country is faring so badly in the current recession scenario. Manufacturing constituted 26% of Singapore's GDP in 2005. The manufacturing industry is well-diversified with significant electronics, petroleum refining, chemicals, mechanical engineering and biomedical sciences manufacturing sectors.

In 2006, Singapore produced about 10% of the world's foundry wafer output. Singapore has one of the busiest ports in the world and is the world's fourth largest foreign exchange trading centre after London, New York City and Tokyo. Singapore has been rated as the most business-friendly economy in the world, with thousands of foreign expatriates working in multi-national corporations. Singapore is also considered to be one of the top centers of finance in the region and the world. In addition to this, the city-state also employs tens of thousands of foreign blue-collared workers from around the world. As a result of a global recession and a slump in the technology sector, the country's GDP contracted 2.2% in 2001.

The Economic Review Committee (ERC) was set up in December 2001, and recommended several policy changes with a view to revitalising the economy. Singapore has since recovered from the recession, largely due to improvements in the world economy; the Singaporean economy grew by 8.3% in 2004, 6.4% in 2005 and 7.9% in 2006. On 19 August 2007, Prime Minister Lee Hsien Loong announced in his National Day Rally Speech that Singapore's economy is expected to grow by at least 4-6% annually over the next 5–10 years. The per capita GDP in 2006 was US$29,474. As of September 2007, the unemployment rate is 1.7%, which is the lowest in a decade, having improved to around pre-Asian crisis level.

Employment continued to grow strongly as the economy maintained its rapid expansion. In the first three quarters of 2007, 171,500 new jobs were created, which is close to the figure of 176,000 for the whole of 2006. For the whole of 2007, Singapore's economy grew 7.5% and drew in a record S$16 billion (US$10.6b, €8.3b)of fixed asset investments in manufacturing and projects generating S$3 billion (US$2b, €1.6b) of total business spending in services. Singapore introduced a Goods and Services Tax (GST) with an initial rate of 3% on 1 April 1994 substantially increasing government revenue by S$1.6 billion (US$1b, €800m) and stabilising government finances. The taxable GST was increased to 4% in 2003, to 5% in 2004, and to 7% on 1 July 2007.

Due to the economic recession, Singapore's economy expanded by only 1.1% in year 2008, much lower than the expected 4.5% to 6.5% growth while the unemployment rate was at 2.8%. The economy is expected to contract greatly by up to 8% in 2009 and unemployment could rise to 5% this year as forecast by several private sector economists. The Economic Development Board is a statutory board of the Government of Singapore. It has been tasked to plan and execute strategies to sustain Singapore as a leading global hub for business and investment.

FREE TRADE AGREEMENTS

Singapore has 14 bilateral and multilateral trade agreements worldwide:

- Association of Southeast Asian Nations Free Trade Area (AFTA)
- India (CECA)
- ASEAN-China (ACFTA)
- ASEAN-Korea (AKFTA)
- Australia (SAFTA)
- European Free Trade Association (EFTA: Iceland, Liechtenstein, Norway, Switzerland)
- Jordan (SJFTA)
- Japan (JSEPA)
- New Zealand (ANZSCEP)
- Panama (PSFTA)
- Peru
- South Korea (KSFTA)
- Trans-Pacific Strategic Economic Partnership Agreement (Trans-Pacific SEP: Brunei, New Zealand, Chile, Singapore)
- United States (USSFTA)

TOURISM

Singapore is a popular travel destination, making tourism one of its largest industries. About 7.8 million tourists visited Singapore in 2006. The Orchard Road shopping district is one of Singapore's most well-known and popular tourist draws. To attract more tourists, the government decided to legalize gambling and to allow two casino resorts (euphemistically called Integrated Resorts) to be developed at Marina South and Sentosa in 2005. To compete with regional rivals like Bangkok, Hong Kong, Tokyo and Shanghai, the government has announced that the city area would be transformed into a more exciting place by lighting up the civic and commercial buildings. Cuisine has also been heavily promoted as an attraction for tourists, with the Singapore Food Festival in July organised annually to celebrate Singapore's cuisine.

Singapore is fast positioning itself as a medical tourism hub - about 200,000 foreigners seek medical care in the country each year and Singapore medical services aim to serve one million foreign patients annually by 2012 and generate USD 3 billion in revenue. The government expects that the initiative could create an estimated 13,000 new jobs within the health industries. Under the Infocomm Development Authority of Singapore (IDA), Wireless@SG is a government initiative to build Singapore's infocomm infrastructure. Working through IDA's Call-for-Collaboration, SingTel, iCell and QMax deploy a municipal wireless network throughout Singapore. Since late 2006, users have enjoyed free wireless access through Wi-Fi under the "basic-tier" package offered by all three operators for 3 years.

CURRENCY

The currency of Singapore is the Singapore dollar, represented by the symbol S$ or the abbreviation SGD. The central bank of Singapore is the Monetary Authority of Singapore, responsible for issuing currency. Singapore established the Board of Commissioners of Currency, Singapore, on 7 April 1967 and issued its first coins and notes. The Singapore dollar was exchangeable at par with the Malaysian ringgit until 1973. Interchangeability with the Brunei dollar is still maintained. On 27 June 2007, to commemorate 40 years of currency agreement with Brunei, a commemorative S$20 note was launched; the back is identical to the Bruneian $20 note launched concurrently.

FOREIGN RELATIONS

Singapore maintains diplomatic relations with 175 countries, although it does not maintain a high commission or embassy in many of those countries. It is a member of the United Nations, the Commonwealth, ASEAN and the Non-Aligned Movement. Due to obvious geographical reasons, relations with Malaysia and Indonesia are most important but the domestic politics of the three countries often threatens their relations. On the other hand, Singapore enjoys good relations with many European nations, including France, Germany and the United Kingdom, the latter sharing ties via the Five Power Defence Arrangements (FPDA) along with Malaysia, Australia and New Zealand.

Good relations are also maintained with the United States, a country perceived as a stabilising force in the region to counterbalance the regional powers. Singapore supports the concept of Southeast Asian regionalism and plays an active role in the Association of Southeast Asian Nations (ASEAN), of which Singapore is a founding member. Singapore is also a member of the Asia Pacific Economic Cooperation (APEC) forum, which has its Secretariat in Singapore. Singapore also has close relations with fellow ASEAN nation Brunei and maintains Army training facilities in the Sultanate.

DISPUTES

Singapore has several long-standing disputes with Malaysia over a number of issues:

- Water deliveries to Singapore
- Mutual maritime boundaries
- Air routes between Singapore Changi Airport and Kuala Lumpur International Airport

The dispute over the ownership of Pedra Branca, an outcrop of rocks, was resolved on 24 May 2008 (Singapore time) by the International Court of Justice between Singapore and Malaysia.

- The Singapore island known as Pedra Branca in Singapore and as Pulau Batu Puteh in Malaysia (names mean "White

Rock" in Portuguese and "White Rock Island" in Malay respectively), is located 24 nautical miles (44 km) off the east coast of Singapore with a land area of 2,000 m (2,392 sq yd). The island also comprises Middle Rocks owned by Malaysia which are two clusters of rocks situated 0.6 nmi (1.1 km) south of the main island. Both countries had staked a claim on the island and were unable to settle the dispute themselves. The case was heard at the International Court of Justice in 2007, with both parties presenting their case. The court delivered its judgment on 23 May 2008 with Singapore having ownership of Pedra Branca and Malaysia owning Middle Rocks. Ownership of South Ledge, a nearby rock formation which can be seen only at low tide is still disputed.

- Relocating the Singapore station of Malaysia's Keretapi Tanah Melayu from Tanjong Pagar to Bukit Timah and moving Malaysia's immigration checkpoint from the railway station to the Causeway.
- Not allowing lay off workers, employed in Singapore shipyards in 1998, to receive their Central Provident Funds (CPF) contributions, which are estimated to be RM2.4 billion.

MILITARY

The Ministry of Defence (MINDEF), currently headed by Minister Teo Chee Hean, oversees the Singapore Army, the Republic of Singapore Navy, and the Republic of Singapore Air Force, collectively known as the Singapore Armed Forces, along with volunteer private companies involved in supporting roles. The Chief of Defence Forces is Lieutenant-General Desmond Kuek Bak Chye. The armed forces serve primarily as a deterrent against potential aggressors and also provide humanitarian assistance to other countries. Singapore has mutual defence pacts with several countries, most notably the Five Power Defence Arrangements.

There is an extensive overseas network of training grounds in the United States, Australia, Republic of China

(Taiwan), New Zealand, France, Thailand, Brunei, India and South Africa. Since 1980, the concept and strategy of "Total Defence" has been adopted in all aspects of security; an approach aimed at strengthening Singapore against all kinds of threats. The recent rise in unconventional warfare and terrorism has cast increasing emphasis on non-military aspects of defence. The Gurkha Contingent, part of the Singapore Police Force, is also a counter-terrorist force. In 1991, the hijacking of Singapore Airlines Flight 117 ended in the storming of the aircraft by Singapore Special Operations Force and the subsequent deaths of all four hijackers without injury to either passengers or SOF personnel.

A concern is Jemaah Islamiyah, a militant Islamic group whose plan to attack the Australian High Commission was ultimately foiled in 2001. Singapore's defence resources have been used in international humanitarian aid missions, including United Nations peacekeeping assignments involved in 11 different countries. In September 2005, the Republic of Singapore Air Force (RSAF) sent three CH-47 Chinook helicopters to Louisiana to assist in relief operations for Hurricane Katrina. In the aftermath of the 2004 Asian Tsunami (or Boxing Day Tsunami), the SAF deployed 3 LSTs (Landing Ship Tank), 12 Super Puma and 8 Chinook helicopters to aid in relief operations to the countries that were affected by the tsunami.

SINGAPORE ARMED FORCES

The Singapore Armed Forces, the military forces of Singapore, takes charge of the overall defence of the country. It comprises three branches: the Singapore Army, Republic of Singapore Air Force, and the Republic of Singapore Navy. The Singapore Army is one of the three services of the Singapore Armed Forces. It is headed by the Chief of Army (COA), currently Major General Neo Kian Hong. The Army focuses on leveraging technology and weapon systems as "force-multipliers". It is currently undergoing the transformation into what it terms a "3rd-Generation fighting force". The Republic of Singapore Air Force (RSAF), the air force branch, guards the airspace of Singapore.

The RSAF was established in 1968 as the Singapore Air Defence Command. It operates four air bases in Singapore and operates its aircraft in several overseas locations in order to provide greater exposure to its pilots. The main aircraft found in its fleet include F-16 Fighting Falcons, CH-47 Chinook and C-130 Hercules. The final branch, the Republic of Singapore Navy (RSN), is the navy of the Singapore Armed Forces, responsible for the defence of Singapore against seaborne threats and protection of its sea lines of communications. Operating within the crowded littoral waters of the Singapore Strait, the RSN is regarded as one of the best in the region. The RSN operates from two bases, Tuas Naval Base and Changi Naval Base, and has a large number of vessels, including 4 submarines, 6 frigates, and 4 amphibious transport docks. All commissioned ships of the RSN have a prefix RSS, which means Republic of Singapore Ship.

SINGAPORE POLICE FORCE

The Singapore Police Force (SPF) is the main agency tasked with maintaining law and order in the country. Formerly known as the Republic of Singapore Police, it has grown from an 11-man organisation to a 38,587 strong force. It enjoys a relatively positive public image, and is credited for helping to arrest Singapore's civic unrests and lawlessness in its early years, and maintaining the low crime rate today. The organisation structure of the SPF is split between the staff and line functions, roughly modelled after the military.

There are currently 15 staff departments and 13 line units. The SPF is headquartered in a block at New Phoenix Park in Novena, adjacent to a twin block occupied by the Ministry of Home Affairs. Police officers typically respond to calls in rapid-deployment vehicles known as the Fast Response Car. They have been staunch users of Japanese-made saloon cars since the 1980s for patrol duties, with the mainstay models in use being the various generations of the Mitsubishi Lancers, Mazda 323s, and Toyota Corollas & Subaru Impreza.

SINGAPORE CIVIL DEFENCE FORCE

The Singapore Civil Defence Force (SCDF) is the main agency in charge of the provision of emergency services in

Singapore during peacetime and emergencies. A uniformed organisation under the purview of the Ministry of Home Affairs, the SCDF provides ambulance, fire fighting and emergency response services to the Republic of Singapore. It also plays a major role in the Republic's disaster relief operations. It is branched into 6 Operational and Training Divisions beneath the Headquarters Element. Of these six, four are known as Operational Divisions, also known as Territorial Divisions, and each cover vast sections of Singapore corresponding roughly to the four cardinal points of the compass.

The SCDF maintains a large fleet of custom vehicles, called appliances, to provide an emergency response force capable of mitigating any and all kinds of fires and disasters. Ranging from the generic fire truck and ambulance to more sophisticated mobile command structures and disaster mitigation vehicles of all kinds, many of the appliances were designed and commissioned by the Force itself rather than obtaining ready-made designs from industries.

NATIONAL SERVICE

Singapore legislation requires every able-bodied male Singapore citizen and second-generation permanent resident to undertake National Service for a minimum of 2 years upon reaching 18 years of age or completion of his studies (whichever comes first), with exemption on medical or other grounds. After serving for two years, every male is considered operationally ready, and is liable for reservist national service to the age of 40 (50 for commissioned officers). More than 350,000 men serve as operationally-ready servicemen assigned to reservist combat units, and another 72,500 men form the full-time national service and regular corps.

DEMOGRAPHICS

Population

According to government statistics, the population of Singapore as of 2008 was 4.84 million, of whom 3.64 million were Singaporean citizens and permanent residents (termed "Singapore Residents"). Various Chinese linguistic groups formed 75.2% of Singapore's residents, Malays 13.6%, Indians 8.8%, while Eurasians, Arabs and other groups formed 2.4%. In 2006 the crude birth rate stood at 10.1 per 1000, a very low level attributed to birth control policies, and the crude death rate was also one of the lowest in the world at 4.3 per 1000. The total population growth was 4.4% with Singapore resident's growth at 1.8%. The higher percentage growth rate is largely from net immigration, but also increasing life expectancy.

Singapore is the second-most densely populated independent country in the world after Monaco. In 1957, Singapore's population was approximately 1.45 million, and there was a relatively high birth rate. Aware of the country's extremely limited natural resources and small territory, the government introduced birth control policies in the late 1960s. In the late 1990s, the population was aging, with fewer people entering the labour market and a shortage of skilled workers. In a dramatic reversal of policy, the Singapore government introduced a "baby bonus" scheme in 2001 (enhanced in August 2004) that encouraged couples to have more children.

In 2006, the total fertility rate was only 1.26 children per woman, the 3rd lowest in the world and well below the 2.10 needed to replace the population. In 2006, 38,317 babies were born, compared to around 37,600 in 2005. This number, however, is not sufficient to maintain the population's growth. To overcome this problem, the government is encouraging foreigners to immigrate to Singapore. These large numbers of immigrants have kept Singapore's population from declining.

Religion

Singapore is a multi-religious country. According to *Statistics Singapore*, around 51% of resident Singaporeans (excluding significant numbers of visitors and migrant workers) practice Buddhism and Taoism. About 15%, mostly Chinese, Eurasians, and Indians, practice Christianity - a broad classification including Catholicism, Protestantism and other denominations. Muslims constitute 14%, of whom Malays account for the majority with a substantial number of Indian

Muslims and Chinese Muslims. Smaller minorities practice Sikhism, Hinduism and others, according to the 2000 census.

Some religious materials and practices are banned in Singapore. The Jehovah's Witnesses, for example, are prohibited from distributing religious materials and are sometimes jailed for their conscientious refusals to serve in the Singaporean military. About 15% of the population declared no religious affiliation.

Education

English is the medium of instruction in Singapore schools. All Singaporeans are required at least primary 6 educations and must attend government schools as part of National Education. Many children attend private kindergartens until they start at primary school at the age of six. Singapore's ruling political party, the PAP, is the largest provider of preschool education through its community arm. English is the language of instruction for mathematics and the natural sciences. For the Chinese community, there are Special Assistance Plan schools which receive extra funding to teach in Mandarin along with English. Some schools also integrate language subjects with mathematics and the sciences, using both English and a second language.

Curricular standards are set by the Ministry of Education with a mix of private schools and public schools. There is no strict public-private dichotomy: the degree of autonomy, regarding curriculum and student admission, government funding received, and tuition burden on the students is further classified into "government-run", "government-aided", "autonomous", "independent", and "privately-funded". In addition, international schools cater to expatriate students, and to a few local students given permission by the education ministry. There are three Autonomous Universities in Singapore; the National University of Singapore, Nanyang Technological University and Singapore Management University. A fourth public university is under consideration as the government looks to provide higher education for 30%

of each cohort. There is another category (Private Universities - Comprehensive); SIM University (UniSIM) provides university education to working professionals and adult learners.

There are also five polytechnics (Singapore Polytechnic, Ngee Ann Polytechnic, Temasek Polytechnic, Nanyang Polytechnic and Republic Polytechnic). Unlike similarly named institutions in many other countries, polytechnics in Singapore do not award degrees. A strange fact in Singapore is that there is no visible difference in salaries of fresh engineering under graduates and that of foreign students who graduate with higher degrees from universities like National University of Singapore and Nanyang Technological University. Under current recession, even a good university degree is unable to fetch a job to aspiring graduates which is another indicator of the weakness of the country's export driven economy. The educational system features non-compulsory kindergarten for three years, followed by six years of primary education leading up to the Primary School Leaving Examination (PSLE).

Four to five years of secondary education follow, leading up to the Singapore-Cambridge GCE 'N' Level or Singapore-Cambridge GCE 'O' Level examinations that assess academic achievement and determine the kind of post-secondary education routes they can pursue. Junior Colleges and Centralised Institutes provide a two or three-year pre-university education route. An alternative, the Integrated Programme, lets the more academically-inclined skip the 'O' Level examination and proceed straight to obtain pre-university qualifications such as the GCE 'A' Level certificate, the International Baccalaureate diploma, or other equivalent academic accreditations. Polytechnics offer courses leading up to at least a diploma for students, while the other tertiary institutions offer various bachelor's, master's, doctoral degrees, other higher diplomas, and associate degree courses. Other institutes include the National Institute of Education (NIE), a teaching college to train teachers, various management institutes, and vocational education institutes such as the

Institute of Technical Education (ITE).

The Economic Development Board (EDB) has been actively recruiting foreign schools to set up campuses in Singapore under the "Global Schoolhouse" programme which aims to attract 150000 foreign students by 2015. ESSEC Business School, a century-old Parisian business school, provides courses specific to Asia. In 2001 INSEAD, a leading business school, opened its first overseas campus in Singapore, and the University of Chicago, Graduate School of Business has a campus in the city as well. The Tisch School of the Arts is the latest to set up a branch campus, opening in 2007. However, the EDB failed to attract and retain the University of Warwick and University of New South Wales, respectively, citing lack of academic freedom and financial concerns.

In 1999, the Ministry of Education started the Programme for Rebuilding and Improving Existing schools (PRIME) to upgrade school buildings, many of which were built over 20 to 30 years ago, in phases at a cost of S$4.5 billion. This programme aims to provide a better school environment for the students by upgrading school buildings to latest standards. In 2005, the Flexible School Infrastructure (FlexSI) framework was implemented through the building of modular classrooms which can be opened up for larger lectures, and allowing a school's staff members to mould their school's designs to suit the school's unique identity and culture. At the same time, an indoor sports hall will be provided to every school so that schools can carry out physical education lessons in inclement weather.

Languages

The official languages are English, Malay, Chinese (Mandarin) and Tamil. The national language of Singapore is Malay for historical reasons, and it is used in the national anthem, "Majulah Singapura". English is the main language of Singapore and has been heavily promoted as such since the country's independence. The English used is primarily based on British English, with some American English influences. The use of English became widespread in Singapore after it was implemented as a first language medium in the education system, and English is the most common language in Singaporean literature.

In school, children are required to learn English and one of the three other official languages. By law, all signs and official publications are required to be primarily in English, although they are occasionally translated versions into the other official languages. However, most Singaporeans speak a localised hybrid form of English known as Singlish ("Singapore English"), which has many creole-like characteristics, incorporating vocabulary and grammar from Standard English, various Chinese dialects, Malay, and Indian languages. The second most common language in Singapore is Mandarin, with over seventy percent of the population having it as a second language.

Most Singapore Chinese are, however, descended from immigrants who came from the southern regions of China where other dialects were spoken, such as Hokkien, Teochew and Cantonese. Mandarin use has spread largely as a result of government efforts to support its adoption and use over the dialects.

CULTURE

Singapore is a mixture of an ethnic Malay population with a Chinese majority, as well as Indian and Arab immigrants. There also exist significant Eurasian and Peranakan (known also as 'Straits Chinese') communities.

CUISINE

Singaporean cuisine is an example of diversity and cultural diffusion, with influences from Chinese, Indian, Malay and Tamil cuisine. In Singapore's hawker centers, traditionally Malay hawker stalls selling halal food may serve halal versions of traditionally Tamil food. Chinese food stalls may introduce indigenous Malay ingredients or cooking techniques. This continues to make the cuisine of Singapore a significant cultural attraction. Local foods are diverse, ranging from Hainanese chicken rice to satay.

Singaporeans also enjoy a wide variety of seafood including crabs, clams, squid, and oysters. One such dish is stingray barbecued and served on banana leaf with *sambal* or chili. Amongst locals, popular dishes include bak chor mee, mee pok, sambal stingray, laksa, nasi lemak, chili crab and satay. All of which, can be found at local hawker centers around Singapore.

PERFORMING ARTS

Since the 1990s, the government has been striving to promote Singapore as a centre for arts and culture, and to transform the country into a cosmopolitan 'gateway between the East and West'. The highlight of these efforts was the construction of Esplanade, a centre for performing arts that opened on 12 October 2002.

An annual arts festival is also organised by the National Arts Council that incorporates theatre arts, dance, music and visual arts, among other possibilities. A first Singapore Biennale took place in 2006 to showcase contemporary art from around the world. The next one will be in 2008 which will feature Southeast Asian works.

MEDIA

Around 78,000 people work in the media in Singapore, including publishing, print, broadcasting, film, music, digital and IT media sectors. The industry contributed 1.56% to Singapore's gross domestic product (GDP) in 2001 with an annual turnover of S$10 billion ($6.6b, €5.1b). The industry grew at an average rate of 7.7% annually from 1990 to 2000, and the government seeks to increase its GDP contribution to 3% by 2012. The "Singapore government" says the media play an important role in the country, and describes the city as one of the key strategic media centers in the Asia-Pacific region.

The goal of the government's Media 21 plan, launched in 2002, is to establish Singapore as a global media hub. In its Annual Worldwide Press Freedom Index for 2004, Reporters without Borders ranked Singapore 147 out of 167. Most of the local media are directly or indirectly controlled by the government through shareholdings of these media entities by the state's investment arm Temasek Holdings, and are often perceived as pro-government.

BROADCASTING

State-owned MediaCorp operates all seven free-to-air terrestrial local television channels licensed to broadcast in Singapore, as well as 14 radio channels. Radio and television stations are all government-owned entities. The radio stations are mainly operated by MediaCorp with the exception of four stations, which are operated by SAFRA Radio and SPH UnionWorks respectively. The Cable and IPTV Pay-TV Service are owned by Starhub TV and Singtel Mio TV. Private ownership of satellite dish receivers capable of viewing uncensored televised content from abroad is illegal.

PRINT

There are a total of 16 newspapers in active circulation. Daily newspapers are published in English, Chinese, Malay and Tamil. Print is dominated by Singapore Press Holdings (SPH), the government-linked publisher of the flagship English-language daily, *The Straits Times*. SPH publishes all other daily newspapers including a free bilingual daily revamped "my paper" - which claim to be the world's first with equal coverage in both English and Chinese with the exception of *Today*, a free English-language tabloid published by the state-owned broadcaster MediaCorp.

Most of these papers have parallel online version. SPH papers that are available online include Straits Times, Business Times, The NewPaper, Mediacorp "TODAY" is also available online www.todayonline.com. There are also several popular magazines circulating in Singapore, like i-weekly, 8 days, Citta Bella, Her World, Brides, Men's Health and FHM Singapore.

SPORT AND RECREATION

Singaporeans participate in a wide variety of sports and

recreational activities. Favorite sports include football, cricket, tennis, swimming, badminton, basketball, rugby union, volleyball and table tennis. Most people live in public residential areas that often provide amenities such as swimming pools, outdoor basketball courts and indoor sport complexes. As might be expected on an island, water sports are popular, including sailing, kayaking and water skiing. Scuba diving is another recreation, particularly around the southern island of Pulau Hantu which is known for its rich coral reefs.

The 55,000 seat National Stadium, Singapore, located in Kallang was opened in July 1973 and was used for sporting, cultural, entertainment and national events until its official closure on 30 June 2007 to make way for the Singapore Sports Hub on the same site. This sports complex is expected to be ready by 2011 and will comprise a new 55,000-capacity National Stadium with a retractable roof, a 6,000-capacity indoor aquatic centre, a 400-metre warm-up athletic track and a 3,000-seater multi-purpose arena. 36,000 square meters of space have also been reserved for commercial development.

Singaporean sportsmen have performed in regional as well as international competitions in sports such as table tennis, badminton, bowling, sailing, silat, swimming and water polo. Athletes such as Fandi Ahmad, Ang Peng Siong, Li Jiawei and Ronald Susilo have become household names in the country. The Singapore Slingers joined the Australian National Basketball League in 2006 and have three Singaporeans in their squad. Despite being the team with the largest support pool in the NBL, they generally get the smallest crowds in the NBL.

Beginning in 2008, Singapore started hosting a round of the Formula One World Championship. The race staged at the Marina Bay Street Circuit in the Marina Bay area and became the first night race on the F1 circuit and the first street circuit in Asia. On 21 February 2008, the International Olympic Committee announced that Singapore won the bid to host the inaugural 2010 Summer Youth Olympics. Singapore beat Moscow in the final by 53 votes to 44.

ARCHITECTURE

The architecture of Singapore is varied, reflecting the ethnic build-up of the country. Singapore has several ethnic neighbourhoods, including Chinatown and Little India. These were formed under the Raffles Plan to segregate the immigrants. Many places of worship were also constructed during the colonial era. Sri Mariamman Temple, the Masjid Jamae mosque and the Church of Gregory the Illuminator are among those that were built during the colonial period. Work is now underway to preserve these religious sites as National Monuments of Singapore.

Due to the lack of space and lack of preservation policies during the 1960s, 70s and 80s, few historical buildings remain in the Central Business District (CBD) - the Fullerton Hotel and the previously-moved Lau Pa Sat being some exceptions.

However, just outside of Raffles Place and throughout the rest of the downtown core, there is a large scattering of pre-WWII buildings - some going back nearly as far as Raffles, as with the Empress Place Building, built in 1827. Many classical buildings were destroyed during the post-war decades, up until the 1990s, when the government started strict programmes to conserve the buildings and areas of historic value.

Past the shopping malls are streets lined with shop houses. Many other such areas have been gazetted as historic districts. Information can be found at the URA Centre in Maxwell Road, where there are exhibits and several models of the island and its architecture. Singapore has also become a centre for postmodern architecture. Historically, the demand for high-end buildings has been in and around the Central Business District (CBD). After decades of development, the CBD has become an area with many tall office buildings.

These buildings comprise the skyline along the coast of Marina Bay and Raffles Place, a tourist attraction in Singapore. Plans for tall buildings must be reviewed by the Civil Aviation Authority of Singapore. No building in Singapore may be taller than 280 meters. The three tallest buildings in Singapore, namely Republic Plaza, UOB Plaza One and OUB Centre, are all 280 meters in height.

RESOURCES

WATER RESOURCE

Without natural freshwater rivers and lakes, rainfall is the primary domestic source of water supply in Singapore. About half of Singapore's water comes from rain collected in reservoirs and catchments areas while the rest comes from Malaysia. The two countries have long argued of the legality of agreements to supply water that were signed in colonial times. Singapore has a network of reservoirs and water catchments areas. In 2001, there were 19 raw water reservoirs, 9 treatment works and 14 storage or service reservoirs locally to serve domestic needs. Marina Barrage is a dam being constructed around the estuary of three Singapore Rivers, creating a huge freshwater reservoir by 2009, the Marina Bay reservoir.

This will increase the rainfall catchments to two-thirds of the country's surface area. Historically, Singapore relied on imports from Malaysia to supply half of its water consumption. However, two water agreements that supply water to Singapore are due to expire by 2011 and 2061 respectively. The two countries are engaged in a dispute on the price of water. Without a resolution in sight, the government of Singapore decided to increase self-sufficiency in its water supply.

Presently, more catchments areas, facilities to recycle water (producing NEWater) and desalination plants are being built. This "four tap" strategy aims to reduce reliance on foreign supply and to diversify its water sources.. In 2008, a water barrage name - The Marina Barrage was built across the Marina Channel between Marina East and Marina South. The barrage aims to provide additional water supply catchments area, improve flood control and serve as an outdoor attraction for tourists and Singaporeans.

TRANSPORT

INTERNATIONAL

Singapore is a major Asian transportation hub, positioned on many sea and air trade routes. The Port of Singapore, man-aged by port operators PSA International and Jurong Port, was the world's second busiest port in 2005 in terms of shipping tonnage handled, at 1.15 billion gross tons, and in terms of containerized traffic, at 23.2 million twenty-foot equivalent units (TEUs). It was also the world's second busiest in terms of cargo tonnage, coming behind Shanghai with 423 million tons handled. In addition, the Port is the worlds busiest for transshipment traffic and the world's biggest ship refuelling centre.

Singapore is an aviation hub for the Southeast Asian region and a stopover on the Kangaroo route between Australasia and Europe. Singapore Changi Airport has a network of 81 airlines connecting Singapore to 185 cities in 58 countries. It has been rated as one of the best international airports by international travel magazines, including being rated as the worlds best airport for the first time in 2006 by Skytrax. The airport currently has three passenger terminals.

There is also a budget terminal, which serves budget carrier Tiger Airways and Cebu Pacific. The national carrier is Singapore Airlines (SIA). The government is moving towards privatising Changi airport. Singapore is linked to Johor, Malaysia via the Johor-Singapore Causeway and the Tuas Second Link, as well as a railway operated by Keretapi Tanah Melayu of Malaysia, with its southern terminus at Tanjong Pagar railway station. Frequent ferry service to several nearby Indonesian ports also exists.

DOMESTIC

The domestic transport infrastructure has a well-connected island-wide road transport system which includes a network of expressways. The public road system is served by the nation's bus service and a number of licensed taxi-operating companies. The public bus transport has been the subject of criticism by Singaporeans, the majority of whom are dependent on it for their daily commuting. Since 1987, the heavy rail passenger Mass Rapid Transit (MRT) metro system has been in operation. The MRT has been further augmented by the Light Rail Transit (LRT) light rail system, and increases accessibility to housing estates. Established in 2001, the EZ-Link system allows contact less smartcards to serve as stored value tickets for use in the public transport systems in Singapore.

More than 2.85 million people use the bus network daily operated mainly by SBS Transit and SMRT Buses, the two main public bus operators, while more than 1.5 million people use either the LRT or MRT as part of their daily routine. Approximately 945,000 people use the taxi services daily. Private vehicle use in the Central Area is discouraged by tolls implemented during hours of heavy road traffic, through an Electronic Road Pricing system. Private vehicle ownership is discouraged by high vehicle taxes and imposing quotas on vehicle purchase.

4

Cambodia in Global Market

In the past two decades, Cambodia has gone through many major changes reflecting the heroic sacrifice of the Cambodian people to protect and to rebuild their homeland, the standard of their living, and the prosperity for their future. With the October 23, 1991 Paris Peace Agreements, Cambodia achieves full right and sovereignty. For the result, the Cambodian people may fervently develop their country with generous assistance from international communities. Before reaching their goal of prosperity, they faced many critical proceedings. With His Majesty vision of Preah Bat Samdech Norodom Sihanouk, the beloved King of the Cambodian people, peace and national reconciliation were finally achieved.

At the second session of the auspicious plenary meeting of the National Assembly, I (Samdech Hun Sen, Prime Minister) have the honor to submit the Royal Government of Cambodia's Platform for approval from the august legislative body, the National Assembly. It is a foundation of governance to ensure peace, stability, democracy and development for the Cambodian people, and to rebuild their country.

POLICIES

DOMESTIC POLICIES

The main goal of the Royal Government is to ensure peace, stability, and national unity. In order to create a political stability conducive to the economic and social development, and the alleviation of poverty, Cambodia has to be state of law. The development of liberal democracy and the respect of human rights must be firmly promoted.

Pacification

The Royal Government adheres to national solidarity. To respect the consuls of His Majesty the King, the Cambodians from all walks of life and political backgrounds from every corner of the world must come together to defense their nation's independence, peace and prosperity. To restore permanent peace and political stability, the Royal Government would welcome the return of the remnant of the Khmer Rouge. It continues to integrate the armed force and the people, who support the policy of pacification successfully implemented in Pailin, Samlot, Malai, Anlong Veng, Preah Vihea, and in other areas. The Royal Government continues to cooperate with international organizations to set up the repatriation program to settle the Cambodian refugees into their society.

It would pay at any price to stop the return of the genocidal regime, and the reoccurrence of the recent past tragedies. The hard-line leaders of the outlawed Khmer Rouge would be put on trial by the court. In the meantime, the Royal Government would reinstate a handful of former servicemen into the Royal Armed Forces. Under the chairmanship of His Majesty the King, the November 13 statement clearly emphasized that the working group in charge of military affairs must immediately and properly implement the agreements set forth in the spirit of the November 12-13 summit. The Kingdom of Cambodia has full sovereignty. It is a unified state, not a seceded state.

Liberal Democratic Process and Respect of Human Rights

The Royal Government adheres to the principle of democratic pluralism and to the respect of human rights for which, it strongly believes they are fundamental to the social progress. The democratization and liberalization of all social fabrics must be rapidly addressed, because they are the essential forces of economic and social developments. The Royal Government assures and protects freedom of its citizenry bestowed in the Constitution, in the Universal Declaration of Human Rights, in the Covenants on Civil and Political Rights and Social, Economic and Cultural Rights, and in the Convention on the Rights of Women and Children. It strongly opposes racial hatred. The overall structure of the state run human rights institution would be upgraded.

Freedom of the Press and of Expression

The Royal Government vigorously supports freedom of the press, freedom of expression and of assembly, which freely contribute to social and political conscience. In order to seek different shade and color of opinions, public forums are encouraged to take place. At the same time, freedom and anarchy should be clearly differentiated. The Constitution provides its citizenry their freedoms to be enjoyed and honored, not to be destructive and intrusive.

The Role of Oppositions

To mobilize the wisdom from all walks of life and backgrounds to build the nation, the Royal Government widely supports the role of oppositions for constructive criticism, and for good services to the nation. The oppositions have full legal rights to perform its political activities. They are fully guarantied by the Royal Government equal social and political benefits, such as freedom, justice, security, and employment.

They may assist Cambodia's young democracy to be fully developed. They do not have to implicate themselves in order to be labeled oppositions. The Royal Government and the oppositions would have to promote jointly the national interest, the social stability, and the welfare of the people, so that Cambodia and her people may enjoy the fruits of long lasting political strength and national stability. The role of the oppositions shall be defined in the law.

The Participation of the Civil Society

The Royal Government and the civil society shall incorporate their principle of state of law into strengthening democracy, liberty, and social law and order. They may not develop the country by conflicting interests between civil and political societies. The civil society shall be a key partner of the Royal Government in the construction of Cambodia. In view, the Royal Government would endorse the multiple activities of the non-governmental organizations and of associations, which have served the Cambodian people nationwide.

It will appropriate special funds and allocate them to the non-governmental organizations in providing services on its behalf to the needy. The Royal Government would welcome the participation of the international non-governmental organizations in the process of rehabilitation of economic development and in the promotion of democracy and human rights. Therefore, it needs drafting a law on the non-governmental organizations and associations.

The Rule of Law

The rule of law is the basic principle of democracy, the sustainability of the government, and of all institutions. It is to ensure freedom, national interest, justice, harmony, and social sustainability. A forceful legal structure to end assaults on human dignity is urgently needed. The enforcement and education of law would be widely disseminated. All men are born free and equal, but they must not be allowed to be above the law. A set of law must be applied equally to all.

Reforms

Presently, administrative, judicial, military and police, and economic reforms are urgently to be addressed. Today, Cambodia's administrative machine is excessive. The Royal Government can not further support it. It would take steps to reform it. It should gradually trim. It should be neutral and sound administration, which is capable to effectively serve the people. The rule of civil servants must be strictly applied. The training program to update the knowledge and skill of the employs must be spontaneously upgraded and maintained. The physical structure of provinces and its cities must be reviewed. The provincial administration autonomy should seriously consider. The management of provinces, districts, communes, and villages should be properly carried out to rules and regulations.

The judicial system and the court are necessary to be entirely overhauled. By law, they ought to be independent, honest, and trustworthy. To succeed their quest, the corporations among the national institutions, such as the National Assembly, the Government, the Constitutional Council, the Council of Magistracy, and the court, should be overcome. Judges' salaries must be adequately raised. Especially, the judges in the Supreme Court must request their summons be properly recorded and executed. However, if there is a judge committing a violation, the Council of Magistracy should immediately reprimand him or her.

The corruption and power abuses, which obstruct the promotion and supports of the people's living conditions, ought to be stopped. The Cambodians, the businessmen, and the investors must not be victimized by those exploitations. The Royal Government of Cambodia considers the fight against the corruption as its matter of priority. The Royal Government would set transparency in every work force. The anti-corruption institution would be soon formed. To ensure the effectiveness in the work force, the following measures would urgently be realized:

- The anti-corruption law against the corrupt,
- The creation of an agency to monitor and to fight corruption,
- The wealth clearance decree,
- The State estates control,
- The encouragement of citizenry to participate in the corruption fight,
- The appropriation of pay raise for the civil servants in accordance to the national budget.

NATIONAL DEFENSE AND SECURITY

The Royal Cambodian Armed Forces (RCAF), the Military Police, and the National Police would fulfill their roles according to the Military and Police rules of order. They must be neutral, obedient, and self-restraint. They must sacrifice their lives to protect the Constitution of the Kingdom of Cambodia. They would bravely defense the national independence, sovereignty, and territorial integrity, to maintain peace, security, and stability, and to enforce law and order. They must end insurgency, terrorism, and secession. They must completely eradicate kidnapping, armed robbery, drug trafficking, artifact smuggling, money laundering, and sexual exploitation of minor children and women. They must properly enforce the law to make their homeland prosperous and safe for all, including diplomats, investors, tourists, and foreign workers.

They would participate in the national development programs. They must be active in the rescue operation to save lives of the people from the natural causes. They ought to curtail the use of illegal weapons, and close down the arms black markets. The service of militia may be reviewed. Some places still need its assistance. For other places, its help is not applicable. However, the demobilization of militia and its disarmament should be highly considered.

FOREIGN POLICIES

Cambodia adheres to policy of neutrality and non-alliance. It indiscriminately establishes relations with all friendly states worldwide. It conducts policies of mutual understanding, equality, respect, and non-interference in other state's internal affairs. Cambodia would fortify bilateral friendship and cooperation with its neighbors. The border issues with its neighbors would be resolved through negotiations, and peaceful means. Cambodia would establish bilateral and multilateral friendships with regional countries, especially with ASEAN. It wants to contribute as it may in jointly building the Southeast Asia to be a region of peace, tranquility, and prosperity.

When it becomes an active member of ASEAN, Cambodia would conduct itself within the principle of the agreements. Cambodia is a member of non-aligned movement. Within the principle of agreements it would increase its diplomatic relationship with other nations, and set up embassies within its financial and human resources. Cambodia with high respect to humanity would conduct itself to be a good member of the United Nations. To solve the problem of illegal immigrants, Cambodia would utilize its immigration law that enshrines the principle set forth in the Universal Declaration on Human Rights. The Royal Government of Cambodia is very grateful to the international communities for their contribution, peace, democracy and prosperity in Cambodia.

ECONOMIC POLICY

The economy is a principle domain to support the national development program, which involves sustainability and macro-economy. It should effectively use its natural and human resources. Cambodia would promote free market economy linked with the program of combat the poverty, and social justice. The economic mechanism runs its course within rules and regulations of free market economy. The Royal Government would not manage the market, but it would support it. The royal Government would grant the private sector the right of self-determination on productivity, investment, and expenditure, and it would intervene much less. For the reasons, it would set legal and administrative structures to ensure freedom and autonomy of the private sector to property right, employment, profession, and the right to compete freely.

It would improve mechanism and structure of economic management to ensure the effectiveness and transparency to cope with corruption and violation of law. That is very important to stabilize the macro-economy, to boost the people's standard of living, and to encourage the investment. It prioritizes the physical agricultural infrastructure, electricity and human resources, which are the basics of overall development. The following goals must be achieved:

1. To speed the economic growth in order to improve the popular living standard and to create more employment. The chief potential to promote the economic growth is to amass and to transform the natural resources and the national products into the products of export. The Royal Government would improve economic rules and regulations and to promote Cambodia to be a goods producer in order to attract more foreign investment.
2. To ensure the stability of Riel currency, to keep the inflation rate at bay, to prevent the loss of revenue and private saving by the Riel fluctuation, and to build confidence in Riel by devaluating with caution the dollar.
3. To increase the export of agricultural and manufacturing products with high expertise and quality.
4. The Royal Government would do its best to alleviate the poverty. The alleviation of poverty is not only the basic of sustainability of the economic development, but it also the priority to implement the social program.
5. To attain the above goals, the Royal Government would seize down the following imbalances:
    1. Between the need and supply, especially on foods, housing, transportation, education, and health care.
    2. Between the revenue and expenditure within the national budget.
    3. Between the import and export.
    4. Between the currency and goods.
    5. Between salary and the standard of living of civil servant and servicemen.
    6. Between the increase in the work force and the employment.
    7. Between the need for national development and the training of human resources.

The Royal Government would continue to carry out the projects, which are identified in the national program of rehabilitation and development of Cambodia. It would focus on the long-term program for the economic and social development in the first five years from 1996-2000. It also attempts to achieve the urgent need for the investment on public sector. Based on these basics and the on going achievements, the Royal Government may carry out the following economic strategies:

- The Development of Human Resources and the Building of Infrastructure

The Royal Government strongly believes in the process of selecting the ones, who are healthy, well educated, well-disciplined, honest, independent, and responsible. In this spirit, the improvement of quality of education, health services, and food security must be strongly promoted by the Royal Government. For the improvement and the globalization of general education, it would prioritize the investment on the vocational training and on higher education. The Cambodian workers would be better equipped with skill and the know-how.

The Royal Government would cooperate with the Chamber of Commerce and other professional institutions to set up the center of transfer of the know-how. The present shortcoming of the national infrastructure tremendously undermines the economic growth of Cambodia. The Royal Government would continue to rehabilitate the national infrastructure. Eventually it would privatize the mass transportation and communication, the telecommunication, and the electrical power supply.

Agriculture

The main economic infrastructure of Cambodia is agriculture. The Royal Government would enhance the irrigation system, because agricultural activities in Cambodia are solely dependent on the weather. Consequently, it is essential to upgrade the General Direction of Irrigation to the level of Ministry of Water Resources and Meteorology. In five years from 1998-2003, it would increase the irrigation capacity from 16.62% to 20%, i.e. an increase of 3.32% to 4% on the farming land, and the increase of irrigation capacity from 374,603 ha. to 450,600 ha. of rice fields.

The water supply would be strictly monitored and distributed. The high quality of clean water must be absolutely maintained. The rubber plantation would be privatized. The Royal Government would encourage a large or small scale of rubber production by the provision of credit and ownership. The Royal Government would consolidate the forest management to ensure its sustainability. It strictly and completely bans illegal logging. It would take the following steps to:

- Cease further investment on wood processing.
- Review all forest concession contracts and cancel non-complied contracts. The forest under the non-complied contract would be used for national parks and habitats.
- Encourage the companies with complied contracts to modernize their factories in order to increase the value of timber, and to create more jobs for the Cambodians The Royal Government must strictly enforce its reforestation policy.
- Review and amend the law on forest management to benefit the investors, who do comply with the rules. Persons, who commit illegal logging and violate the forest law, must be brought to justice.

Industries

The Royal Government would encourage small and large industries to fulfill its tasks. It would focus on strategy of producing export goods rather than import ones. The liberalization of international trade makes the local products difficult to compete in the foreign markets. The small industries produce its output enough for domestic use. It strive all efforts to make the textile industries and agricultural industries to be the core structure of Cambodian industries. The Royal Government promotes the research and exploitation of petrol, natural gas, and other minerals, which becomes the potentiality of the national economy. It would develop soon the hydropower in order to ensure adequate electric supply with low cost and to meet its economic goal.

Trade

The Royal Government would enhance its policy of trade liberalization. It would facilitate the free circulation of goods. The price and quantity of goods would be simplified from one region to another in order to promote the growth of its production. It would also broaden international trade relation by bridging the domestic markets to foreign markets. Finally it would promote the integration of regional and global trade.

Tourism

The Royal Government would promote the development of tourism and make it to become tourism of culture and nature. It would heighten the private and public investments targeting at building up tourist infrastructure. It would ensure security and political stability. Tourist work has to be linked by the preservation of natural cultural heritage and natural environment.

Foreign Economic Policy

The Royal Government adopts a precise political guideline of its external economy conforming to the liberalization of international trade, and integrating national economy into the world economy. Through this policy, Cambodia prepares itself to attract and to face regionally and globally the process of economic internationalization. At the same time, the competitive productivity and capacity of Cambodian economy in the international markets will be enhanced through the application of mass production, which decreases the unit price of production and expertise based on the availability of the domestic resources.

Cambodia, however, will face the influx of foreign finished products, which rejects a number of industries in the country. The pressure of the integration process of the regional economy, in which Cambodia expects to join ASEAN and the World Trade Organization in the near future, will add more burden to the national budget through the fall of the tax revenue, and import duties. These financial activities would change the economic structure of Cambodia. The Royal Government is optimistic and prepares to amend its legal procedures to accommodate the economic integration.

Investment Policy

The Royal Government of Cambodia promotes the internal and external investments through the application of the principle and the encouragement of the investment policy of the Kingdom of Cambodia. It strengthens its cooperation with friendly countries and their institutions in order to attract more investments, development assistance, trade status as most favorite nation from the developed countries and the expansion of the markets.

To have a good environment for the investment, the social political stability and the stability of the macro-economy must be ensured. The principle and the guidance of the investment policy must be firmly adhered. The Royal Government of Cambodia may reform and strengthen the institution, which is responsible for the activities of the investment, especially for the improvement on the formality of the application for the investment undermining the illegal activities and corruption.

Financial and Monetary Policies

The Royal Government must ensure the effectiveness of the execution of its financial and monetary policies. The fiscal policy recently improved has not yet been properly carried out. The national budget, which has a duty to evaluate, to collect, and to distribute the national resources, is the most important tool to handle the economic and social policies of the Royal Government of Cambodia. Therefore, the national budget must be disbursed distinctively for the support of public services, and for the handling of public projects with the economic sense of prudence, conscience, and proficiency.

The Royal Government must give the priority to the promotion of productivity, the private investment, the social programs, and public health care. The future ASEAN membership of Cambodia would influence tremendously the reform of the revenue of the national budget. The national revenue by taxation on the import and export goods will be decreased. For that, it would strengthen all facets of tax control and broaden the internal tax revenue base in order to encourage the entrepreneurs to be in the investment process, and to achieve the budget surplus for which it is to be the sources of internal credit, such as for the public investment and for the financial intervention to pay raises for the employees of the government.

To achieve the effective control over the budget and fiscal policies, the Royal Government of Cambodia must immediately take the following steps:

- Use every measure at all costs to combat tax evasion.
- Strongly prohibit revenue collection and shelter, and disbursement infringing the budgetary system.
- Abolish tax exemption, which is not stipulated in the investment law, the law on fiscal policy, and the law on the annual financial management.
- The Ministry of Economy and Finance must strictly check and control goods before loading in order to properly tax the merchandises, while its services are being effectively conducted with high consideration of time consumption.
- Carry out strict measure of austerity, especially against the unneeded expenses. The financial resources from privatization must only be used for the public investment such as the infrastructure, or the counterpart fund of the credit fund from the financial institution.
- The fund used other than infrastructure purpose must be prohibited.

The Royal Government undertakes its political will to impose punishment on fraud, illegal transfer of fund, and corruption. To ensure the stability of buying power of Riel currency, the Royal Government would set the spending rate of the national budget to be below the rate of the national economic growth, and the rate of reserve fund of the banks. The interest rate conducive to the promotion of private saving and the intervention of the National Bank in the domestic monetary markets in to stabilize the rate of Riel exchange. The attempts of the Royal Government of Cambodia to cut down the economic imbalance will encounter numerous difficulties, because the limited financial resources force it to prioritize the use of the economic measure. But often the economic aim being decisively successful requires a variety of economic tools to come together at one time.

At the same time, the lingering economic crisis and the declined economic growth in the region will impact the flow of the foreign investment and the domestic growth. The Royal Government would overcome those economic stumbling blocks in order to attain its economic goal, because of its last achievements. This task needs the joint participation of national and international sectors to improve national economy and to strengthen the capacity building, the work spirit, ethics, and social obligation of public servants.

CULTURE, HEALTH, SOCIAL OBLIGATION

The Royal Government initiates tough measure to restore and to promote culture heritage and national civilization, to end the declination of national culture, to highlight the social ethics, and to promote the national cultural characteristic and progress. For that, the Royal Government has to expand the education of culture and civilization, to promote the general understanding of the national identity and pride, and to stop the flow of the foreign culture, which affects the national culture. On health matter, the Royal Government would promote health services to public and private sectors, disease prevention, mother and child care, fight against the contagious disease, and health check up and treatment in State hospitals and clinics.

On social issues, the Royal government would upgrade the standard of living of the people and to ensure the equal benefits for the people from all walks of life. Primarily, the Royal Government would cut down to the maximum of the vulnerability, and increase the chance for the poor and indigent citizens to be able to participate in the social and economic programs. It would firmly carry out the labor law and the international convention on labor unions in order to secure the right and privilege for the workers, employees, and employers. It would establish a good working condition to benefit the handicapped persons, the orphans, the widows, and the indigent men and women, so their livings could be better conditioned. It would defense the right of women and children according to the universal convention.

It would engage the women in politics and in other social and economic fields. It would assist the minority to involve in restoring the economic, social, and cultural heritage. To succeed the social rehabilitation and development, there is an important factor to be addressed; that is the task of building social conscience, confidence, and self-determination, which produce quality work. The idea and stand on ordinary productivity to improve the skill and the knowledge of know-how in agreement with the rules of development must be encouraged.

5

Flows of Ideas and Cultures

TIMELINE

Mainland Southeast Asia consists of the present day states of Myanmar (Burma), Thailand, Cambodia, Laos, and Vietnam. Maritime or island Southeast Asia includes the Malay part of the peninsula and a large archipelago divided between Indonesia and the Philippines.

PRECOLONIAL ERA

c. 500 B.C.E. Indian trade with mainland Southeast Asia begins, leading to the spread of Hindu-Buddhist ideology and the influence of Sanskrit and Pali on local languages.

c. 1 C.E. With the spread of trade into the islands, west and central maritime Southeast Asia comes under the influence of Hindu and Buddhist traditions.

1st millennium C.E. Mon-Khmer people settle Irawaddy Valley, Bangkok Plain, and Mekong Delta; Khmer site of Angkor Wat (ninth century) typifies court of Hinduized Southeast Asian state. Red River Valley (southernmost extent of Chinese Empire) occupied by Vietnamese. Chams (Malayo-Polynesian language group) inhabit coast from the Red River Valley to the Mekong Delta.

Early 2nd millennium C.E. Burmans moves into the Shan Hills from the eastern Himalayas; conquer Mon-dominated

Irawaddy River Valley. Thai and related Lao move into what is now Laos and Thailand from Southeast China.

1300 C.E. Islam expands into island Southeast Asia from the Indian Ocean, following trade routes; Muslims introduce Arabic as they convert local populations.

14th–18th centuries. Vietnamese push south, dominating Chams and taking the Mekong Delta from the Khmers.

16th century. Spain annexes the Philippines, bringing Christianity and Spanish and blocking the eastward spread of Muslim conversions. Portuguese and then the Dutch occupy the Spice Islands.

18th century. Four ethnic groups dominate mainland Southeast Asia by this time: Burmans (Irawaddy River Valley), Thais (Bangkok Plain), Lao (northern and central Mekong Valley), and Vietnamese (eastern lowlands). The contemporary states of Myanmar (Burma), Thailand, Laos, and Vietnam take their names from these ethnic groups.

COLONIAL ERA

1824–1885. British acquire Burma, which becomes an Indian province in 1885.

1858–1885. French take over the Nguyen dynasty of Vietnam; French becomes the language of administration in French Indochina (present-day Vietnam, Laos, and Cambodia). French introduce the printing press to Vietnam; the first French-language bulletins appear in 1861. Malay (later the Indonesian national language) develops a popular literature, spreading ideas of modernization and nationalism from the late nineteenth century on.

1885–1945. Western schools rapidly expand by the early twentieth century. First Vietnamese (French-language) newspaper is printed in 1917. First Thai publishing houses are established in the 1930s. In Vietnam a remarkable expansion of literacy in *quoc-ngu,* romanized Vietnamese script, takes place between the 1920s and 1940s. Early nationalist movements develop throughout Southeast Asia in response to colonialism and the introduction of Western thought.

1945–1954. Most of Southeast Asia is decolonized in the aftermath of World War II.

POSTCOLONIAL ERA

1954–1975. The expansion of radio in the 1960s and 1970s creates a community of listeners in Southeast Asian countries for the first time. The Vietnam War ending in 1975 with the fall of Saigon, results in massive devastation, population loss, and displacement within mainland Southeast Asia as well as an unprecedented international refugee flow.

Mid-1980s. Television is introduced to Laos and Bali. The refugee diasporas stimulates use of new media, such as video. Literary analysis and the first women scholars emerge in Laos during the late twentieth century.

1990s. Television viewing greatly expands with the advent of satellite television.

2000. Cell phones, fax machines, computers, and cybercafés permeate city life. The Thai language, in both spoken and written forms, increasingly dominates neighboring Laos.

In Laos and Northeast Thailand in the 1930s, writing on palm leaves became obsolete. In the late twentieth century a new field of Lao literary analysis emerged in which female as well as male Lao scholars participate. The last two decades of the twentieth century brought modern mass media within reach of most Southeast Asians, though access varies. Television first appeared in Thailand during the 1950s but was not available outside the capital until rural electrification took place in the late 1970s.

During the 1980s color television sets and then videocassette recorders became common, and by the next decade television viewing had greatly increased. In Bali (Indonesia), famous for its popular theater, the effect of television on live theater was so great that eight out of ten theater troupes vanished during the 1980s. Siam's (present-day Thailand) confrontation with Western colonialism in the nineteenth century led to a concern with boundaries and remodeling of the Siamese administration system after the model of Dutch and British colonial practice. One of the first Asian countries to use new media to further national development, Thailand has promoted an "official" national cultural identity for at least ninety years through its public education system and mass literacy in Central Thai.

By the late 1980s television programming was used to introduce new, non indigenous patterns of consumption, such as the presentation of Christmas gifts. Due to Thai control of modern mass media, the Thai language in both spoken and written forms increasingly dominates neighboring Laos. Whereas Thai and Lao are closely related, the Thai language modernized more rapidly; Lao scholars are still debating the standardization of its writing system. Communication of ideas on the popular level in mainland Southeast Asia in the early twenty-first century is largely within an Asian sphere of influence; for example, Thai boxing and beauty contests, Hong Kong dramas dubbed into Vietnamese or Thai.

Foreign ideas and the English language have begun to enter Thailand to some extent as a result of the increase in tourism after 1987. The influence of Southeast Asian refugees on both their host countries and countries of origin should not be ignored, particularly now that former refugees can visit or even return permanently to Southeast Asia; new ideas include more rights for women, increased individualism, and democracy. The political legacy of the Vietnam War remains a part of global, particularly U.S., consciousness.

KUALA LUMPUR

The particular brand of developmentalism engineered and nurtured by former premier Mahathir Mohamad throughout the 1980s and 1990s has indelibly transformed the Malaysian social imaginary as the country shifted from an agrarian to an industrializing and service-based economy. Concomitant with this shift has been a re-imagining of the country's social fabric as evidenced by globalizing tropes such as "Vision 2020", "Bangsa Malaysia" (Malaysian race), "Malaysia Boleh" (Malaysian Can!), and "Truly Malaysia, truly Asia".

As the capital city of the country, cosmopolitan Kuala Lumpur arguably manifests most visibly the imprints of these transformations. In this milieu, significant changes and makeovers in the built environment - infrastructure, skyline, streetscapes etc. – have been accompanied by projecting the country as "truly Asian" – a microcosm of the geographically expansive and diverse region of Asia. Sections of Old Kuala Lumpur are continuously being re-imagined and re-branded in tandem with the re-making of the New by the interventions of City Hall and big businesses.

Firstly, examine the contested processes involved in the cultural re-making of the "Little India" quarter of Kuala Lumpur giving particular attention to the perspectives of an array of sidewalk vendors who populate that area. The statistic top-down approach with the pioneering but low-keyed efforts of the itinerant Gerai Orang Asli (Indigenous People Stall) which markets the crafts of some 17 indigenous people groups and bypasses the intervention of middlemen and state sponsorship.

Whilst one depends on the spirit of individual voluntarism and goodwill to animate its activities, the other is a rationalized attempt at engineering cultural diversity. In what ways do these disparate strategies and energies contribute meaningfully to the fostering of cultural enterprise? How have they in turn enhanced livelihood opportunities? What lessons can we draw from the intersection between statistic and non-statistic initiatives?

FROM TRADITION TO MODERNITY IN MANDALAY

Throughout the centuries, the Burmese capitals have been shifted from one place to another under the orders of the rulers. Mandalay, situated in the dry zone of central Burma, is the last of a long series of successive capitals of the Burmese kingdom. Each time, when the capital was moved to a new location, the royal palace, the whole court, the people, including monks, merchants, handicraft makers, etc, were also moved carrying their traditions as well. In fact the building of the last Burmese capital of independent Burma, results from a holy dream of King Mindon (1852-1878).

For three years (1857-1860) the chosen site of the new capital was a vast building site where thousands of independent labourers, servants and slaves were working. Most of the Mandalay Quarters, built with the help of Italian and French architects, survive to this day. Difficult of access during under the colonial regime, damaged by the bombing of the Second World War, the old capital was further isolated under the Socialist regime of the Burmese Way to Socialism (1962-1988). From 1989 onwards the commanders governing the town have followed the directives of a junta promoting a full time development aiming to drive the country toward modernity. Constructions of villas, condominiums, hotels, markets, shopping centers have followed, boosting the local economy.

Moreover a considerable effort to improve the transportation infrastructure, in and around the town, has been made. Finally the embankments of the river Irrawaddy, which are protecting the capital from flood, have been reinforced while the port for logs has been shifted further south from the conurbation of Mandalay-Amarapura. These developments have been accompanied by the arrival of a number of Chinese migrant entrepreneurs encouraged to invest by the regime. The impact of their economic activities, sustained by a reservoir of skilled Burmese workers, on the landscape of the old capital and the Burmese traditions will be reviewed.

At a time when France and its empire were engulfed in the first world-war, the city-port metropolis of Saigon was becoming what Lucien Febvre called an historical 'space of possibilities', within which a complex process of imposed acculturation and social interactions led to new expressions of political consciousness, both individual and collective.

This fertilization in turn drew from a hybrid political genealogy that mixed French republican and anarchist traditions with neo-Confucian Vietnamese behaviour. A unique blend or Métis sage thus facilitated the autonomy of individual political action and expression, and with it, the introduction into the public realm of new themes of debate. The paper will briefly sketch Saigon's socio-economico-cultural map in the 1920s.

It will then attempt to draw a link, from the Social to the Political, by concentrating on new phenomena of individual social consciousness and the resulting patterns of socialization, laying the foundations of an autonomous Habermasian political public sphere. In so doing, the paper aims to contribute to the emerging debate over the importance of modern metropolis in Southeast Asia and beyond, for their role in shaping the kind of environment conducive to the emergence of a public political culture of debate and diversity.

CHANGING LIFE STYLE AND ATTITUDE OF CAMBODIAN ILLEGAL MIGRANT WORKERS IN THAILAND

The trauma of civil war and the ensuing process of peace and economic development in Cambodia have stimulated a continuous flow of hundreds of thousands of Cambodians immigrating illegally into Thailand in search of new job opportunities and higher wages. These Cambodian illegal immigrants are working almost everywhere in Thailand especially in Bangkok and in the provinces, as unskilled construction workers and fishermen. Drawing from my Masters thesis the Living Conditions of Cambodian Illegal Migrant Workers in Thailand, this chapter will examine the changing attitude of illegal migrant construction workers in Bangkok.

In particular, it will examine how Cambodian rural migrants think and feel about city life-styles in Bangkok; how they have adapted to city life, and how Cambodians own life-styles and attitudes have changed as a result of their new experiences. These changes are a result of material influences: from their regular exposure to Thai people around them and to the media. The development of these behaviour patterns and their retention of the notions they feel unlike Thai people who they see as always looking down on them and treating them very indecently.

In conclusion, the paper argues that the material effects (their behaviour changes through dress, etc) are stronger than their negative feelings about the Thai people. In other words, their feelings of difference to Thai people, and their negative perspectives of Thai people, are disjunctive with these Cambodian illegal migrant construction workers' actual life style and attitudes.

Commercial Places as Part of Urban Culture in SE Asian Cities: A Lesson from Bangkok: The accelerated urban growth and change brings forward questions of cultural continuation and sustainability. Commercial activity can be a good "barometer" to detect such changes. Commerce colors all aspects of everyday city life. Shopping areas provide insights into the ways in which societies and cultures work.

Commercial places welcome the encounter between merchants and clients as yet another expression of the way human societies operate. The commercial places reflect many aspects of the culture of the city; they show what people like, what they consume, what they need, how they dress, what they eat, how they behave ... They expose the dynamics of the global flows of ideas and capital, and thus indicate the extent to which globalization affects a particular society. This chapter explains the importance of indigenous urban commercial places for the urbanity of the cities. The emphasis is on "fluidity" of commercial spaces in South East Asian cities, their flexibility, spontaneity and ability to adapt to new situations.

The specific case presented is one of the most important market places of Bangkok, the Chatuchak Weekend Market, the biggest and arguably the most diverse market in South East Asia. The example of Chatuchak shows how the indigenous form of commercial place as "market place" can go further than just a "local" market. Chatuchak market which, with its successful Internet site expanded even to cyberspace, demonstrates the extreme case, where the quality of a simple market place attained significant roles at both national and international economic levels.

The paper touches upon some specific 'identity' characteristics or discourses of the Chatuchak market and offers a brief discussion of the relationship between the market-as-offer and market-as demand, the phenomenon of mutual framing and definition between what is on sale and the ever-changing tastes of consumers, both of which are increasingly exposed to the forces of globalization.

Variations on a Shopping Mall: An Exploration of Mobile Marketplaces. A market is a place where buying and selling takes place.

Yet this seemingly simple business transaction has expanded into layers of institutions professing to bring complex matrices of information from branding to visual merchandising to market research, all to bring the seller closer to the consumer, or vice versa. The most ubiquitous marketplace remains the shopping mall. From Bangkok to Phnom Penh, to Singapore, shopping malls not only proliferate, they are getting bigger and bigger, and have lately become showcases for national pride (i.e. Siam Paragon in Bangkok, Thailand, and The Mall of Asia in Pasay City in the Philippines).

As symbols of modernity, sites of leisure, aspiration, and entertainment, they are indispensable institutions in urban South Asia. For all they profess to do, malls have not replaced other types of markets. This chapter is an attempt to understand various ways in which the marketplace mediates everyday life in a Southeast Asian city. In particular, it explores suburban Kuala Lumpur where self-organized markets, from 'night markets' to 'wet markets' to the 'thieves market,' to a few mobile carts huddling next to a road junction, continues to thrive. Some of the self-organized markets are set up on the ground, on the sidewalks, from the trunk of cars, or on tabletops with fluorescent lights powered by portable generators.

Most, if not all, of these markets are known only through word of mouth. What gives these self-organized markets life? What is the social contract that keeps the night markets, the thieves market, and the mobile markets viable? These places of commerce occupy otherwise public spaces such as roadsides and parking lots. Like the monsoon rain, the timing of these markets is predictably imprecise. Wet markets open in the mornings, but others open once a week, and only at nights. Thieves' markets get closed down, but there are always people milling about until the police leaves. Needless to say, such marketplaces demand constant negotiation and renegotiation of time and space. Their resilience to legal frameworks, formalized institutions, and even competition from shopping malls, provide clues to the viable and diverse urban futures in Southeast Asia.

CITIZENS' URBAN MOVEMENTS IN INDONESIA

Through out the last decade, citizens groups have been formed to address a multitude of urban issues: land, housing, eviction, environment, arts space, elections, heritage, HIV-aids, budgetary transparency, freedom of religion, ethnic identity, minorities rights, etc. Some of them are specifically urban in both issue and the scope; some are parts of national movements such as in environment. Some of the organisations and movements that they advocate had been formed during Suharto's regime; some are newly formed after the 1998 crisis.

In either case, changes in national and global context bring new challenges and drive the movements and organisation to reposition them. They are in fluid a situation now. This makes a mapping and some reflections on the diverse streams of citizen's urban movements in Indonesia urgent and useful to provide insights for the future. As Indonesia is entering a new era of decentralisation and local autonomy, while urbanization has been irreversibly increasing, an understanding of how organized citizens movements on urban issues might help the country achieve a better quality of life.

How do they reflect urban diversity? How can they contribute to its sustainability? What are the likely strategies? How is it helping in social and cultural capital formation? What are the weaknesses and potentials yet to be cultivated? How do they respond to changing national and global contexts?

URBAN DEVELOPMENT AS A THREAT TO LAND TENURE SECURITY

Since the free market economic policy was introduced to Cambodia in 1989 and its recent integration into the international and regional economic and politic, extensive investments in

Cambodia have stimulated growth while exacerbating social inequality. Starting with the demands on land and housing presented by the influx of 25,000 people with UNTAC in 1991-1993, and as a result of the lack of regulation and measures to manage public and other vacant land in this city, many informal settlements took place. More than 80% of total national investments now take place in Phnom Penh. Economic opportunity and rural poverty have stimulated high migration to the city.

Continued poor urban planning, high demand for housing and land markets, and real estate development have seen an expansion of informal settlements in this city. These informal settlements are mostly located along public gardens, railway tracks, lakes, ponds, rivers, roof-tops, old abundant government buildings, abundant roads, roadsides, and around government building compounds, etc. Those informal settlements with better physical and less economic potential locations enjoy better tenure security.

Settlements with poor physical and in prime economic potential locations face increased instances of forced eviction. Although they play an important role for economic development in this city, residents of these informal settlements are viewed as anarchic peoples in anarchic settlements by developers, authorities, and also by most of the general population. Finally, it will suggest possible suitable solutions and make recommendations to solve those tenure security problems in ways that are acceptable to all key stakeholders: Government, NGOs, private sectors, and the communities themselves.

While efficiency, productivity and flexibility were the testimony of growth of the 20th century, the driving growth factor of the 21st century is creativity. A creative city is home to a diverse array of creative businesses, organisations, groups and individuals who contribute and propel the success for the city. A creative city is an attractive place to live and work; it attracts visitors and is capable of regenerating its economic base. Diverse human capital resources have replaced other factors of production such as location, natural resources and market access, as the tangible urban assets critical for developing a creative city.

Furthermore, the Digital Revolution has not only accelerated the speed of information dissemination, but has redefined the relation of space and time; thus creating a global marketplace for a myriad of goods and services. Challenges created for cities by the new economy are formidable and need to be addressed urgently. With globalisation, Southeast Asian cities are also faced with significant social and economic transformations, as well as typical urban issues of poor housing, unemployment, traffic congestion, and quality of the environment. Despite these obstacles, it is imperative that cities formulate clear objectives and strategies to strengthen their diverse intellectual and creative assets; enhance the quality of life and economic prosperity, in the context of new economy challenges and opportunities.

Georgetown, the capital of Penang state was the earliest British settlement in Southeast Asia in the 18th century. The people of Georgetown and their unique lifestyles constitute the living culture thriving within the heritage enclaves of the inner city. Today, concerns have been raised on the destruction and relocation of traditional social cultural attributes of Georgetown, including street vendors, petty traders and craftsmen, due to high rentals, declining inner city population, and changing lifestyles. The paper examines efforts undertaken by the Penang Municipal Council in providing a conducive living and working environment for the city residents, shoppers, tourists and traders alike, to ultimately improve the quality of life for the city populace.

The roles of the private sector, NGOs and the community are also highlighted to gauge grass root support. In the long run, it is critical that Georgetown's built environment and cultural properties be planned and managed in ways that complement its historical patterns and traditions in order to enhance the city's economic profile and sustain its socio-cultural diversity. This pre-requisite would contribute strongly towards the establishment of Georgetown as a creative city in the new economy.

This chapter will explore the impact of rapid urbanization on an island that is within the capital's tourist orbit and is currently valued for its diversity and 'rural' character inscribed in its traditional livelihoods and architecture, both of which are now under threat by precisely those processes of modernization that valorises them as 'traditional' and therefore of commercial, tourist value. It will examine representation and adaptations of the past in Phnom Penh suburbs, focusing on water based communities. The paper will highlight the ways in which rapid urban development has affected life around the capital, as rural sites such as Koh Dach are pulled into the peri-urban fringe.

About fifteen kilometers Northeast of Phnom Penh, the island of Koh Dach possesses more than 50 pre- war houses of which were built more than 80 years ago. Most of the 2,000 households on Koh Dach engage in farming, weaving and tourism, and it has become a popular tourist attraction, especially along the waterfront. However, little attention has been paid to the heritage value of the island's traditional houses, and those closest to the Island's transport and tourist hubs have seen extensive and un-coordinated renovation in recent years. Plans for a new bridge linking the island to the mainland will hasten this modernization.

Traditionally, many settlements in Cambodia as elsewhere in Southeast Asia occurred among main waterways. In Phnom Penh as elsewhere, these old patterns have been overlaid by a rapidly developing road system, particularly in and around urban areas. In this context, what characteristics of housing and living style can we identify as Cambodian (Khmer)? This chapter seeks to ask that question by focusing both on how people perceive and how and to what end they might preserve those forms and values they and others identify as "traditional", through the promotion of traditional or cultural landscape conservation. The paper will consider some planning strategies for cultural landscape conservation in Koh Dach.

CULTURAL DIVERSITY FOR SOUTHEAST ASIA

The Philippines plays an important role in the promotion of cultural diversity in Southeast Asia. Few might have known it but its Palawan conservation experience is worth replicating for the region. Pawalan is great not only as a diving haven. It is also a home to two of UNESCO's designated World Heritage Sites, the Tubbataha Reef Marine Park and the Puerto Princesa Subterranean River National Park and a number of locally-declared natural wildlife sanctuaries. These resource potentials, however, are threatened by fundamental factors that are necessary for any development effort to be realized. There are infrastructure projects, tourism, investment programs, and livelihood opportunities, to name a few.

All these have, in one or many ways, caused massive movement of goods, services, and peoples with major social and cultural significance and consequences. It is thus crucial to look into this development phenomenon and its socio-cultural impact in relation to promoting cultural diversity and the management of Palawan's cultural heritage. It must be noted that with the massive influx of local and international tourists, conservation effort of these valuable World Heritage Sites and of the province's natural environs is a tremendous task.

This will not only give a glimpse of a well-defined agenda for cultural diversity, but this will certainly enlighten policymakers, reform agents, program implementers, and community leaders of an alternative pro-active paradigm for action. A collective effort of all sectors concerned to seriously pursue a blueprint for cultural diversity under a sustainable development paradigm for Southeast Asia, just like what is being done in Palawan, is a crucial legacy that will ultimately make "development" a tool that will enhance Southeast Asia's competitive lead in global cultural diversity contest.

Particularly, this chapter delves into the cultural diversity experience of Palawan, Philippines where marriage between culture and development are revealed. This provides an impetus for audience to know that culture and development may not necessary work contrary to each other and that, in fact, both can effectively complement to achieve best results and hence, the promotion of genuine and more humane outlook for development.

The framework that describes four fundamental influences are culture, markets, history, and geography in terms of an essential underlying tension between modernity and tradition. This approach helps to situate individual cities within a framework that juxtaposes culture and markets as alternative systems of valuation. Likewise, historical and geographical influences are linked through a space-time interplay drawn from the work of David Harvey. The framework to develop tentative analyses of the underlying vortex of city shaping forces impinging upon three different cities in Southeast Asia: Jakarta, Singapore and Kuala Lumpur.

CITY PLANNING IN HYDERABAD AND KUALA LUMPUR

The problem with rapid urbanisation is not so much that there are vast numbers of new people in the city, but those public planners, social commentators, journalists and the reading public (readers of journalism, commentary and policy) see these arrivals as a problem. In contemporary cultural studies arguments have been put forward that revolve around the slogan: urbanization causes hybridity – referring to the cultural frisson and mix that is both a resource for a vital creative economy and something in need of an interventionist solution.

This smacks of the twin fantasies of exoticization – "ooh, look, cultural differences" – and commodification – "they are differences we can sell". That the planning and zoning of cities now includes routine acknowledgement of diversity, and embraces institutional forms and supports to mix such diversity with creative industry, is the current benchmark of capitalist development thinking. This thinking has a heritage that reaches back through the past sixty years of social engineering – the examples in this presentation will be the life-world-creative industry mix, showcased in recent so-called 'technopolis' projects, such as the MultiMedia Super Corridor in Kuala Lumpur, Malaysia and the digital economy redevelopment of Hyderabad, in India.

THE VALUE OF CULTURE SHOCK IN INTERNATIONAL URBAN DESIGN

Urban design practice is more globalised than ever. Urban designers are increasingly asked to make propositions for places and cultures which contributes valuable expertise, the issues of cultural relevance and sensitivity of their interventions are of critical importance. The global flow of ideas and expertise is very much one-way. Theories, doctrines, methods and practices developed in the West (and represented as "global") get implemented in the East, often without necessary cultural contextualization and at the detriment to the local quality. At the same time, cultures of the East have insignificant impact on urban thinking and development in the West. How should urban design professionals act in such situations?

How should the educators prepare graduates for meaningful encounter with difference and the other? Those studios addressed real-life in East and South East Asia. They were co-organised with overseas partners and conducted in collaboration with local institutions. The fieldwork was used to help students experience otherness; develop better understanding of both the host and their own cultures, and cultural nuances in doing and teaching design. This chapter consists of three interrelated parts. The first part summarises the origin and philosophy behind those travelling studios.

The study of the city is strongly influenced by the use of dichotomies, such as Gemeinschaft and Gesellschaft, mechanic and organic solidarity, town and countryside, centre and periphery, formal and informal sector, and globalization and localization. Famous examples of classic oppositions applied in urban studies are Gemeinschaft and Gesellschaft by Tönnies (1887), and mechanic and organic solidarity by Durkheim (1893). These concepts are analytical constructs used to understand the social transformation occurring in an industrializing and urbanizing society. Tönnies argued that

Gemeinschaft relationships are found mostly in the countryside and are characterized among other features by mutual help and dependence, as well as communal feelings rooted in family and neighbourly relations.

In contrast, *Gesellschaft* relationships are considered to be more individualistic in nature. They are often based on functional and contractual agreements and imply tension, sometimes culminating in conflict. Tönnies argued that in the course of time *Gemeinschaft* relationships are replaced by *Gesellschaft* relationships. Durkheim saw traditional society as characterized by mechanical solidarity rooted in correspondences between individuals in a society. These correspondences between individuals diminish when society becomes more differentiated as the consequence of an increased division of labour, which implies organic solidarity between individuals.

The distinction between town and countryside was elaborated in the 1950s when empirical research proved the existence of differences between rural and urban societies in the United States with regard to family size, mortality, level of education, ethnicity, and marital status. In the 1970s this dichotomy was complemented by the more abstract concepts of centre and periphery. This elaboration offered the possibility to pose the question of whether the town always functions as the centre of development. Moreover, it opened ways for more general approaches of international and intranational relations, for example, in the framework of studies on imperialism with models based on centers existing both in centre and periphery nations as well as peripheries located in the centre and periphery nations.

In the 1970s formal and informal sector research began to flourish. This approach implied a distinction between activities of a formal, contractual, and registered nature, contrasted with informal, familial, and non-registered activities. The underlying question was whether informal activities, were these to be recognized and accepted by the government, could become a stronger factor in the development process than when they were simply neglected or, conversely, hampered by the authorities as the official policy was restricted to the formal sector activities only.

In the 1990s and at the turn of the century, a new dichotomy has come to the fore as a consequence of discussions on globalization and localization. The space in urban areas incorporated in global flows of capital, ideas, and personnel is contrasted to the space of place, characterized by a localized character and exclusion from globalization tendencies. This means that the distinction between the space of places and the space of flows has become a new focus for scholarly attention with regard to mega-urbanized regions in the world in general and in Southeast Asia in particular.

This tenacity of dichotomized theorizing in urban studies is astonishing in an era in which the metropolises of Southeast Asia are developing into mega-urban regions. These regions represent a new form of urbanization incorporating a great variety of areas and life-styles. They include old inner cities, slums, industrial areas, suburbs, greenery, agriculture, recreational centers, new towns, extensive communication and transportation networks and so on. This pluriformity of land use, social communities, and ways of living in first instance would give rise to the expectation of more complex theorizing.

However, the complex and rapidly changing urban realities are determined to such a large extent by processes of globalization that this new theoretical construction of opposite concepts is becoming accepted more and more as crucial to the understanding of the present-day urban transition. In this chapter we shall begin by exposing two theoretical frameworks, one on mega-urbanization and one on the informational society, and then present some data from and examples of Southeast Asian cities. A more detailed description of the place-local dimension is followed by an exploration of the flow-global dimension of Southeast Asian cities.

TOWARDS A NEW MINDSET

One of the well-known scholars studying Southeast Asian cities is T.G. McGee. He has discussed a great number of topics ranging from traditional forms of urbanization in the region to modern mega-urban developments. In his work on recent trends with Robinson, he states that mega-cities in Southeast Asia are rapidly extending beyond their boundaries. 'This process has particularly effected the largest cities but is also now occurring in the largest secondary ones, such as Chiang Mai in Thailand, Bandung in Indonesia, and Cebu City in the Philippines. Metropolitan regional growth tends to sprawl along major expressways and railroad lines radiating out from the urban cores, and leapfrogs in all directions, putting down new towns, industrial estates, housing projects, and even golf courses in areas hitherto agricultural and rural. In such areas, regions of dense population and mixed land uses are created, in which traditional agriculture is found side by side with modern factories, commercial activities, and suburban development'.

The concept of extended metropolitan region or *desakota* zones has been coined for this amoebic-like spatial form of region-based urbanization, which seems diametrically opposed to the city-based urbanization to which we are accustomed. These urban regions have several components, such as the 'city core', the 'metropolitan area', and the 'extended metropolitan area', the last constituting the patched area of mixed agricultural and non-agricultural activities listed above. Pertinently, mega-urban regions, according to McGee and Robinson, may follow divergent patterns of spatial growth. An example of the 'expanding state model' is the growth triangle of Singapore, also involving part of Malaysian Johor and Indonesian Riau.

Kuala Lumpur is a case in point following the 'extended metropolitan region model' and Jakarta, Manila, and Bangkok are examples of 'high-density extended metropolitan regions'. These new urban phenomena cannot be analysed with ideas developed for the reality of the ancient town or the old metropolis in mind. Many of these ideas are obsolete and are inapplicable to mega-urban regions. The large size of cities, for example, need not be a problem in itself. Contrary to the general run of feelings, such regions can also be sustainable and need not be economically parasitic.

Cogently, these regions are certainly not only cities of the poor, although many poor live there, but it is proved that the poor often have better chances and are better off in cities than they are in the rural areas. Faced with these disclosures, according to McGee, a new mindset is needed. We have to abstract what is relevant and pertinent from many old ideas and dichotomies, which have developed into myths and prejudices. New insights leading to a completely different urban reality are required.

URBAN REGIONS IN THE INFORMATIONAL SOCIETY

The work of Castells can probably provide us with such a new mindset for the study of mega-urbanization. In previous publications Castells has already dealt with urban regions. In his latest work, *The Information Age: Economy, Society and Culture,* consisting of three volumes, covering *The Rise of the Network Society, The Power of Identity, and End of Millennium,* he has put his ideas into an encompassing theoretical framework. In this section we shall begin by discussing this framework in brief, after which we shall go deeper into Castells' analysis of space in general and urban space in particular.

Since the 1970s two parallel processes have taken places that have fundamentally changed the way societies are organized world-wide. On the one hand, there have been revolutionary technological changes: the development and use of microchip technology as a carrier of information, of computers, and networking between computers to store and transmit information. Digital technology has opened up an entire range of new modes of communication. At the same time, driven by a profitability crisis in the Fordist mass production system, the capitalist mode of production has been in the process of restructuring.

The vertically integrated giant enterprise was no longer the most advanced way of organizing production. Deregulation, privatization, and globalization of production and distribution, in combination with the use of new information technologies, have led to a new economic structure in the form of a network. In this network, the economically dominant regions, social groups, and functions are interconnected in real time - through these new information technologies - and are interdependent. Flows of capital and information circulate between these regions and social groups.

Castells analyses the social implications of this technological revolution and the restructuring of capitalism in a comprehensive way. His central thesis is that the transformation process taking place has two dominant characteristics: (1) the network becoming the dominant morphology of all aspects of social life and (2) the uneven diffusion of this network morphology throughout the world. The possibilities of the new information technologies have given rise to speculation with regard to the future of cities. These technologies could make urban areas redundant. As activities can be performed and co-ordinated from a distance, they would no longer be bound to a specific locale.

All major activities, like working, shopping, and banking could be performed from within the sitting-room. Indeed the introduction of new information technologies means that spatial contiguity is no longer a prerequisite for time-sharing social and economic interaction. Yet, one of Castells' statements is that urban regions will not disappear. They will even grow in size and number. Cities will remain important in the future. In the cities business centers can find the highly skilled professionals and the suppliers they require. At a practical level, once real estate investments have been made in city centers, enterprises are reluctant to move away. Nor is the victory of technology absolute, Castells argues that important business deals are usually not made via the Internet, but still require face-to-face contact.

Finally, most opportunities for personal services, leisure, entertainment, and education for the elite are found in metropolitan areas. However, Castells argues that, because of the parallel transformations briefly described in the previous section, the logic of urban regions has been fundamentally transformed. He does not present us with simple models or easy futurology, but describes a complex pattern of change.

The new urban form is characterized by simultaneous concentration and deconcentration; globalization and localization. A dual structure is emerging in which some cities are included in a global, interdependent network dominating economic, political, and social life, while other cities are excluded from this network.

This network is hierarchical though flexible in nature. The dual structure is versatile, some cities or parts of cities becoming included in the network, and others excluded. Below we shall discuss these characteristics of contemporary urban form in more detail. The form of a city is related to the functions it serves. The spatial organization of these functions has changed in accordance with the parallel transformations described above. With it, urban form has changed as well. We shall discuss at this juncture the locational pattern of advanced services and manufacturing in urban regions. Advanced services are at the heart of the global economy.

Information technologies allow for both the world-wide dispersion of these services and for the deconcentration of these services at the city level. The latter process is mainly related to 'mass processing' and 'execution of strategies decided in corporate centers'. On the other hand, there is a simultaneous concentration of these services in a few urban centers. Looking at the matter of international finance for example, New York, London, and Tokyo play a leading role. With regard to the location of manufacturing industries, there is continuity in the dominance of major metropolitan areas. Yet, new high-tech zones are also being developed, and have acquired an important place in the world economy.

These dominant manufacturing and advanced service areas and 'milieux of innovation' are interconnected in a global network and are interdependent. Besides global cities, which play the leading role in world economics, there are also regional, national, and local centers connected to this network. Between these nodes of the global economy, there is a constant exchange of capital, information, and images, which circulate the world in split seconds. This is, for example, the case with transfers of stocks, shares, and currencies on the capital market. A second example is the exchange of information, images, and music via the Internet. In this global network 'no place exists by itself, since the positions are defined by flows'.

'The emphasis on interactivity between places breaks up spatial patterns of behaviour into a fluid network of exchanges that underlies the emergence of a new kind of space, [which Castells calls] the space of flows.' The composition and hierarchy of this network is not fixed but subject to 'endless changing movements of co-operation and competition between firms and locales'. It is precisely the versatility of this network structure that is characteristic of the new spatial organization of dominant economic activities. Given this the hierarchy of the different places thus can and does change. We see this, for example, in the rapid inclusion in the world economy of some parts of China, like the Pearl River Delta.

While a number of flows converge in the centers of the global economy, other places or cities are bypassed. The most important determinant in this respect is the differential ability of regions, societies, or groups to master the new information technologies. Difficulty in this respect is an important source of international and intranational inequality. The main economic differences are no longer found between the North and the South, but within these regions. Some countries in the so-called Third World are developing very fast, while others are being left behind. South Korea, for example, has increased its Gross Domestic Product per capita more then tenfold, from the average level of Africa in 1950 to the level of Greece, Ireland, and Portugal in 1992.

Within countries some social groups or territories are also developing, while other stagnates. A large, often uneducated, part of the world population is excluded from the global network or adversely affected by it. This, what Castells calls the Fourth World, can be found both in the developed and developing world alike. It is not a lack of economic means as such, but disconnectedness from the global network that determines a new type of poverty, namely exclusion from the dominant social and economic processes in society. The excluded can be found in developing countries, but also in ghettos of American and European cities. Those who are included live in the West, but also in the capitals of African, Asian and Latin American countries.

In other words there is a dual structure in the world economy and present-day spatial organization. Besides the dominant spatial logic of the space of flows of those areas that are connected to the global network, there is another logic that of the space of places, of the disconnected, marginalized cities and regions. The spatial logic of the two is fundamentally different. Whereas locations belonging to the space of flows only exist in relation to other places connected to the global network, those belonging to the space of places are self-contained. The form and identity of the latter are distinct, historically and culturally rooted. In contrast, the form and identity of the spaces of flows express sameness.

This is, for example, articulated in architecture. The major business centers, such as international hotels and airports often look alike, their architecture trying to supersede culture and history. This post-modern architecture, according to Castells, is characteristic of the space of flows, while the architecture of the space of places is more culturally and historically rooted. According to this author, the elite, belonging to this space of flows, also 'create a lifestyle and ... design spatial forms aimed at unifying the symbolic environment around the world'. At the same time however, these cultural codes serve as in- and out-group boundaries, drawing a line between those connected to the space of flows and those living in the space of places.

This dual structure of contemporary society, in the form of a contrast between the space of flows and the space of places, is articulated in mega-cities. These agglomerations of ten million or more inhabitants constitute a new urban form which, Castells argues, will be characteristic of the third millennium. These mega-cities are the main centers of economically and politically dominant functions of the global economy. Playing the major role in the global network described above, and being globally connected to other dominant (mega-) cities; at the local level they disconnect the people and regions within their own borders and hinterland that are unnecessary to this global network. In the following sections, after sketching the historical diversity of Southeast Asian cities, we will elaborate on both the places and peoples that are connected and those that are disconnected from the network in Southeast Asia.

URBAN DIVERSITY IN TIME AND PLACE

The region of Southeast Asia is very diverse and although the overall level of urbanization is still modest in comparison that in Western countries, nevertheless large numbers of people are living in the big cities. Thailand has even acquired fame as an example of a country with a multi-million primate city: the capital Bangkok exceeding many times in size the other large cities in the country. In fact, it is sometimes usual to speak of an uneven urban structure or an urban gap, because of the lack of middle-sized urban centers in this country. The urban development in Southeast Asia has passed through several phases.

The three stages, namely traditional cities, colonial city-formation and postcolonial dependence-urbanization, are represented either directly or indirectly in the present-day situation of mega-urbanization. In the pre-colonial period in some parts of Southeast Asia, such as the Philippines and New Guinea, traditional settlements were small, generally not larger than villages. Other countries in the region, however, have experienced high levels of civilization with substantive early city formation. These traditional cities are generally divided into two types, namely inland and coastal cities.

Two examples of famous traditional cities in the region are Angkor, capital of the an old Khmer Empire situated in present-day Cambodia, and Sriwijaya, the capital of the like-named realm probably located near present-day Palembang in the Indonesian island of Sumatra. The first is a typical inland city based on the extraction of agricultural produce, and the latter a coastal town with trade as the main source of livelihood, although indubitably directly or indirectly inland cities were also related to trade and coastal cities to agriculture. The city of Angkor was the capital of an ancient Khmer state that functioned from the ninth to the fifteenth century in the region of present-day northwestern Cambodia. The archaeological site is located near the city of Siemréab. At its peak the influence of the ancient kings ranged from present-day China and Vietnam to India. The city was a centre of administration and religion, and is particularly known for two temples, Angkor Wat and Angkor Thom.

It was abandoned in 1431 after being captured by the Thais. The layout of the city was a representation of a cosmic Hindu-Buddhist landscape with the mount of the gods in the centre encircled by the habitats of humans and spirits on the continents and oceans. Kostov says that Angkor re-enacts this sacred configuration 'in a rigidly orthogonal plan and a lavish, ornate architectural style'. 'The Bayon in the center, the largest temple of the city, is the mountain of the gods, Mount Meru. Surrounding it is the enclosure of the royal palace, followed further out by the walls and a wide moat, corresponding to the lower elements of the cosmological universe. The moat was crossed by five stone causeways. This royal city formed a square almost two miles (some 3 km.) on each side. The towers above the four axial city gates, directed toward the four cardinal points, had the same crowns [....] as did the gate towers of the central temple.'

Outside the city were situated several water reservoirs. These artificial lakes served to irrigate a large areal of rice fields. The common people lived in densely occupied villages outside the walls amidst these rice fields. In contrast to Angkor, very little is known about the city of Srivijaya, which was the capital of the enonymously named ancient kingdom in Sumatra. It was probably located near present-day Palembang, although Jambi also might have been the capital of this kingdom for a period. A report on the results of an archaeological research project in Palembang that started in 1991 was published by the Departemen Pendidikan dan Kebudayaan in 1993.

It mentions Palembang, Java (Libor), Jambi, Kedah, and Muara Takus as possible sites of the capital of Sriwijaya. The reason for this lack of data is that most of the buildings were made of perishable materials, little of which has survived. The city, most probably the palace area, was surrounded by a brick wall. The ordinary population lived either outside the confines of the wall, or on rafts moored to the banks of the river. The hinterland of the city was sparsely populated and was barely cultivated. Chau Ju Kua describes the position of the ruler in Sriwijaya as follows: 'When the king goes out, he sits in a boat; his body has a *mau-pu* (*sarong*) wrapped around it. He is sheltered by a silk umbrella and guarded by men bearing golden lances.

The people either lived scattered about outside the city, or on the water on rafts of boards covered over with reeds, and these are exempt from taxation. They are skilled at fighting on land or water. When they are about to make war on another state they assemble and send forth such a force as the occasion demands. They (then) appoint chiefs and leaders, and all provide their own military equipment and the necessary provisions. In facing the enemy and craving death they have not their equal among nations.' The influence of Sriwijaya was far-reaching and it reached its peak in the thirteenth century.

At a certain time it was probably what is termed a binodal state consisting of the city of Sriwijaya in the south on the Straits of Malacca and the city of Kedah in the north on the Malaya Peninsula. As it owed its origins to a trading empire, its major function was as an entrepôt. Its importance can also be deduced from the fact that it sent ambassadors bearing tribute to China and maintained cloisters in South India. The ruler owned ships. Ruler and the aristocracy were engaged in trade and taxed the transit trade; as well as deriving income from holding the staple rights. This meant that passing traders and ships were forced to sell their goods there. The trade commodities included tin, gold, ivory, spices, fine sorts of timber, and camphor. War and piracy contributed to the means of livelihood. However, these activities also had a shadow side.

In 1025 the mighty Cola State of South India attacked Sriwijaya. The capital of Sriwijaya was not just a capital and commercial city; it also functioned as a cultural centre. In AD 671 there were already more than a thousand Buddhist monks resident there.

Sriwijaya probably evolved in the seventh century. At the end of the thirteenth century war broke out with Majapahit in East Java and Sriwijaya was forced to surrender some of its power. In the fourteenth century it was even forced to become a Javanese vassal. In the wake of an insurrection, it was punished by a Javanese fleet but, for the most part, the Javanese left the kingdom to its fate. The advent of Islam caused the final eclipse of this Buddhist-Hindu kingdom. Many left the capital and very few traders still came there.

The European colonization of Southeast Asia from the west was very diverse, because the Portuguese, Spaniards, Dutch, English, and French were active in the process, and some areas, such as Thailand, were not colonized at all. At the beginning of the process enclave settlements were built to create bases for the support of trade. Later, settlements with a mixture of the Western and local population, often in combination with other ethnic groups, such as Chinese, Indians, or Arabs, came into being. Cities assumed a dualist structure with Western colonial wards and indigenous areas. Besides the enclave trade towns' garrison towns generally with a trade function were also established. Later these settlements played a role in the greater colonization of the region. Batavia is a good example of this process.

In 1619 the Dutch created this fortification and trade post on the site of a quite important local port town. Batavia grew up after the complete slighting of this indigenous princely settlement. The town was probably laid out after a map made by the Dutch town planner Simon Stevin. It was an unequivocal copy of the Dutch towns at that time with canals, drawbridges, canal houses, step-gables, a church, church bell-ringing, and streets paved with cobble stones. Batavia was shaped around a central axis, a main street that connected the castle to the town-hall and left room in between for beautiful vistas from the town centre. The system of canals was rectangular, as was the case in Amsterdam at that time.

Along defensive works like the castle, which in fact was a fortification, and the town walls, lines of Dutch canal houses complete with their characteristic flights of steps were found there. Batavia was a typical frontier town suffering a permanent lack of labour and materials. Because of existing tensions with the states of Mataram and Banten, no Javanese were tolerated in town for a long time. The Dutch were afraid of a revolt from inside. Batavia also was a slave town. The need for labour was supplied by slaves brought in from such places as India and Bali. Slaves were used as porters (*kuli*) in storage houses and on construction works, and as craftsmen. Prisoners-of-war and criminals were also used as labour.

The distinction between freemen and non-freemen was the most crucial criterion in the stratification system of Batavia, apart from the differences in race between Europeans, Indo-Europeans, foreign Orientals, and the indigenous population. This last group, the Indonesians, lived outside the town walls of Batavia in *kampung* shady with many fruit trees. At the inception of the settlement the Chinese lived in town, but were no longer allowed to live there after the so-called Chinese massacre of 1740. They had to settle in the Chinese camp outside the town wall, on the site of present Glodok. During its first stage Batavia flourished and was praised by Valentijn for its beautiful buildings, shady canals, straight streets, many different markets, and lively trade. Population growth as well as the water pollution and endemic illnesses as malaria later caused an urban exodus.

Daendels, who was governor general from 1808 to 1811, was the catalyst of the process of suburbanization that marked the second stage of Batavia. His departure to more salubrious Weltevreden caused many Europeans to follow suit. Weltevreden was situated around a large square, on which the palace was located. Besides this large square, there was a smaller one that was initially more important because of the various sorts of public buildings such as the palace of Daendels, the Concordia Club, and the Roman Catholic Church. Probably the layout of Weltevreden was to some extent inspired by the traditional Indonesian town. The architecture also showed Indonesian influences, particularly those derived from the *priyayi* house. The cool, roomy mansions had an open look, evoked by their verandas.

The spacious gardens created a pastoral atmosphere. In the old town, a business district began to emerge made up of the offices of the important enterprises, banks, and import and export firms. The Chinese camp had a town-like character, because of the rows of terrace houses and shops. Greater Batavia developed a dualistic structure consisting of the lower old town and of the more highly situated suburb, Weltevreden. These two parts were connected by the Molenvliet and a small strip of Indische mansions. A number of kampung was situated between the two parts. A certain mutual adjustment was taking place between East and West, on the grounds of which it would be fair to speak of Batavia as an Indische town in this phase.

This town was strongly characterized by a process of acculturation, resulting in a mixed culture, called an Indische culture. It originated from the contacts between the Dutch and the Oriental and Indonesian official classes (the *priyayi*), in the public domain and with Indonesian concubines (the *nyai*) in the private domain. Above all it was these women who were responsible for the assimilative character of the Indische culture, because they taught it to their children, who, by the way were classified as European if legally acknowledged by their European father. Inevitably, these women informed their husbands about Indonesian cultural elements that were part of the Indische culture, especially those to do with food, clothes, spiritualism, traditional medicine and its practitioners, and the shadow play (*wayang*).

The Indische culture formed the dome over a more or less integrated social order. Its values were centered on 'a belief in the basic goodness of the European Christian male, an admiration for the Indonesian women, a view of legal status as an attribute of character and an identification of light skin with beauty and virtue'. Disruption of this unity by the rise of nationalism, growing contradictions between European groups and because of the problem of the Indo-Europeans only occurred much later in the colonial period. In its economic domain Batavia combined the functions of coastal and inland town. It was primarily was a governmental and military centre, as were the other Indische towns.

It functioned as a rendezvous, as a trade centre for the archipelago, organized trade to the West, and provided storage, transit, and market facilities. It also was the centre of tax collection for the rural population, which was mainly constituted of forced deliveries and statute labour. Batavia was the gateway to the Orient for the Dutch, and so was Malacca for the Portuguese and Manila for the Spaniards. The city of Manila developed from a fishing port to the most important Spanish military and maritime basis. Malacca became important to the Portuguese after the occupation of 1511.

According to McGee 'The imposition of Portuguese rule led to an increase in the city's population for there is evidence that the Portuguese encouraged Chinese immigration and the number of traders who settled permanently in the city increased considerably. But Portuguese rule did not lead to any radical changes in the social structure of the city. The Bishop replaced the Imam, the Governor replaced the Sultan and the Portuguese citizen possibly assumed more importance in the social structure than his Malay counterpart, but the merchants still retained their importance in the city's society. Nor did the morphology of the city change dramatically apart from the addition of some stone buildings and walls of Fort A'Famosa.'

In the industrial period the world market grew in importance. Besides maintaining trade interests, the colonies became more involved in the delivery of raw materials and simultaneously flourished as consumer markets for such commodities as textile. The colonial towns were steadily directed to an ever greater degree towards the interest of the mother countries and in this third phase the social stratification became caste-like, putatively because of the increasing number of European males and particularly women. The colonial harbour cities were comptoirs, functioning as intermediary between their hinterland and Europe.

This pattern laid the basis for the dependent urbanization, which characterized these cities after the Second World War. Even Thailand which retained political independence developed, as was said before, a skewed urban structure with Bangkok as the dominating primate city. The three phases of urban development - traditional towns, colonial cities, and dependent urbanization - are important to remember to appreciate the changes that are occurring in the present era of globalization, characterized by autonomous mega-urban development at the regional level.

As a matter of course, the older phases directly or indirectly influence the present-day situation, for example, Palembang is keeping the memory of Srivijaya alive for city promotion. Ruins of traditional towns have become cynosures of modern tourism everywhere. Colonial architecture is also dominant in many cities and considered to be of great value to city life and beauty, and the cities resulting from dependence urbanization are still functioning as capitals in modern times, incorporating and partially maintaining the old layers of development.

Nevertheless, notwithstanding these continuities, the major leap which has now been taken into an era of region-based mega-urbanization is evident. Many questions may be posed about the meaning of the present socio-spatial transition and resulting urban configurations. The distinction presented above between the dimensions of place and the flow may be helpful in unravelling this new phase in the process of urbanization.

THE SPACE OF PLACES

As described above, Castells makes a distinction between

the space of flows and the space of places. The first is part of a global network of flows of capital, information, images, and power; the latter is excluded from this network. In this section we will discuss 'the excluded' in urban areas and their spatial organization. It almost seems to be a *contradictio in termines* to speak about the 'excluded' in the present-day world in which societies are becoming increasingly interdependent. The isolated tribes which anthropologists used to search for have practically disappeared. Indeed, it is becoming more and more difficult for societies to withdraw from outside influences. In this sense, all places and societies are 'included'.

As mentioned earlier, Castells puts the dichotomy in a different way. Whereas most societies are somehow influenced by broader processes outside their own borders, not all societies or peoples are influenced in the same way and to the same extent. In Castells' eyes, being 'included' equals having the ability to exert some influence on, or being a major player in these global processes. Access to and the ability to work with information technologies is he believes indispensable. In this regard, some cities are more dominant than others.

This can be examined empirically by comparing the number of flows of capital, information, and images that converge in some urban areas, while bypassing others. In the last two decades, the dichotomy between what used to be called the First and the Third World has been dissolved into a much more complex, flexible but nevertheless still dual structure of the interconnected space of flows on the one hand, and the marginalized space of places on the other.

The most important differences are no longer found between the First and the Third World, but within these regions. Some Africans belong to the richest people in the world, but a considerable percentage of American children live in poverty. Marginalized places and people can thus be found in the Western and non-Western world alike. This complex dual structure is also apparent at the level of cities in general and mega-urban regions in particular. From a socio-economic perspective these regions are often extremely diverse. They include parts which are highly developed and capital-rich, characterized by a predominance of advanced services, elite housing, and leisure facilities. Other parts of these regions are often socially and economically marginalized.

These areas attract few high capital investments; consequently the people living there often have a low educational attainment, live in run-down houses, and have fewer perspectives for personal development. The space of places and the space of flows in mega-urban regions are not always geographically separated. They can sometimes also be found side-by-side in the same neighbourhood. In this section we will focus on the characteristics of the space of places, and the space of flows will be discussed in the following section.

What do the places that are bypassed look like? Castells defines these places as self-contained and which have an identity and architecture that is historically and culturally rooted. This stands in contrast to the uniformity of the space of flows. A place which can serve as an example in this regard is Pisangan Baru, a poor-to-lower middle-class quarter in Jakarta, one of Asia's largest metropoles. It is one of the 'old established *kampungs*', in colonial times Pisangan Baru used to be the east gate to the city. Swallowed up in the vast urban expansion, at present-day the neighbourhood is absorbed into the metropolitan area. The local Betawinese who used to live there have to a large extent out-migrated.

Their places have been filled by migrants from all over the archipelago. Even today the population mobility is still high. The area, inhabited by mainly young, poor and lower-middle class households, is among those with the highest population density in the city (about 57,000 people per square kilometer). The low economic status and high population density of the neighbourhood are reflected in its physical outlook. The layout of the streets and houses seems to be without structure. The neighbourhood is made up of a labyrinth of pathways and alleys, sometimes just wide enough to let one person squeeze through.

Quite a number of paths are made of concrete but others are sandy tracks which often turn to mud in the rainy season. The numerous gutters and streams are often clogged with plastic and dirt. The neighbourhood layout seems to have evolved gradually over time, seemingly without a predefined plan. The pluriform nature of the housing only adds to this unique identity of the neighbourhood. This hotchpotch of constructions consists of relatively large and well-maintained concrete houses, side-by-side with small, run-down wooden, bamboo, or brick constructions. The poorest inhabitants of all live in tiny, one-room wooden shelters besides the railway line. Each of the houses has its own form. Like the neighbourhood itself, the houses also seem to have been developed gradually over time.

When the owners have saved enough money, wooden walls are replaced by brick ones or a storey is added. Other houses are divided into two living quarters, providing room for a newly wed daughter and her husband. This heterogeneous nature of the houses in combination with a high density of buildings and twisting alleys sometimes makes it hard for outsiders to tell where one house ends and another begins. A large part of social life takes place in the streets and alleys where people, especially the women, sit and chat in front of their houses, sort rice, sell snacks, watch over the children, do their washing and go to the local market a few corners away. Some of the men also try to make money in or around the neighbourhood, as the owner of a small shop or a stall-holder, as a motor taxi driver, market vendor, carpenter, or second-hand goods trader. All this leads to a blurring of the distinction between public and private.

This chaotic configuration of Pisangan Baru makes it virtually impossible for an outsider to map this area. Social boundaries may also contribute to its inaccessibility, especially for the richer fellow citizen. Around the neighbourhood, and especially near the railway station, there is a high level of street prostitution, a widely spread but socially unaccepted phenomenon. Social control is high, because most of the houses are small; the inhabitants spend a lot of their time outside at their front door.

As a consequence, they notice everybody who passes by and will be especially aware of non-residents. The richer Jakartans often describe the people living in poor areas like Pisangan Baru as dangerous, rough, uneducated, and undeveloped, and their living quarters as dirty and unhealthy, and will try to avoid these areas when possible. Through *kampung* improvement programmes the government is making an effort to upgrade the physical infrastructure of areas like Pisangan Baru. Sand paths are turned into concrete ones, small, twisting alleys are widened and straightened, gutters and streams are cleaned. It is sometimes suggested that these programmes also function as a government attempt to gain more control over these areas.

This government penetration is not always appreciated by the inhabitants, as they sometimes have to give up some of their private property for public infrastructure. Given the above, at a first inspection, Pisangan Baru seems to fit Castells' description of a space of places: a self-contained area with a historically rooted unique identity. However, we would like to challenge the black-and-white division between the space of flows and the space of places. We would like to argue that Pisangan Baru - and probably also other places which would appear 'excluded'- is much more related to the rest of the city, and as such to global capital flows and political power processes than Castells would like us to believe.

For one thing, Pisangan Baru is not self-contained. While in it being inaccessible for outsiders, the neighbourhood is located fairly strategically with regard to transportation and infrastructure facilities. It is situated behind Jatinegara railway station, and along major (toll) roads, connecting the area with other parts of the city. Motor taxis, three-wheeled motorized vehicles, a variety of mini buses and large buses, and taxis, make virtually all destinations accessible by public transport (although using the cheaper, crowded buses in the perennially traffic-jammed Jakarta can make travel a quite strenuous undertaking).

This strategic location provides the possibility for a fairly easy exchange between people and products of the neighbourhood and other parts of the city. Many of the inhabitants have either a radio or television, which enables the exchange of information, ideas, images, and sounds. A combination of Western advertisements and soap operas, Asian 'kung fu' films, plus national news and cultural programmes resounds throughout the houses. Moreover, Indonesia has an efficient, nation-wide telecommunication system, connecting the Indonesian people living dispersed over the archipelago with each other and with the rest of the world.

In every neighbourhood, including Pisangan Baru, there is *wartel* (*warung telekomunikasi*), where people can make local, regional, and international phone calls and sends faxes. In the evenings, the office is always full of people waiting to use these facilities. Cogently, as mentioned above, Pisangan Baru has a heterogeneous population largely consisting of migrants. This migration to the Jakarta metropolis is related to global economic and political forces. Especially since the 1970s the migration to Jakarta has accelerated. People from all over Indonesia were attracted by the economic growth the city experienced during these oil boom years.

While quite a number of these migrants have their money making activities in or around the neighbourhood, others have found jobs in the formal sector outside, for example as parking attendant, lower-ranking civil servant, nurse-assistant, and waitress in Dunkin Donut's, or as a bank employee. While indeed Pisangan Baru and the lives of its inhabitants are related to global flows of capital and information, and to global politics, Castells would argue this does not imply that they themselves belong to the space of flows. While related to this space of flows, they remain dependent and marginalized.

This assertion became painfully obvious during the 1990s Asian economic crisis, which struck Indonesia hard. For the inhabitants of Pisangan Baru this economic crisis meant, among other problems, rising prices of food and other basic necessities, increasing costs of private health care services and over-the-counter medication, and rising unemployment. Most of the households have changed the composition of their daily menu since the onset of the crisis. An often combinations of the following food-stuffs were either no longer eaten at all, or were bought in smaller quantities: chicken and meat, fish, eggs, fruit, and milk for children.

While some no longer bought milk anymore for their children, others found it so important that they managed their budget to still be able to buy it. In some of the households there was no financial need to change the diet, but others were already living on such a minimal diet that it left little possibility for any further reduction. In a small number of households not only has the composition of the daily menu changed, but the quantity of food intake has also be adjusted since the onset of the crisis. The members of these households either skip meals, or reduce the amount of rice that is eaten per meal. Some of the households have also changed their health behaviour as a result of the rising prices of health care.

The changes mentioned most often were a shift away from private to public health care, and a shift from the consultation with a doctor to the use of self-medication. There appeared to be a clear inverse relationship between household wealth and the impact of the economic crisis on a household. Wealthy households have experienced only little impact of the crisis, while poor households have been struck hard. Summing up, on the one hand Pisangan Baru is not self-contained, or what Castells calls a 'black hole', but is very much related to global flows of capital, images and power. On the other hand, this neighbourhood remains vulnerable to the impact of these flows, deprived of the ability to steer their direction.

Having said this, we think that another nuance has to be

made. While none of the inhabitants of Pisangan Baru has major political or economic power, there are inhabitants who nevertheless might be regarded as 'included' when taking into account their access to information technologies and ability to work with these is taken into account. The few university students who live there, for example, all have access to computer and Internet facilities on their campus. A few high-skilled professionals also live in Pisangan Baru. Some of these are computer experts, with PCs in their homes. They thus have access to information and people from all over the world. Therefore, we would like to argue that it is not possible to make a clear-cut distinction between space of places and space of flows.

This is even more the case in Malaysia, one of Indonesia's more developed neighbours, with regard to information technology. This technology is more widely diffused here than in Indonesia. In Malaysia, in a small town with nothing much as an attraction, one-day's travel by slow train from the capital city, one can still find public Internet facilities with many fast computers with a good Internet connection. There one can see schoolchildren, boys and girls (the latter both with and without veils) from as young as ten years sitting behind the computers with their eyes glued to the screen, using the Internet chat-rooms and making contact with the opposite sex. While these Internet cafés are private initiatives, they are sometimes also stimulated by a community request for computer education.

In Malaysia one can also find tiny restaurants where local people come to eat cheap local food, served by veiled women, where customers watch a (probably illegally copied) VCD with a video clip of one of the latest Western song hits, titled 'sex bomb', showing scantly clad women. Castells has expressed his concern for an increased disconnection between the space of flows and the space of places. He believes that if no efforts are undertaken to build some 'bridges' between the two, they might become 'two separate universes'. We would prefer to argue that there is no black and white difference between the included and excluded, and that when differences are very large indeed, numerous efforts are undertaken to build 'bridges'. The activities of many NGOs may serve as an example of this.

For instance, a Jakarta-based NGO works with prostitutes gives them empowerment training and workshops concerning sexual health. They are brought into contact with Dutch prostitutes, and have enabled them to compile a book with photos taken and poems written by the prostitutes themselves. To which extent do these people belong to the space of flows or the space of places? Is the Malaysian schoolboy using Internet included or excluded, and what about the computer expert living in Pisangan Baru? They have access to information technology and the ability to use it, but do they really have influence on global economic and political processes? Who actually does? Does a person belong to the space of flows when he has access to Internet or when he has some stocks or shares?

THE SPACE OF FLOWS

As said before, the space of flows is that part of society that is included in the global streams of money, people, and ideas. Most prominent, of course, is the financial market system that is completely interconnected and makes it possible to buy and sell shares somewhere in the world around the clock. The international companies and organizations with their global networks also fall in this category. The hotel chains, airport lobbies, and shopping malls for the travelling business elite are good examples of the space of flows. Their architecture often has the special characteristics of Post-modernism, sometimes completely detached from the cultural area in which it is situated, such as Singapore airport terminal, but sometimes it also combines this atmosphere with localized features, such as Jakarta international airport terminal where the halls are decorated in different regional styles.

Hotels may also have this localized expression on a globalised frame, such as the international Hilton hotel chain.

The promotion of condominiums and the modern urban compound development in Jakarta before the crisis of the 1990s may also serve as an example of the space of flows imagery. In launching this capital in the framework of enabling strategies backed by the central and local governments, private initiative in housing construction has enjoyed strong support in the past decade.

In the first place, this has pushed condominium construction, often combined with shopping malls and other services and, in the second place; it has stimulated modern Western-style urban compound development, both aiming mainly at the provision of high-class housing environments. This increase in real estate development has triggered off an advertising boom geared to sell the houses and apartments. The presentation of these 'great works' of the 'private initiative period' in urban development, as we call it, seems to be very informative.

One such advertisement for so-called Greenview apartments offers:

'A contemporary, modern, and cosmopolitan life-style with a classic nuance for which all the facilities, such as swimming pool, jogging track, tennis court, and attractive spaces for festivities and formal meetings, are present. This is rounded off by a fully equipped business centre with telephone and fax facilities, and meeting rooms. All this located near the city centre and in the middle of the prestigious area of South Jakarta'.

This advertisement comprises a drawing of a number of high-rise buildings with the swimming pool scintillating in the middle and the edges decorated with parrots. It also has pictures of people playing tennis and golf and of other people busy jogging. These people are all Europeans. Do they constitute the target group or the reference group? In the advertisement 'Town house for rent. Enjoy living by the sea from as little as US $1500. Complete with service and facilities', an elegant Indonesian girl is portrayed diving into the water near the Waterfront Housing Estate which, because of the

European-like, single family dwellings as some sort of a 'horizontal condominium', is probably better adapted to the Indonesian housing specifications and wishes.

The 'Luxury Prapanca Apartment' advertisement does not refer to the target group. Under the tall high rise building it reads:

'Virtually everything you look for in a spacious luxury apartment is right here in the heart of Prapanca Area - Kebayoran Baru. With elegant atrium, fully equipped fitness centre, swimming pool, squash court, whirlpool, sauna, mini tennis court, mini golf driving range, golf putting green, and 24-hours security and maintenance services, we have truly set the standard for a better place to stay.'

A compound development delivering free-standing, single family dwellings is found in East Jakarta and advertised as a garden area. The small mansions have concomitantly small gardens and the whole ward gives the impression of a European garden city area. Other compound developments have terrace housing, which heightens their Western ambience. These condominiums and modern compound developments transform the city into a conglomerate of protected islands owned by the rich in a sea of *kampung* and offices with a connecting infrastructure that leaves much to be desired, and this type of development can be characterized as the privatization of public space.

In Castells' terms these privatized areas are clearly the connected ones. The advertisements for office buildings and services related to these dwelling developments also provide rich insights into the development of the urban context. By its manipulation of positive contrast this advertisement put out by PT Bhumyanca Sekawan clearly shows the defects of the urban environment in which this self-contained unit is located.

The global influence in urban development in Jakarta is also beautifully illustrated by the new town, Lippo City, near

Bekasi, which is intended to house one million inhabitants. The master plan for this 'city of tomorrow which is here today', according to one of its fancy brochures, is 'the work of internationally recognized city planner Meng Ta Cheang, whose award-winning designs for new cities in the Netherlands, Germany, China, and Malaysia have had substantial impact in the field. His Singapore-based firm is associated with OD 205 Architects, a firm which has its headquarters in the Netherlands and is now involved in major urban development projects around the world.' This city is completely devoid of Indonesian decorations and symbols.

This picture of modern, global, and connected urban development should be completed by the phenomenon of the mall. Many of these have been developed in cities at different levels such as Singapore, Jakarta, and Denpasar. One example is Metro Pondok Indah in South Jakarta. This is an enormous, three-storey complex with luxury shops, restaurants, a cinema complex, and video games hall. The shops cover almost all possible sectors from electronics to furniture, clothing to toys and office equipment. There are shops for Western wedding frocks and sports shoes. They are modern and colourful. Like the real estate projects, they almost all have English names: Shop in Body Care; Sports Station, the Sport Supermarket; 101 Shoes Shop; Royal Textile & Tailor; Sizzle Steak, Seafood, Salad; California Pizza. One exception is the French café Oh La La. The toilet area is indicated in English as 'restroom' and the doors have 'man' and 'woman'.

The shopping centre is most frequented by young people. They stand there, talking in groups, eating ice-cream, looking over the balustrade at the escalators and at lower levels of the building. Couples date there and young families enjoy their day out. Everybody is nicely clothed, sometimes even extremely well-dressed, but always attired, visitors sometimes wear leisure clothing but they are never dirty or slatternly. The building is very clean with shining tile floors. There is an abundance of services and guards are found in every nook and cranny. In front of the main entrance on request somebody loudly calls the drivers with their cars to pick up the owners, so that they do not need to walk any distance or go in search of their vehicle.

All around the building are beautiful lawns and extensive parking spaces. Informal sector activities are completely banned from the scene. In 1995 a policy was launched to call a halt to the proliferation of English names, encouraging the use of Indonesian names in malls and real estate advertisements. This policy is a nice example of reaction to globalization tendencies, in this case of a national character. Another example of Post-modern 'connected' architecture in Southeast Asia is the PETRONAS twin towers at Kuala Lumpur. This pair of Malaysian round skyscrapers is among the tallest buildings in the world.

The towers stretch 452 metres above street level and have eighty-eight stories of occupiable space. They are connected by a sky-bridge at the forty-first and forty-second levels. The building was designed by the Argentine-born American architect, Cesar Pelli, who has also developed tall buildings in London and several cities in the USA. PETRONAS was constructed in association with local firms and completed in 1996. The towers house the headquarters of the Malaysian National State Petroleum Company, but this Southeast Asian 'Arc de Triomphe' also provides ample room for other offices and services.

The skyscraper as a typical American icon has assumed a special character in this Malaysian setting, as it is situated in a large park with a swimming pool and is connected to a giant mall and a concert hall. In fact, the whole area serves as a-city-within-a-city with integrated and mixed functions comprising commercial, retail, hotel, residential and entertainment facilities. This concept of a skyscraper is in strong contrast to the American one. In the USA skyscrapers are generally located in built up areas in the middle of other tall constructions. In their decorations the PETRONAS towers are also adapted to the local setting. They are embellished with patterns of Islamic art, with a liberal use of gold and silver colours and splendid light filtered through green glass.

The Kuala Lumpur twin skyscrapers are prominently part of the space of flows as becomes clear from their elaborate communications system. They are a connected space and the people using them are included in the space of flows by a fully structured cabling system. According to the developers, one of the special features to enable this connectivity is the raised flooring to facilitate cabling. The hub of the system is the Central Telecommunications Office. It serves as a local communications exchange and gateway to the outside world. The network comprises vertical and horizontal cabling and connectivity to telecommunications carrier companies. It is designed as a local loop communications system within the boundaries of the whole project. Several exchange routes ensure network availability and reliability.

This type of tall building has been and is being constructed all over the world and is part of a global process of development and competition. The local people and elite are proud of these icons of modernity. They are the means by which to put the capital city and even the nation world-wide on the map, to attract foreign companies, and to boost the image. Singapore, Hong Kong, Tokyo and many other cities for a shorter or longer time were the proud host to the tallest building of the world in competition with the earlier Western examples, such as the World Trade Centre and Empire State Building in New York.

Other cities such as Jakarta have been trying to be included in the globalization process on a more modest scale by developing the largest mosque of Southeast Asia, the Istiqlal Mosque, or a smaller tall building, such as the one that is planned to mark the former location of the airfield of Jakarta, the new town of Kemayoran. The case of Bangkok is interesting in this context of the analysis of the total urban configuration. The capital of Thailand is, according to Korff (1993), composed of several parts rooted in different historical periods with divergent meanings for the inhabitants. The old centre has a traditional, 'sacred' meaning and encompasses the city pillar as the guardian spirit of the city, the royal chapel related to the monarchy and the state, and the open square, Sanam Lung, used for ceremonies and on certain occasions ritually symbolizing the world mountain.

Western modernizing influences have marked the administrative and infrastructural developments in the city. Besides Thai and Western styles, architectural diversity also includes Chinese characteristics. The opposite of the 'sacred' part of the city is the 'profane' core shaped by democratic values and encompassing the parliament building and ministries. Bangkok, Korff argues, has reached a high level of synthesis between tradition and modernity. However, during the past few decades several modern commercial centers have evolved and the city is increasingly being dominated by modern market mechanisms.

The capital is becoming 'a department store of localities' and is losing its coherence in meaning. The morphological, social, and cultural fragmentation is accompanied by the rise of Post-modernist architecture. This evokes a familiar picture of Southeast Asian mega-urbanization. The development of Bangkok is proceeding towards hybrid, flexible urban structures of localized places and globalized flows under the dome of new architectural forms defined by powerful market forces in the space of flows. The new pair of concepts formulated by Castells, namely space of place and space of flows, leads as we have shown to a different description of the urban societies in Southeast Asia than that which has been considered adequate and more or less conventional so far.

It is the connectivity with modern communications media and particularly the Internet and its consequences that are becoming the focus of research. By the application of these concepts the dichotomy of included and excluded as well as local and global appears to be compulsive. Or perhaps stated more adequately, the analysis is pulled into a 'thick description' made up by the framework set by these three pairs of concepts. Communications and architecture in a developing informational network society on a global scale become the focus of attention. It is not formal registration versus informal activities, or town versus countryside, or communal relationships versus more individualized ways of living that are studied, but connectivity on a global and local scale with its spatial and societal effects.

Besides this new and promising focus, the problems of such a description and analysis are also undeniable. Questions may arise related to the absoluteness of being in the space of place or the space of flows. For it is also true that the excluded may easily enter the space of flows on a communal basis in Internet cafes or by buying small numbers of shares on the stock market, while the included may refrain from such usage in practice, preferring a local, disconnected lifestyle. The included may be tightly knit to the excluded in all sorts of ways and even dependent on them in a positive way by services and a negative way by threat and crime. So, it is not completely clear what precisely is meant by inclusion and exclusion and a specification of direct-indirect, passive-active, and individual-communal inclusions are needed.

These concepts have not been fully reflected upon, defined, and operationalised yet. The space of place and the space of flows are strongly related and even intermingled in modern mega-cities. Probably all sorts of intermediate places are also being developed in this transition period. Moreover, in the foreseeable future the speed of technological innovation will lead to cheap communication media that are working on speech and need no fiber cabling so that in fact the whole world will most probably be included. Then, this inception phase of the informational society will prove to be short and the resulting pattern of exclusion and inequality and globalization and localization consequently not long-lived.

Whatever the new research questions may be and how difficult they are to study and answer, the promising side of this description of Southeast Asian cities is that a combination of a new approach and a new phenomenon has come into being. The new pairs of concepts have to be matched with the evolving processes of mega-urbanization in the region. In our view this combination is a precondition for an interesting and stirring phase in the development of urban research.

6

Grassroots Globalization and the Research Imagination

More obscure still is the approach offered by the reliably enigmatic literary theorist Fredric Jameson (1998), for whom globalization is "an untotalizable totality which intensifies binary relations between its parts-mostly nations, but also regions and groups, which, however, continue to articulate themselves on the model of `national entities` (rather than in terms of social classes, for example)." Jameson, however puzzling, is just getting warmed up: "But what we now need to add to the other qualifications implicit in the formulation-binary or point-to-point relations already being rather different from some plural constellation of localities and particulars is that such relations are first and foremost ones of tension and antagonism, when not outright exclusion: in them each term struggles to define itself against the binary other".

And so on. If much of this stuff can be characterized as "globaloney," to use Claire Booth Luce`s punchy term, which has recently been recycled by economist Paul Krogman, we believe that there is nonetheless something identifiable and analytically valuable about the concept of globalization. In this chapter on globalization in Southeast Asia, we shall try to lay out precisely what and, in so doing, will both delimit and historicize this process. We will even throw in an apposite Southeast Asian binary of our own: Davos Man versus the orang ulu. In a very broad way, we all instinctively know or at least think we know what globalization is.

The problem is pinning down the concept in analytical terms. Rather than looking to Louis Armstrong for inspiration here-when asked about the definition of jazz, the great trumpeter famously responded that "if you gotta ask, you`ll never know"-let us take a shot at specification. Despite the vaporous quotations cited previously, there has in fact been some very useful writing on globalization and its effects. According to one, the globalizers have "given a cosmopolitan character to production and consumption in every country." As a result, all old-established national industries have been destroyed or are daily being destroyed.

They are dislodged by new industries, whose introduction becomes a life and death question for all civilized nations, by industries that no longer work up indigenous raw material, but raw material drawn from the remotest zones; industries whose products are consumed, not only at home, but in every quarter of the globe. In place of the old wants, satisfied by the productions of the country, we find new wants, requiring for their satisfaction the products of distant lands and climes. In place of the old local and national seclusion and self-sufficiency, we have intercourse in every direction, universal interdependence of nations. And as in material, so also in intellectual production. The intellectual creations of individual nations become common property.

Moreover, the globalizers "by the rapid improvement of all instruments of production, by the immensely facilitated means of communication, [draw] all, even the most barbarian, nations into civilization. The cheap prices of [their] commodities are the heavy artillery with which [they batter] down all... walls." A good start, if a bit wordy and a touch dramatic. Oh, yes, a bit on the venerable side, too: the preceding quotations are not from William Greider or Edward Luttwak but from Marx and Engels`s Communist Manifesto, written over 150 years ago. These two scientific socialists certainly captured the spirit of globalization, even if they used different lingo: the group we refer to earlier as globalizers they prefer to call the bourgeoisie.

However powerful Marx and Engels's descriptive language - language that they employ to "burst asunder" the "integument" of globalization, er, capitalism - other, more rigorous or at least testable and thus falsifiable definitional approaches are possible. For example, in defining globalization, one can emphasize change and process and, in so doing, stress increases in the absolute size of transnational flows of labor, capital, products, services, and the like or, more fruitfully, increases in the relative importance of these flows. Krugman, for one, often looks to the relationship between the rate of growth in world trade and the rate of growth in world production as a proxy measure of globalization; that is, if the former is consistently higher than the latter, the process called globalization is occurring.

Far be it from us to criticize definitional concision-in principle, we all are for parsimony but reducing globalization to a quantifiable ratio of one sort or another is a bit exiguous even for our tastes. Rather, we prefer to interpret long term growth in the relative importance of world trade, for example, as a manifestation and expression of deeper, more complex, and ultimately more meaningful qualitative changes in the structure, organization, and operation of economic life. Along these lines, the Organization for Economic Cooperation and Development defines globalization as "the geographic dispersion of industrial and service activities (for example, research and development, sourcing of inputs, production and distribution) and the cross-border networking of companies (for example, through joint ventures and the sharing of assets)".

Not elegant, perhaps, but rich in descriptive and even anatomical power. In this regard, social theorist Manuel Castells (1994) emphasizes interdependence, scale, scope, and simultaneity, defining the global economy as "an economy that works as a unit in real time on a planetary basis". Thomas Friedman (1999), too, stresses the qualitative: globalization comes into existence when "everyone" feels the pressures, constraints, and opportunities attending the relative increase in importance of world trade, and the "democratizations" of technology, finance, and information associated with the same.

Here, Friedman follows much the same path taken by Fernand Braudel, when the great French historian was working on the origins and spread of capitalism. In Capitalism and Material Life (1973) and elsewhere, Braudel stressed everyday people and everyday life: capitalism can be said to have come into existence in a particular place when a sufficient number of people were sufficiently affected by "capitalist" markets, behaviors, and mentalités as to render alternative "markets," behaviors, and mentalités increasingly unimportant, insignificant, or even obsolete. Can we not just substitute "globalization" for "capitalism," "global" for "capitalist" and fill in the blanks?

Probably not, but by combining certain quantitative ratios-relative increases in transnational flows of one sort or another over a sustained period of time-with some of the qualitative measures discussed previously, we can rein in, if not capture completely, the wild conceptual beast known as globalization. The mere mention of wild conceptual beast offers a nice segue into Southeast Asia per se. Even as we write, there is considerable disagreement over the proper bounds of Southeast Asia, indeed, over whether or not a coherent, readily identifiable, culturally discrete geographical entity called Southeast Asia can even be said to exist.

The very term "Southeast Asia," for example, became common only during World War II, when it was used with reference to the Japanese-occupied parts of Asia south of China. Prior to that time, the area-at least in the West-was either packaged generically and climatologically as Tropical Asia or Monsoon Asia or, instead, subdivided, spliced, and diced into sub-regions known as "Further India," the Malay Archipelago, Indochina, and the East Indies, along with a residual outlier: the Hispanicized Philippines. To the Chinese, on the other hand, the area east of India and south of China was known traditionally as Nan-yang, the (lands of the) Southern Ocean.

In the academy, it was only with the publication of D.G.E. Hall's trailblazing History of South-East Asia in 1955 that the rubric in question began to resonate widely. It should be noted, moreover, that however broad his conceptual embrace, Hall excluded one part of the region, the Philippines, from consideration. In later editions of his History, Hall did include the Philippines, however, and most scholars have more or less followed his lead ever since. In retrospect, it is not difficult to understand the late entrance of Southeast Asia onto the nominal or even notional scene. For several centuries, much of the area had been under the political control, whether titular or real, of one or another of the European imperial powers.

Through both formal and informal means, these powers worked hard to establish and enforce close economic, political, and cultural ties between themselves and their respective colonies or in some cases groups of colonies. At the same time, these same powers worked formally and informally to impede, if not prohibit, similar ties between neighboring parts of the area organized under different European flags. As a result, the various constituent parts of what we now call Southeast Asia often had much closer links with European metropolis than they did with one another. To employ, albeit in a slightly different way, a concept associated with the distinguished South-east Asianist Benedict Anderson: imperial logic militated against an "imagined community" in the region and, indeed, against even a commonly accepted regional name.

To be sure, we do not wish to imply that, but for what Giovanni Arrighi (1978) has called the geometry of imperialism, Southeast Asia and Southeast Asians would fit together hand in glove, or, given the area's climate, perhaps we should say foot in thong. The historical experiences of, let us say, Brunei and the Philippines, Myanmar and Singapore, Java and Laos are none of them particularly close.

This said, the area's common geographical and climatic features, the innumerable contacts, migrations, and cultural exchanges between the area's peoples over the millennia, and the fact that the entire area was shaped to a greater or lesser degree by the same extraneous or at least extra-regional forces Indian and Sinic civilizations, Islam, and, more recently, the West gives substance to the claim that Southeast Asia can legitimately and profitably be examined, analyzed, and interpreted as a discrete geopolitical area, if not an undifferentiated whole.

Thus far in this chapter, we have attempted to "unpack" to use the debased currency of the academic realm the meanings of two concepts: globalization and Southeast Asia. Our task now is to bring these two concepts together, which is more problematic than may appear on the surface. For example, one of the central narrative lines in recent years in both the business weeklies and even in professional journals in business and economics has been the purported incorporation of Southeast Asia into the "global market." Countless stories have appeared documenting either the rise of Singapore - one of the original Asian "tigers," along with Taiwan, South Korea, and Hong Kong - or, at some remove, the attendant ascent of regional "dragons" such as Thailand, Malaysia, and Indonesia.

The unstated premise, the unarticulated assumption behind many of these stories is that these areas (and still others in the region, such as Vietnam and the Philippines) were experiencing something completely new. In the least adroit versions of the story, Southeast Asian economies are depicted as traditional, backward, and inefficient until a series of exogenous changes in transportation, communications, and production technology began to affect them in the 1970s and 1980s, courtesy of Western multinationals, thank you. More sophisticated narrators conceded that parts of the region were deeply involved in world markets, mainly as exporters of raw materials, as far back as the late nineteenth century, this time courtesy not of Western multinationals but rather of looser and less formal institutions and instruments associated with Western merchant capital.

Not everyone has accepted these views, of course. A cadre of specialists on the economic history of Southeast Asia has long argued that the region was a focal point for both trade and transnational flows of labor and capital for centuries prior to the age of high imperialism, which began in the second half of the 19th century. The early modern period offers a case in point. Focusing on Southeast Asia's key role in three great trades during this period that of the Indian Ocean and the South China Sea, along with the more celebrated but quantitatively less significant "East India" trade with Europe – these scholars put the lie to glib contemporary assertions that Southeast Asia was somehow a late - comer to extra-regional, dare we say "global," economic activity.

Indeed, in recent years, some of these specialists have gone further still, pushing for a fundamental reinterpretation of world economic history during the early modern period, which reinterpretation places Southeast Asia not on the periphery but at the very center of international trade and exchange. These revisionist scholars are not just reeling in the usual suspects either. For example, although they acknowledge both the symbolic and the real commercial importance of the Chinese eunich admiral Zheng He, whose seven expeditions through the South China Sea and Indian Ocean between 1405 and 1433 stand up well to comparison with anything done during the period known in the West as the Age of Discovery, they are more interested in broader trends, particularly in the scale and scope of production and exchange in the East vis-à-vis the West.

These scholars differ considerably on many empirical details. Moreover, some make extremely bold, perhaps even rash, claims and adopt strident tones. Even after allowing for the same, however, in light of their overall findings, it is difficult for anyone to deny the fact that Southeast Asia was much more prominent in world trade during the early modern era than was previously assumed.

Indeed, commodities, capital, and labor may have flowed in greater quantities and across greater distances to and from Southeast Asia between 1400 and roughly 1800 than to and from any other region in the world. Similarly, these scholars and others have demonstrated that throughout the 19th century not just after 1850, when the British and French began to consolidate and formalize their imperium on the mainland Southeast Asia was a principal arena in the global economic scheme.

By the 1870s, the region's importance was obvious to all, as the "Victorian Internet" the transoceanic telegraph cable linked the region ever more closely to growing extraregional markets, particularly in Europe, and technological improvements and cost reductions in transoceanic navigation facilitated ever greater economic streams and flows. As European, South Asian, and East Asian capital poured in, Southeast Asian commodities rice, sugar, cotton, coffee, tin, teak, and rubber poured out. Labor poured in, too, largely from South India and South China. Until the worldwide depression of the 1930s and World War II, much of Southeast Asia was as global as any part of the world. Indeed, many textbook cases of so-called open economies are drawn from the region: Burma, Malaya, and Thailand, to name but a few.

Once past the trials and tribulations of postwar decolonization and nation building, many parts of Southeast Asia attempted to reclaim their erstwhile prominence in the international economy. By the 1970s and 1980s, a number of areas had done so, leading to oh so much talk of tigers and dragons in both the East and the West. Does all of this mean that the authors of this chapter are craftily attempting to deprecate, depreciate, and debunk the au courant notion that "something happened" in the last decade or so? That Southeast Asia was as embedded in the global economy in 1600 or 1900 as it is in 2000? That Southeast Asia, to paraphrase country-and-western artist Barbara Mandrell, was global when global wasn't cool? Hardly.

All we have hoped to do in this section is to establish the fact that Southeast Asia has an economic history that began prior to the fall of communism and the triumph of neo-liberalism, the fact that some parts of the region were central to the world economy well before Jamestown was settled in 1607, and the fact that the region's global importance has generally been underestimated since that time. One could, in fact, call this section "Southeast Asia Slouching Toward Globalization," in other words. This said, let us turn to the main business at hand: Southeast Asia's economic history since World War II, particularly over the past decade when globalization became a so-called fact on the ground.

GROWTH, INTEGRATION, AND THE 1997-98 FINANCIAL CRISIS

The 10 countries of modern Southeast Asia straddle a vast geographic area, bounded by Australia to the south, India to the west, China to the north, and the Pacific Ocean to the east, and are populated by some half a billion people. With the exception of Thailand, they were all European colonies at one time (and under Japanese rule in the early 1940s). Following independence in the decades after World War II, some have evolved into modern competitive democracies (Thailand, the Philippines) or have elected governments under single dominant party rule (Malaysia, Singapore) or Communist governments (Laos and Vietnam). Indonesia, Malaysia, the Philippines, Singapore, Thailand, and Vietnam constitute Southeast Asia's larger or more developed economies.

The remaining four include the tiny oil-rich sultanate of Brunei and the region's three poorest members Laos, Cambodia, and Myanmar (Burma). Little will be said of this latter group, due to lack of data as well as their marginal importance to our theme-the globalization of Southeast Asia. Amid national exhaustion and bankruptcy of the former colonial powers at the end of World War II, the United States emerged as the new hegemony. It had long replaced Great Britain as the world's great maritime nation, and it alone commanded the economic resources for the postwar reconstruction of Europe and Asia.

Moreover, as impresario of the new global economic system created with the establishment of the World Bank and the International Monetary Fund in Washington, D.C., the nation's leaders felt compelled to assume primary responsibility for promoting stable and sustainable international economic growth. Clearly, U.S. policy preferences in the postwar period should be viewed at least in part in the context of the depression of the 1930s, particularly as reactions against the destructive autarkic economic policies of that period. It is equally clear, however, that U.S. commitments in Asia in the postwar period were also sustained by the strategic imperatives of the Cold War.

That is to say, without U.S. perceptions of an overarching strategic interest in the prosperity and stability of Asia as a bulwark against Asian communism, it is difficult to imagine that the remarkable economic performance in Southeast Asia would have occurred as it did. Modern, internationally oriented economic growth was thus established in Southeast Asia in the context of an open, multilateral trading system based on the General Agreement on Tariffs and Trade the linchpin of the new international economic order.' Since the mid 1960s, one of the great changes of modern history began with the rapid growth of several Asian economies.

Indeed, East Asia including a large part of its Southeast Asian component has grown faster on average than any other part of the world over the past three decades. Beginning with Japan, waves of rapid economic growth cascaded down first to the newly industrializing countries (NICs), or the Four Tigers South Korea, Taiwan, Hong Kong, and their Southeast Asian counterpart, Singapore. Rapid growth soon followed in the so-called next tier NICs, all in Southeast Asia: Indonesia, Malaysia, and Thailand. More recently, Vietnam and the Philippines joined the group of rapidly growing economies, after both carried out belated economic reforms in the late 1980s or early 1990s.

In the three decades up to 1995, per capita income grew at an astonishing 7.2 percent annually in Singapore and about 5 percent in Indonesia, Malaysia, and Thailand, in contrast to South Asia's 1.9 percent and Latin America's 0.9 percent. Alone among the market economies of Southeast Asia, the Philippines performed poorly in per capita income growth: its average annual growth rate of 1.2 percent over the 30 year period converged with the poor performance of its developing country counterparts in South Asia and Latin America. Due to the excesses of the Marcos regime in its later years, and the decline in central authority during the following Aquino administration, moreover, the Philippines did not share in the region's high growth performance of the 1980s and early 1990s either.

With the exception of the Philippines the long-time "sick man of Southeast Asia" Southeast Asia`s economic growth has been exceptional, with annual rates in the 5-7 percent range for the decade 1980-90. Growth rates were even higher averaging around 7-8 percent annually during 1990-96, again with the exception of the Philippines. The Philippines has only recently begun to exhibit the rapid growth rates its counterparts in Southeast Asia have long enjoyed, averaging over 5 percent annually over the years 1994-97, as the government of President Ramos began to implement economic reforms that included deregulation, privatization, and the liberalization of the trade and foreign investment regimes.

Two factors prevented reunified war ravaged Vietnam from participating in the economic boom in Southeast Asia of recent decades: externally, the economic and political alignment with the Soviet Union, and the invasion and occupation of Cambodia in 1978; internally, the rigidity of Marxist-Leninist doctrine and state control over the economy. In late 1986, however, the sweeping events besetting the Soviet Union and Eastern Europe abroad and recurrent economic crises within the country forced drastic reversals in policy, signaled by fundamental reforms under the banner of *doi moi* (renovation). In the space of five years, Vietnam made a decisive break from a long history of war, central planning, and economic crises. Since then, it has registered among the region's most impressive growth rates in output and in exports, albeit from very low bases.

Although the policies and growth patterns of the Southeast Asian countries differ significantly, one commonality among them is that their economies have been significantly more open, measured by the ratio of total exports and imports of goods and services to gross domestic product (GDP), than are the economies of their counterparts in South Asia or Latin America. Not surprisingly, Singapore and Malaysia, reflecting their long histories as open, trade-oriented economies, have trade (exports plus imports) that much exceeds the size of their domestic output, but the other Southeast Asian countries also have significantly more trade-oriented regimes than their counterparts in Latin America or South Asia. The openness of the region is further underlined by the rapid growth in exports, significantly exceeding the global average, over the past two decades.

The Southeast Asian adoption of a trade-oriented model of development, in contrast to the closed approach of Latin America, is evident in the rates of export growth achieved. The export-oriented growth experience of the Southeast Asian countries has not been a mere continuation of primary commodity export patterns that became established as a result of incorporation into the colonial order from the seventeenth century onward. Manufactured exports as a share of total exports from the region have grown rapidly over the past two decades. Southeast Asian countries have emerged as an important base for offshore production by multinational corporations. The export-oriented strategy of the key Southeast Asian countries typically began with the manufacture of low-skill, labor-intensive goods but gained momentum with the emergence of the semiconductor industry, which increasingly set up offshore assembly plants.

By 1975, according to one estimate, East Asia including key export processing zones in Malaysia and Thailand employed over 90 percent of worldwide offshore electronic assembly plant workers. Even more striking than the globalization of product markets of recent decades and the trade flows that have sustained it is the global integration of capital markets. While global trade has expanded twice as fast as world output in the second half of the 20th century, foreign direct investments have grown four times as fast.

Southeast Asia has been a particularly important destination for foreign direct investment, attracting considerable sums from outside the region, which have enhanced its export performance and contributed to its long term growth potential.

It is remarkable, and a testimony to the extent of the region's openness to global flows of capital and technology, that relatively small countries such as Thailand and Malaysia and even tiny Singapore have each attracted more foreign investment than all of South Asia together. (Of course, in the converse, it is also remarkable how closed the Indian subcontinent has been to the global economy.) Over this same period, the six key countries of Southeast Asia received foreign investments that amounted to over 70 percent of the total invested by foreigners in all of Latin America and the Caribbean and to over 7 times the total invested in all of South Asia. The globalization of Southeast Asia in its economic dimensions, then, has been robust and intensive.

With the exception of Myanmar, Laos, and Cambodia, the paradigmatic strategy for the market-based Southeast Asian economies is export-oriented growth, deepening integration into the global economy by encouraging foreign direct investment. This strategy contrasts sharply with the classic (now abandoned or repudiated) Indian and Latin American developmental models espousing state ownership of industry and the "commanding heights" of the economy, together with the encouragement of import substitution behind protectionist barriers.

Yet in 1997, after three decades of sustained and rapid growth when Singapore had achieved developed country status; when Indonesia, Malaysia, and Thailand were rapidly increasing the wealth of their citizenries; and when even Vietnam and the Philippines were beginning to be labeled "high performers"- financial crisis and economic recession struck with a fury that shockedob servers and participants alike. With the financial shock wave emanating from its epicenter in Thailand which floated the baht in July 1997 after a futile attempt to support the currency the contagion spread with a speed that seemed incredible. By early 1998, the Indonesian Rupiah was down more than 80 percent against the dollar, and the currencies of Thailand, Malaysia, and Philippines all fell by 30-50 percent. Within months of the baht flotation, the stock markets of all four saw losses of 60 percent or more in dollar terms. The "Asian flu," or what Paul Krugman (1999) has wryly called "bahtulism," had set in.

On the eve of the crisis in 1996, when warning signs were already apparent in Thailand's financial and real estate sectors, no one could yet imagine that Thailand or Indonesia were only months away from going, cap in hand, to the International Monetary Fund for massive financial bailouts. To be sure, some analysts, most notably Alwyn Young (1992) and Paul Krugman (1994), were already raising questions about the "economic miracle" in Southeast Asia, particularly about the degree to which this "miracle" was based on capital and labor mobilization rather than on increased factor productivity. And clearly, the region was no stranger to financial instability or recession: Indonesia and the Philippines suffered from financial shocks in 1983, Thailand in 1984, and Malaysia and Singapore saw economic downturns in 1985.

However, in contrast to previous occasions, the depth of the 1997-98 downturn in currencies, equity values, and output and the simultaneity of the impact across key Southeast Asian economies set this crisis apart. Indeed, the massive losses of wealth built up in previous years and the hardships imposed on millions of people in societies that lacked institutionalized welfare safety nets constituted a water shed for Southeast Asia. Much has already been written on the Asian financial crisis. From the perspective of the globalization process in Southeast Asia, some key attributes of the crisis stand out. From the early 1990s, a rising share of global capital flows has consisted of short term portfolio funds.

Today, both lending and equity markets are globally integrated, and as a result, there has been a delocalization of finance as global funds have become increasingly important as ready sources of capital and credit. The decades of rapid economic growth in Southeast Asia led to, in the words of economist Max Corden, "an euphoria stage of the investment and borrowing boom". Thus, while, on the supply side, large funds scoured the globe for short-run opportunities, the economic boom in Southeast Asia led, on the demand side, to a binge of corporate borrowing. Increased capital inflows fueled rapid credit expansion, lowered the quality of credit, and inflated asset prices, which encouraged further capital inflows in a frenzied boom evident in escalating property prices and increased construction in the cities and in rising equity values in the stock markets of Southeast Asia.

Contributing in a significant way to the financial crisis were the formal and informal currency pegs that discouraged both lenders and borrowers from hedging. Highly leveraged corporate sectors and large unhedged short term debt made countries such as Thailand and Indonesia highly vulnerable to changes in market sentiments. By late 1996, pressures on the baht had emerged, and they intensified through the first half of 1997. This occurred against a background of an unsustainable current account deficit (caused by a slowdown in export growth, which in turn was related to the baht's peg to an appreciating U.S. dollar), rising short-term and unhedged foreign debt in the corporate sector, and increasingly apparent financial sector weaknesses.

Weaknesses in bank and corporate governance and the lack of market discipline, with lax and poorly enforced prudential regulations, encouraged excessive risk taking. There existed close and often corrupt relationships between governments, financial institutions, and corporate borrowers, which worsened the problems. Weak accounting standards, poor disclosure practices, and lack of prudential oversight reflected such crony arrangements. The lack of appropriate commercial norms of accounting and risk assessment hid growing weaknesses until it was too late. With mounting exchange rate pressures, and ineffective interventions by Thailand's Central Bank, the baht was floated on 2 July 1997 and promptly collapsed.

With astonishing rapidity, the contagion of sharply negative market sentiments, rapid withdrawals of foreign private capital, bank runs, and drastic economic downturns spread to Indonesia (and South Korea in northeast Asia). The financial shock and its immediate aftermath led to one of the most fundamental changes to have occurred in modern Southeast Asia: the demise of President Suharto's regime of 32 years in an Indonesia that towers over the rest of the region in geographical size and sheer weight of population (over 200 million people). Malaysia and the Philippines, less exposed to short-term foreign debt than their neighboring counterparts, were less affected but nevertheless experienced steep falls in currency and stock market values and in economic activity.

If global economic integration, domestic economic deregulation, and rapid advances in technology especially information and communication technologies are the three great pillars of modern globalization, then Southeast Asia can certainly be said to have manifested them in its postwar economic history. The postwar decades of rapid material advance led to an ever deepening integration of Southeast Asia into the global economy. Market-oriented reform, partly as a response to the requirements of the deepening integration into competitive global markets, was carried out in the Southeast Asian economies, albeit at different speeds and comprehensiveness in each of them. Economic reforms involved not only trade liberalization but other complementary steps as well: domestic economic deregulation for attracting foreign investments, and privatization of public-sector enterprises.

Globalization is leading to a push for ever greater transparency in the government and corporate sectors. Securities and corporate analysts, rating agencies, and the business media gather and provide data and analysis to track economic and business performance with ever more powerful analytic tools and ever faster channels of communication. The revolution in information and communication technologies, combined with the phenomenal growth in the global capital market since the mid-1990s, has profoundly affected-negatively in the recent financial crisis and will continue to affect the economies of Southeast Asia. Globalization took on a virulent form in the Asian financial crisis, and it constitutes a profound challenge to the region's governments and corporate sector.

Indeed, as Lawrence Summers (1999) points out, managing international economic integration may be the preeminent challenge facing policymakers around the world. In a world of capital mobility, governmental capacity to tax capital or regulate industry has eroded. This constriction in the state's capacity to carry out discretionary macroeconomic policy may well be perceived as a positive development in modern political economy.

By requiring credible commitments to make policy and regulatory behavior of the state transparent, international capital markets-and the associated technological infrastructures in information and communica-tions have raised the domestic political costs of incompetence, inefficiency, corruption, and fiscal irresponsibility for governments everywhere.

The Asian financial crisis has clearly shown that short-term capital flows were excessive and destabilizing to both borrowers and lenders alike. Thailand's foreign corporate debts, short-term and unhedged, were a particularly risky form of global integration. Yet it would be a pity if the lessons learned from the events of 1997-98 led policymakers to impede capital flows from global markets to Southeast Asia. In this regard, Malaysia's response to the crisis-the establishment of capital controls and the expenditure of much rhetoric regarding the "conspiracies" associated with Western capitalism-seems a dubious case in point. If anything, the recent events in Southeast Asia point to the importance of establishing robust domestic financial sectors that keep pace with rapid economic growth and integration into global capital markets.

The mainstream economics explanation of the growth experience of Southeast Asia has been based on the "Washington consensus": that is, the pursuit of economic policies based on outward orientation, macroeconomic prudence, and domestic liberalization. This means, in common parlance, first, trade a lot; second, avoid inflation and maintain sensible and stable exchange rates and interest rates; and third, promote competition and, in general, let the private sector thrive.

The crisis events of Southeast Asia qualify the basic message of the Washington consensus with an important rider: that it is important to sequence liberalization of domestic capital markets to match the development of adequate regulatory and supervisory capacity of financial regulators. Are the governments in Southeast Asia equal to the challenge of establishing appropriate rules and institutions for effective systems of corporate governance, incentive compatible property rights, and transparent accounting and prudential standards in both public and private sectors? The answer to this question will largely determine the extent to which Southeast Asia emerges from its recent turmoil stronger and better able to confront the challenges of inevitable globalization in all its manifestations.

SINGAPORE'S EMERGENT ENVIRONMENTAL-POLITICAL LANDSCAPE

In his 2004 inaugural speech Singapore's Prime Minister Lee Hsien Loong expressed a desire and intention to make Singapore a more "open" society. Often typified as an authoritarian state, Singapore has in the past been noted for its dearth of human rights, including a lack of citizens' freedom of expression, and association. Moves towards greater openness, freedom of expression, and tolerance are therefore welcomed by many Singapore citizens, civil society groups, and NGOs, as well as proponents of democracy around the world. Yet, what this declaration of pending openness signals in practice, and the processes through which it will be attained, are very much open to question.

As Rodan (2003) cautions, expansions of new or alternative spaces of political concern and practice in Singapore should not be taken at face value. They instead beg careful interrogation as to their qualitative nature and significance for political practice. Such an interrogation in turn necessitates engagement with empirically informed discussions about the current nature of the Singaporean polity, to illuminate the complex socio-political contexts that such moves occur within—a case this chapter makes through two main arguments: one primarily methodological, the other an empirical commentary on one aspect of the Singapore polity.

To begin with the former, this chapter argues that contextual understandings of the Singapore polity are enabled by the use of qualitative research methodologies. These allow engagement with governance as a process of shifting, contingent, and emergent socio-political relations. Too often a priori theorizations foreshadow discussions on the complexities of how, why, and in what ways governance is expressed in Singapore. Instead of yet another rework of the concepts of the state and/or civil society, this chapter suggests that explorations of discursive and bodily practices of political actors effectively illuminate the nature and the workings of existent political spaces in Singapore, situating it within a small but not insignificant literature on Singaporean spatial governance.

The theoretical approach adopted here is a post-structuralist understanding of social relations, in particular a Foucaultian perspective on power that eschews analysis of sovereignty to instead look at how power is constituted through practice—that is, how it forms political subjects and systems through a multiplicity of forces and processes. In this framework, the idea of hegemony is problematized. The state is thus rendered a "work-in-progress" that must constantly ensure its survival through discursive and material tactics of re-creation. For example, the Singapore government is repeatedly argued as possessing impenetrable and non-negotiable powers. Yet, in its speeches, documents, and policies the refrains of "survival", impermanence, and no-nonsense bottom-line rationalizations are ever present, suggesting its supposed iron grip of power is more fragile than is often acknowledged.

This chapter discusses the practices of Singaporean

environmental NGOs to complement and extend the already substantial literature on environmental policies and regulations in Singapore. Its basic aim is to better understand how and why these NGOs attempt to get the environment on the public and political agenda in Singapore. Although there is definite contention as to whether NGOs can be said to exist in Singapore, the phrase here represents organizations not directly run by government apparatus on a day-to-day basis. In this sense, NGOs are conceptualized as organizations whose discourses and practices are part of emergent, multi-level socio-spatial relations rather than fixed entities on the political landscape, characterized by static relations.

This chapter focuses primarily on the motives and political interactions of environmental NGOs. Through this focus, it is argued that NGO volunteers are motivated by a desire to forge stronger feelings of belonging, of being Singaporean in a way that connects them to the land and with each other. These feelings are not merely repetitions of governmental attempts to inscribe idealized forms of national identity onto citizens through institutional reach and norms.

They instead speak to the creation of political spaces that suggest a Singapore different from the one imagined in government discourse. This brings NGOs into ambiguous relations neither with government and state actors, being neither "inside" nor "outside" the boundaries of the state. (This condition is explored on different planes by Lenore Lyons ["Transient Workers Count Too?" in this issue], who looks at foreign domestic workers in Singapore and Ooi Can Seng ["State-Civil Society Relations and Tourism", in this issue], who analyses the ways in which tourism has opened up local civil spaces.)

For NGOs, this is a mixed blessing. On the one hand, it enables the forging of discernible spaces of alternate practice. On the other, it means NGOs are unable to rationalize and predict the outcomes of their interactions with government, which in turn presents some potentially powerful barriers to greater openness in Singapore. In making this argument, the remainder of this chapter is structured as follows. First, research methods are outlined, followed by a discussion of the Singapore polity and the environment's place within it. Then, two main empirical sections focus on the motives and practices of NGO volunteers, and the types of socio-political relations that currently exist between environmental NGOs and state actors, followed by some concluding remarks.

It focuses in particular on one NGO—the Green Volunteer Network (GVN), although other NGOs are also discussed briefly. The GVN is the volunteer arm of the government-initiated Singapore Environment Council, established in 1995. It was chosen as the initial case study for this research as it is a relatively new organization fast gaining public standing in Singapore with a young volunteer body, and some access to government decision-making apparatus. The qualitative methodologies employed in this research are rationalized by the argument that post-structuralist epistemologies best answer the initial research question that stimulated this work, that is, how do environmental NGOs operate in Singapore on a day-to-day basis?

Within the social sciences, qualitative methods are employed under an array of theoretical positions, and the one adopted here is situated in moves to re-centre the research participants as knowledgeable and active agents in political life, whose narratives and experiences offer one take on contemporary sociality. Part of this approach is to focus not so much on what is being represented by speech, thus raising the spectre of whether subjects' narratives can be taken as "true" or not. Rather, the focus is on what is being done, examining practices not only as bodily experiences but seeing speech as a form of political practice that itself constitutes social life and the subject.

This research utilizes two main qualitative methods. First, in-depth, semi-structured interviews explore volunteers' life stories, motivations, experiences, and opinions. For this, 15 GVN volunteers were interviewed, who are all female and under the age of 30. Also, the two full-time salaried GVN staff were interviewed, who are both male, one in his late twenties and the other in his fifties. Whilst at face this does not present a large sample, it is an adequate representation of GVN's core group of volunteers who regularly contribute to the workings of the group. It should be noted that many of these interviews were not recorded due to background noise levels but extensive notes were taken during and after each interview. Thus few verbatim quotes were available for use in the empirical sections of this chapter, which relies for the most part on interview notes.

Interviews were also carried out with members of the Nature Society Singapore and the Environmental Challenge Organization (ECO), a youth NGO set up in 2003 to promote awareness and education of environmental issues in Singapore. Second, participant observation was undertaken to observe GVN volunteers' practices. This was carried out at the GVN offices, where time was spent talking informally to staff and volunteers. Also visits to some of Singapore's remaining nature areas such as the island of Pulau Ubin off the north coast of Singapore, enabled observations of key conservation spaces. The discussion in this chapter is based on coding of the interviews and field notes, using open coding techniques.

GOVERNANCE, CIVIL SOCIETY, AND THE ENVIRONMENT

First, it is important to briefly outline the nature of Singapore polity as argued in existing literature. Whilst academic arguments often differ, there exists a general agreement that during the one-party rule of the People's Action Party (PAP) since independence, a "growth consensus" has been successfully forged. Here, the state enables citizens to increase their material wealth, and access public service. In return, citizens participate in a "development-first" mode of governance. This mode allows them to contribute to economic prosperity without the demands of political plurality, facilitated through the non-confrontational and highly regulated party political system that tolerates limited criticism from inside and outside the nation.

In this developmental state, the rapid loss of sites of

ecological importance is underpinned by the transformation of the environment from "nature" to part of an ordered urban quality of life, where a "garden city" image and lifestyle sustains economic growth. "No-nonsense" environmental policies and the forwarding of a sustainable Singapore such as the "Singapore Green Plan 2012" thus frame Singapore as a "dean and green" city, where the government attempts to truncate environmental concerns by interweaving the environment into discourses of nation-building, leisure, heritage, efficiency, and economic survival. Such a mediation of public life is in turn facilitated by a considerable blurring of boundaries between the government, state, and civil society, with non-government actors absorbed into the state through the intertwining of interests, careers, and roles.

This enables the externalization of governmental norms, to create and control sets of institutions to reproduce its own values and practices. Purportedly little political and civic activity takes place outside the "octopus-like" reach of the state, underwritten by legislation that prevents non-state sanctioned political activity taking place. As Clammer has underlined, even the current array of grassroots and community groups are part of the state apparatus, "set up and controlled by the government to channel, monitor and control public expression of political and social needs". This state of affairs is not stable, however. Of late, the Singapore government has attempted to show itself as responsive to social change, with an enlargement of the "middle ground" of politics.

"Participatory" styles of government that include citizens in political processes have been promoted to ensure an array of opinions and needs are included during decision-making. This expansion of political space, however, does not signal a wholesale move towards Western-style democracy. Instead, governance changes to date have been in keeping with the distinctive ideological foundations of the Singapore government—patriarchal, allegedly Confucian-based, and intolerant of criticism. For example, the establishment of a "Speaker's Corner" was heralded as a move towards freedom of speech.

Initially any potential speaker had to gain permission to speak by providing 30 days' notice of intent to the authorities. Although this time restriction has since been relaxed, the infamous "out-of-bounds" markers are still in place, forbidding comment on socially sensitive issues. Yet, as Dalpino cautions, this continuation of an authoritarian approach to governing should not prevent a thorough enquiry into the nature of the changing political landscape in Singapore, in particular in reference to NGOs:

> Western policymakers and democracy activists often gloss over, or ignore altogether, the phenomenon of apolitical NGOs in authoritarian systems. There are several reasons for this oversight. The first is a blank slate approach, or the assumption that associational life is alien to societies under authoritarian rule. In this view, regimes are immune to or refuse to tolerate all public pressures, and citizens lack any concept of social organization. Thus civil society can only awaken under democratization, most likely with a jump-start from the international community. (Dalpino 2000, p. 53)

Dalpino here critiques the mostly "Western" intellectual disinterest in apolitical NGOs in authoritarian states. Other commentators have expressed similar indignity at assumptions that underpin discussions on NGOs in Singapore. In particular, the framing of the nation as an "illiberal democracy" with a managed civil society denies the processes of negotiation and evolution of socio-political initiatives that currently take place. Indeed, the NGOs discussed in this chapter present one case of such negotiation and evolution, being simultaneously "inside" and "outside" the government, signalling the complexity of the polity omitted from many overly structural models of its institutions and processes that often populate the literature.

NEW ENVIRONMENTAL CITIZENS

In 1995 the National Council on the Environment was renamed and reconstituted as the Singapore Environment Council (SEC), in part to eradicate its image as mere window-dressing for the government. Today the SEC is officially a non-government and non-profit organization of "public character" it remains the activator of the government's non-regulation environmental agenda. It is partially government-funded with its Board consisting of an array of "bureaucratic players", echoing the above thesis of government and non-government actors and values inter-twined. Several years later, the SEC launched the Green Volunteer Network (GVN) to provide support in carrying out its agenda of fostering "greater appreciation of the environment amongst the community as a whole".

The GVN's purpose is to make available to Singaporeans a range of practical activities and programmes to "turn awareness into action". It receives partial funding from the state for agreed-upon projects, which have to be cleared by the Board, whilst being free to seek outside funding for other projects. The GVN is arguably part of broader governmental attempts to foster "civic society" through an active citizenry operating within the chosen realms and practices of the government. The GVN, therefore, sits comfortably within the government's agenda of forwarding environmental goals in Singapore such as being active and responsible without asking why environmental degradation and destruction is occurring in the first place.

The GVN does not have a single-issue or overtly political focus in its activities, which include nature appreciation walks and treks; road-shows, talks, and green fairs for general public awareness; reforestation and park/swamps cleanup activities; "eco-green" camps; and also fund-raising. These activities do not directly threaten the government's control of environmental issues, complementing rather than contesting the government's vision of an efficient, sustainable, and clean Singapore. However, the GVN's unique configuration of attributes places it in an interesting position in the Singapore political landscape.

It has a non-specialist volunteer membership, unlike the most well-known environmental NGO, the Nature Society, which has a predominantly specialist membership of ecologists and botanists. The GVN is government-sanctioned whilst being allowed to develop some level of independence through seeking funding and carrying out its own programmes. It also does not have a predefined constituency unlike the para-religious and ethnic "grassroots" community groups so prevalent in Singapore, but is open to anyone that wishes to take part. It shares many environmental concerns with the government, for example, both place emphasis on the preservation of the island's few remaining natural places. At the same time, there are significant ideological differences.

For one, the Singapore government has a predominantly "use-value" perspective on Singapore's undeveloped places, viewing them as either providing services to Singaporeans or being development-sites-in-waiting. In contrast, environmental NGOs argue that natural places have intrinsic aesthetic and ecological value, and are worth saving for their own sake, and for the sake of future generations of Singaporeans. The environment as a social issue thus presents a fascinating entry point into an exploration of the changing nature of the Singapore political landscape.

IDENTITY, COMMUNITY, AND THE ENVIRONMENT

The "octopus-like" thesis of the Singapore polity does not suggest that the project of inscribing citizens' with particular values is ever wholly successful or complete. Despite claims that Singaporeans have become endemically apathetic in relation to political issues, non-governmental political spaces do exist in Singapore that are often hard to discern from top-down forms of analysis. These spaces do not cluster so much around party politics—a demarcation that enables the government to silence critics, by stating that those outside the political system have no right to comment on it. Instead they cluster around the future of Singapore as a place of passion and connection.

Singam (2000) provides an apposite example. She outlines the work of the NGO AWARE (Association of Women for Action and Research), which has had some degree of success in making gender equality issues part of the Singaporean social agenda. Singam argues that young Singaporeans emigrate as they feel little affinity or sense of belonging in their homeland. However, when some become involved with NGOs, new connections to communities and country are forged and felt. Along similar lines, Singaporean artists and architects have called for citizens to feel passionate about their homeland in embodied ways, and in terms and forms not defined by the state. Such a drive for connection, for passion that is at once personal and shared, arguably underpins the ambitions of GVN volunteers.

For example, when asked about their perceptions of GVN's work, volunteers quickly pointed out they did not work for the government or towards any government aims. Indeed, several volunteers baulked at suggestions that they purposefully enact or were surreptitiously co-opted into a government agenda. Instead, volunteers perceived their work as a means to rethink their Singaporean identities. They expressed apprehension over the future of Singaporean community life. They cited how greed, lack of care for others outside of immediate family circles, and the privileges of living in a relatively clean, safe, and well-serviced environment had engendered de-sensitized individuals. As one volunteer interviewee put it:

Groups such as the GVN are very important. Singapore is a place of privilege and I really want other people to know that it is not like this all around the world, that other things exist outside of these privileges and that they have to see the real picture of the world.

For this GVN member, the "real picture" is one where environmental destruction, community degradation, and loss of identity go hand in hand. This requires that a society be forged where individuals are more aware and concerned about the needs on their own doorstep, not only environmental, but also social and economic ones. Given the noted de-politicization of Singaporeans, this might be read as a desire, on the part of the GVN volunteers, for a process of re-politicization. But this is not directly the case.

Volunteers were only too aware that in general Singaporeans are not interested in party politics or overtly political stances, as one volunteer interviewee underlined in the following example:

> People stay away from politics in general in Singapore. If you approach people on the street about an issue they will walk away and not want to know. I saw the opposition party handing out leaflets and trying to get attention in a shopping centre but nobody was paying them any attention. I took a leaflet and when I got home, my mother told me off. She said I should not do that, to not get involved with that sort of thing.

Volunteers' aims are therefore not political as defined by the Singapore government but socio-political in terms of a shared and community life. In the above quote from Interview 7, the volunteer evokes a nation where care for others—with the environment being one of these "others"—is genuine. This stands in distinction, but not direct opposition, to the government rhetoric of volunteerism. As a volunteer interviewee put it:

> The government may be big on getting people to volunteer, they may talk a lot about it, but they don't create the conditions that allow people to do it in reality. There is no time away from work and they do not encourage people to do anything other than consume. Groups are doing it because they are getting points from school, they are not doing it for the love of it.

This suggests that the volunteering model being propounded in Singapore is transparently rhetorical and self-interested. The GVN volunteers were by contrast keen to forge an approach to volunteering wherein the "community" has meaning beyond this rhetoric, where Singaporeans are able to forge their own identities, and to shape the meanings attached to social issues. The processes volunteers mobilized to hopefully incite such feelings and meanings were those of "education". Although this at first suggests government-sanctioned modes of social change, as well as the transference of knowledge through the repetition of facts, another type of education was being forwarded here.

By taking children and adults out to Singapore's nature

reserves and parks, and by talking about the ecological worth of Singapore through showing and doing, volunteers took part in bodily enactments of the care they hoped to foster and create. Not only was this care enacted and felt through doing, it became a modus operandi for some volunteers as they came to embody this sense of connection with Singapore's environment. As a volunteer explained:

> GVN's approach is very determined. It is not something that volunteers just do in their spare time and forget about at others, but something they carry with them at all times and they try and share with others. It does impact upon people.

In itself, these actions are small, as are their overall impact on the Singapore political landscape. However, they do speak to alternate political spaces existing alongside—not in conflict or in co-option—purported hegemonic spaces of the state. These are spaces where, through care and connection with the environment, a different Singapore is imagined outside of state discourses—one that evokes an enthusiasm for nation not captured or invoked by the duty-bound discourses so prevalent in the Singapore polity.

Before moving onto the next section, it is worth briefly asking whether these new volunteer identities may be part of a "post-material" condition, where concerns for "others" become the manifestation of new lifestyle politics that depart significantly from traditional political practices. Although there are substantial theoretical critiques of such a thesis—which brevity forbids direct engagement with here—there are striking parallels between this and the "new rich of Asia" thesis. For one, five of the GVN volunteers interviewed were well-educated trainee teachers. They drew distinctions between their generation, which has the time and space to explore social and environmental issues, and their parents' generation, which lived through the often difficult forging of Singapore as a nation, where concern was with personal and national survival. However, this does not automatically translate into GVN volunteers being part of a post-material and/or "new rich" thesis.

For one, the role of the middle class in environmental protection in Southeast Asia has been at best ambiguous. The middle class and the PAP in Singapore are argued as "shoring" each other up, with the former seeking autonomy from the PAP as consumers not as political subjects. Indeed, the middle classes of Singapore are reported as caring less about the environment. As one commentator has noted, the wealthy of Singapore can afford to, and do, jet off to Malaysia for the weekend to enjoy nature. It is the "heartlanders"—those who live in public housing estates "and whose interests and horizons are largely limited to the local" —who are the ones that will lose out in the medium-to-long term.

As such, it is not intellectually rigorous to neatly categorize or explain away the practices of environmental volunteers in Singapore. Instead, nuanced forms of political space are discernible by the appreciation of how practices, that at first glance appear in keeping with state discourses, are rather embodied attempts to forge a different Singapore and indeed, different Singaporeans. The GVN volunteers attempt to foster perceptions of the worth and place of the environment in Singaporean society that differ from, but do not directly conflict with, those of the government.

They do in fact utilize the vocabularies and practices of the government such as notions of environment, education, volunteering, and citizenship. They therefore do not seek to modify the language of volunteering but rather the motives and desired outcomes of its practices. One question that logically follows on from this argument is what impacts do these practices have on the political landscape, and how do they feed into, and/or how are they effected by ongoing changes in governance processes in Singapore?

SPACES OF INFLUENCE AND LIMITATION

GVN volunteers were keen to point out that in Singapore changes do not happen quickly, and they were optimistic that it was still early days for them as an organization. The recruitment of new volunteers continues apace, with an on-paper membership of over one thousand. Their range of activities continues to expand, with nature walks and other events regularly fully booked. Plus, they have achieved some impact at the government level. They take part in the networks that constitute the far-reaching "tentacles" of the government through state apparatus. At the same time, they prevent becoming fixed onto one position on the political landscape. This does not mean that volunteers were optimistic of their abilities to effect widespread political change.

For one, there was a great deal of resignation that the government as an institution was unlikely to change. GVN does not wish, however, to bypass or overcome the government, to take action on its own that will force the hand of the government and the state. This is a risky tactic in Singapore and threatens to dissembled organizations such as GVN from their multiple networks of influence. Rather, GVN volunteers framed their political relations as being fluid, issue-contingent, and not definable to a single position, which provides them with some room to move within political spaces. To provide examples, GVN is invariably part of the "octopus-like" networks of influence that pervade Singaporean social and political life. Through its Board of Directors, personal contacts, work with other agencies and its relationship with the SEC, it sits well within the government sphere of influence.

Volunteers are mindful of this position and negotiate their way through these networks to prevent being too far "inside" or "outside" that state. For example, whilst it may seem advantageous for the GVN to foster a close working relationship with government agencies, the GVN instead seeks to work with them only if it is convenient, advantageous, and does not result in loss of control over an issue. Another example is how volunteers use their extant contacts and networks to gain access to information, pass opinions along to state actors about key issues, and gauge reactions to certain opinions or planned actions—deflecting any direct confrontation with government but still finding a political voice within these governance networks.

By being able to attract external funding, often from the private industry—such as a native tree planting campaign sponsored by Ricoh in 2004—the GVN has space to enact its own agenda not circumscribed by the potentially differing agenda of state actors. Here, the octopus-like quality of the Singapore polity that is so often diagnosed as singularly oppressive is turned to the advantage of the GVN. Whilst their position in governance networks does present restrictions on behaviour it also enables the GVN to informally acquire information and to choose which networks to activate at which time.

As well as such informal practice, staff members are part of a semiformal "consultation" process, such as a closed-door prime ministerial question-and-answer session. Also, other formal routes for voicing concerns are used, such as letters to the Forum pages of the Straits Times.

Involvement in such processes is also common for the Nature Society of Singapore (NSS), the key Singapore conservation NGO established in 1954. Since the early 1980s the NSS has lobbied against the destruction of the nation's biodiversity, and has gained some foothold to influence and/or inform government decisions, evidenced by some of their recommendations being incorporated into the 1990 Green Plan. Members of ECO have also taken part in youth feedback forums, where government ministers are made publicly available to hear the comments and opinions of interested parties.

Taken together, these practices place environmental NGOs such as GVN and NSS in politically ambiguous roles, of operating simultaneously in different spheres of influence whilst subtly extending ideological vocabularies to introduce normative inflections into Singapore's environmental discourses. Whilst they do not wish to, and realize the futility in challenging the government head-on, they wish to be affective of the political landscape in Singapore through the mobilization of a variety of channels of influence, the contingencies of which allow the GVN to remain unfixed and fluid as a definable political animal on the Singaporean political landscape. How then might ongoing changes to governance practices in Singapore impact and/or be effected by such practices? Will more "openness" be good news for these NGOs?

At face value, the obvious answer is yes—more opportunities to feed into government opinion and decision-making can only be beneficial to the environmental cause. However, the ways in which this openness is operationalized will be instrumental to the future ability of NGOs to provide an effective voice in Singapore. For example, interviewees explained how involvement in government processes both empowers and limit, with the latter the most apparent in so-called consultation processes. As increasingly popular tools of public communication by the PAP, these consultation processes involve NGOs being invited to make some input into predetermined issues. Once consulted, NGOs are then expected to stay publicly silent on an issue—from the government perspective, they have been heard, and so there exists no need for further discussion on the matter.

Consequently, NGOs do not know what happens to the information and opinion they provide, and can only gauge their impacts once final decisions are announced. Here the downside of political ambiguity becomes apparent. Interviewees spoke of the constant need to react to government agenda, which leaves little public space to be proactive, and set the public agenda on key issues. As such little political public space exists in Singapore, interviewees suggested that NGOs have developed a culture where there is little time, energy, resources, and willingness to work with other NGOs, often furthered by uncertainty about other NGOs' motives and connections to government.

This disallows NGOs to forge coalitions around key issues, a state of affairs intensified by a political climate where NGOs joining forces publicly could easily be considered a thoroughly political manoeuvre, and one that threatens government control of public issues. Thus the conflation of openness with more behind-door consultation will do little to help the environmental cause in Singapore.

Instead, they will further the factionalism, and heighten the reactive and ambiguous climate that pervades. Even public consultations arguably serve to only disseminate the specific concerns and tensions, rather than being legitimate political platforms for free comment on unscripted issues. Environmental NGOs are facing some big challenges ahead. The uncoordinated coalition that formed around the desire to prevent development on the Chek Jawa mudflats on Pulau Ubin in 2001 shows the potential power of public voice to make a difference to the Singapore environment. With this development merely stalled and the future of Pulau Ubin in still in question, the outlook of the nation's few remaining biodiversity hot-spots do not appear positive.

If this new climate of openness does not provide the space for NGOs to work together, and to feel confident that they can anticipate governmental reactions to their campaigns and wishes rather than shadow-boxing in a climate of uncertainty, environmental NGOs can only continue to fight a rearguard action, and continue to negotiate the pervasive political ambiguity of the Singapore polity. There is no doubt that Singaporean socio-political relations have become more open to alternative constructions. The GVN is less than a decade old, while new and more contentious "environmental" NGOs have also begun to emerge, such as Animal Concerns Research and Education Society (ACRES). At the same time, the paradoxes at the heart of government ideologies have become more visible; for example, calls for creativity and innovation in business are being contradicted by restrictions on any creative deconstructions of how and why Singaporean society operates.

However, care must be taken not to assume this heralds the arrival of liberal democracy, the emergence of civil society and/or the crumbling of authoritarianism. This chapter has argued that "other" political spaces already exist in Singapore, brought about through the bodily practices and motivations of environmental NGO volunteers. This is made possible by socio-political relations that are less rigid and structured than some theorizations suggest, wherein both informal and semi-formal governance networks provide spaces for political negotiation. At the same time, these networks, and the uncertainty they engender, limit NGO abilities to have efficacious impacts.

With no clear, delineated rights of public voice or freedom of association, organizations cannot work together with the assurance that they will not breach the government's bounds of acceptability. As a result, some NGO volunteers may eventually become politically disenchanted, withdraw from the public arena and thus privatize their concerns and contributions. In this scenario, current practices and aims of the GVN are temporary and will have little impact on environmental perceptions and being in Singapore.

However, there is a case, and indeed a need, to stay optimistic. For one, the conclusions here beg the question as to whether they apply to other NGOs in Singapore. In what ways would the findings detailed here differ for NGOS in other sectors, such as AWARE, and newer, non-government-sanctioned NGOs such as ACRES (Animal Concerns Research and Education Society)? There is further work to be done to trace the historical nuances of Singaporean NGOs, to consider how their practices have shifted over time in relation to not only the state but also other actors. Thus, more process- and practice-based forms of research are required to uncover how the political landscape is negotiated, and where NGOs may or may not create influence, with more focus on the micro-level processes and less on debates about the boundaries of all-pervasive structural determinants of perceptions and practices in Singapore.

To return to the argument made at the start of this chapter, to understand how proposed and actual changes to Singapore governance impacts on socio-political relations there must be pre-requisite in-depth appreciations of current practices, both within and without organizations such as NGOs. Only then can the impacts of moves towards greater "openness" be fully appreciated and scrutinized for their effect on Singapore's political landscape.

7

Tourism and Its Social and Political Repercussions

South East Asia is the generally accepted name for a series of island and peninsulas which lie east of India and west of China. South East Asia is blessed with abundant sunshine and plentiful rain. With the exception of North Vietnam and a few mountain locations, virtually all of South Asia falls within the 27-36 C annual temperature range. There are, however, seasonal variations in rainfall and temperature due to changing wind and pressure systems. Warm, humid climatic conditions have given rise to lush tropical rain forests teeming with a wide variety of plant and animal life. Beside the climate, South East Asia nations shares similarities on the archeological background.

Archeological evidence for the origins of some prevalent South East Asian decorative motifs may be seen in beautifully ornamented ritual bronze artefacts, such as kettle drums, weapons and bells, which have been uncovered from many sites throughout the regions. The highly stylized designs found on bronze objects from the late Chou period of China (eight-third century BC) also had some influence on South East Asian decorative motifs in terms of asymmetrical layout of design and the merging and modification of motifs to fit in with an overall schema. This influence is most evident on some textiles from Borneo and Sumatra. This corner of the world is also remarkable for its incredible diversity of ethnic groups, each of which has its own language, customs, mores, and religious belief. South East Asia today has a sprinkling of hunting-gethering Negrito people, such as the Atea of the Philipines, The Semang of Malaysia, and the Orang Kubu of Sumatra.

Austroloid people are also thought to have passed through South-East Asia during the early migration period. Traces of these people may be seen in the current racial stock of Timor and Flores. Meanwhile the majority of the present day indigenous population are basically Mongoloid, consisting of various people who migrated from South China and the Tibetan border areas at various times. The earliest and most far reaching influence which was to permeate South East Asia was that of India. Many local rulers adopted such Indianized ideas as a belief in a god-like king at the head of a hierarchical administration system, an ancestral genealogical pedigree system, the lunar-solar calender, astrology, and various of Hindu ritual worship. Buddhism was brought from India by traders.

The basic proportions and much of the iconography for South East Asia religious art come from India cannons of design. Classical Indian art motifs, such as crowned snakes, the Makara water monster, the Kala monster face mask, the garuda bird (the mount of the Hindu God Vishnu), peacocks, the lotus, the 'vase of plenty' and the wishing appear on South East Asia textiles. Local languages have been greatly enriched by the loan from Sanskrit, the ancient and sacred language of India. Indian epics, such as the Mahabarata and the Ramayana and the Buddhist Jataka Tales, form the basis of classical theatre in South East Asia.

The Ramayana is performed as a puppet play in southern Thailand, northern Malaysia and Java, and as a dance drama in Burma, Laos, central Thailand and central Java. Puppet figures from these epics (called wayang) appear on the textiles of Bali and Lombok in Indonesia. During the early years of Ming Dynasty (1368-1644), China took a more active interest in South East Asia. The influence of China culture can be seen in ceramics. Chinese ceramics have been imitated in brassware by the Maranao people of southern Philipines, while some ceramics motifs have been widely copied on South East Asian textiles. Images of Dragon from stoneware jars may occasionally be seen on warp ikat clothes from Sumba. In Bali and Thailand, the banji, or swastika, motif is a pattern regularly encountered on silk weft ikat.

It may also be seen in a supplementary weft on Lao, Shan, and Kachin textiles. Meanwhile the influence of Muslim to South East Asia may be seen in the soft, loosely woven double ikat-pattern patola cloth, sometimes called cinde. Patola textiles became symbols of wealth and prestige. The royal weft ikat cloth of Thailand and Cambodia is similar with the weft ikat cloths from Inle Lake in Burma and some sarongs, such as the malong andong of southern Philipines. The European influences by the spread of Western hygiene, improved sanitation, and health care have led to a decreased death rate and lead to the increase in population.

While education and the spread of Western ideas and technology have been responsible for much material progress, they have contributed to a cleavage between new and traditional ways of life. The influence of the textile motifs can be seen in the use of garden flowers in cloth from Arakan and Amarapura in Burma, Laos, Javanesse Batik and Timor. South East Asian shares some similarities from the ancestors, artefacts up to the influence brought by India, China, Muslim and Europe. However, the South East Asia nations have the same backgrounds. The similarities lead to the unity among the nations.

At a World Trade Organisation (WTO) conference in Male on the Maldive Islands in February 1997, Seungdam Choi, director of the Korea Tourism Research Institute, commented that tourism in South Korea had a 'bad connotation because it was too consumer-oriented'. Now, he explained, the government was looking at it 'as an industry', and one calculation was particularly important in this new perception: 14 foreign tourists coming to Korea add up to selling one car. This is a perspective that points to tourism as an activity determined by the essential logic of capitalism. Since tourism has been recognised as a priority in most Asian economies, inter-sectoral comparisons of profitability play a crucial role.

Indeed, a study of tourists' motivation, behaviour and experience would be insufficient without an understanding of tourism as an extension of commodification of modern life and an integral part of modem consumer culture. International tourism promotion is driven by supply and demand within the capitalist market economy, and both tourist-generating and receiving societies are subject to the dictates of this international system. As Watson and Kopachevski observed, '... people now live in a world in which tourism and tourist experience are major components. Such a world is one in which image, advertising, and consumerism - as framed by style, taste, travel, "designerism", and leisure - take primacy over production per se, and in which commoditisation is shaped and honed by specific, influential groups in society utilising a mixture of social, cultural, and political resources' (1996, 284).

In contrast to the notion that tourism growth is an epitome of freedom, choice, self-fulfilment and the realm of the 'authentic', modern tourism has often been seen as a reflection of 'supernational institutional will' and a consequence of 'the structural control over one's life, work, consumption, lifestyle and social relations'. According to Rojek, in modern capitalist society, 'the time and space allocated for work and leisure can be determined by mathematical precision', and 'leisure activity is explored as a way of filling in the consumers' empty time'.

Those who have the economic and political power to instil a sense of materialism and consumerism in society, are also able to shape tourists' consciousness, values and tastes. 'Mass tourism can also be interpreted as relations of power, and is... susceptible to the standardisation and homogenisation of all massified experiences, including both at the ideological and at the level of consumption. To the degree that this happens, individual thought, choice and action are destroyed'.

ALL-PERVASIVE

The development of South-East Asian tourism clearly illustrates how all-pervasive the commodification of tourism can be. The products of the industry which make the tourist experience - or that which Urry has dubbed the 'tourist gaze' (1990) - are an amalgamation and packaging of formerly diverse elements for consumption, including places, services - e.g. transportation, accommodation, dining, recreation, and entertainment - natural and cultural features, hospitality and ambience. At the end of this system of administered consumerism, the product incorporates what Asian tourism critics have denounced for many years as the 'sale' of whole countries involving entire societies, their culture, their environment and their identity.

Usher, for example, described the Thai government's promotional campaign 'Visit Thailand Year 1987' as 'an extravaganza of shameless commercialism' which 'depicted everything up for sale - from spotless white beaches to luscious jungles, from colourful cultural events to beautiful Thai women...'. Malaysian social critic and president of the Consumers' Association of Penang (CAP) Mohamed Idris raised the issues of modernisation based on Western values eclipsing Asian societies and changing people's leisure behaviour, describing the Malaysian situation as follows:

'In the past, most people would spend their free hours playing with their children, going on family picnics, or visiting their relatives and friends... Most people would enjoy some hobbies that would deeply satisfy them. Some would go for walks in the countryside, climb hills, swim in rivers and seas, and go fishing... Leisure would thus bring people close to nature, build healthy bonds within the family and with the community, deepen one's knowledge of humanity and the world, and manifest one's human creativity and feelings.

'Some people still do these things, but more and more of our leisure time is being taken up by new types of activities. Many people just plonk themselves on a chair and watch TV or video shows... If it's not TV or video, many people also now spend their free time in some kind of "fun for the moment". Society has become much commercialized. Advertisements have influenced people (particularly the young) to find enjoyment in quick thrills, new short-term sensations and trendy appearances'.

Idris' viewpoints suggest that the changes of leisure behaviour of Asians are not very different from those in the West. But there is the reminder that in many Asian countries, the transformation from traditional to modern society - accompanied by dramatic urbanisation, industrialisation, growth of technology and science, mass movements of people and the development of new social and personal opportunities - has happened in a period of less than two decades and been largely driven by external forces.

DISORDER AND ALIENATION

The imposition of modern values on rapidly developing Asian societies appears to have had especially disintegrating effects and created a sense of disorder, alienation, fragmentation and uncertainty of people's experience. The processes of commodification and homogenization, along with the mass circulation of new ideas, images and information, have been comprehensive and penetrating, with little margins left to prioritise traditional conventions, cultural customs, family and community values.

The 1977 Pacific Asia Travel Association (PATA) slogan for the Asia-Pacific travel and tourism industry, 'The consumer - the only person who matters', seems to have become reality in the Asian newly industrialised countries (NICs) which have embraced Western consumer culture and lifestyles. In his book Megatrends Asia, Naisbitt described the remarkable shift from export-led to consumer-driven economy in the region and highlighted the emergence of the middle classes as prime movers to spread consumerism:

'The average Asian's living standard is bursting out of "survival" into consumption. Incomes are increasing dramatically... If Asian consumers continue their 6 to 10% annual expansion of the last decade, their middle classes will double and triple in the next decade. The Asian middle class, not counting Japan, could number between 800 million and 1 billion people by 2010, resulting in a stunning $8 to $10 trillion in spending power. That's in the neighbourhood of 50% more than today's US economy...

'Asia's young population is in its consumer spending prime. Each of the little dragon nations of Hong Kong, Singapore, Taiwan and South Korea has more than 65% of their population between 15 and 65 years of age. The percentages are also high for countries in developing Asia. Thailand, Indonesia, Malaysia, China, India, and the Philippines range between 59 to 66%... 'Asia's middle classes are changing the economic, social and political landscape of the region. They are better educated, are marrying later and having fewer children. The young, urban middle classes of Asia are as sophisticated as any in the world. They lead sophisticated lifestyles and want sophisticated products and services. They are looking for quality as part of a self-conscious search for quality of life'.

According to Naisbitt, the upsurge of regional tourism is a major characteristic of this Asian consumer revolution:

'Suddenly, people in Asia can afford to travel, and exposure to satellite television has piqued their curiosity about faraway places - and not so faraway places... Ten years ago, executive-class cabins and lobbies of five-star hotels were the domains of Caucasians on holiday and Western business travellers working for multinationals in Asia. Frugal Asians, who used to fly coach for business and stayed at mid-price hotels, are increasingly taking those executive-class seats and checking into the region's upscale hotels. A new generation of middle-class Asians intent on visiting friends and family is creating an extraordinary opportunity for the mid-price hotels. Most growth is from Asians travelling to other Asian countries'.

Notwithstanding that such descriptions fail to take into account the vast historical, socio-economic and cultural differences in the region and within individual countries, they partly explain why the last decade of high economic growth has driven conspicuous consumption to new levels and tourism has become a middle-class rite throughout the region. Traditionally, a large proportion of the South-East Asian middle classes are ethnic Chinese who have accumulated wealth through family businesses such as retail trading. But over the last decade, professionals, managers, executives and medium entrepreneurs have generally witnessed a high degree of social mobility in countries like Singapore, Malaysia and Thailand. Particularly the class of the so-called Asian 'yuppies' - young professionals and entrepreneurs - whose spending power can be up to 20 times more than the average citizen's has grown in leaps and bounds.

A considerable number of people have also made easy fortunes as stockmarket players, and land and real estate speculators. It is especially these 'nouveau riche' whose highest hope in life is success, measured in terms of material possessions and expressed in free-spending lifestyles - including tourism. According to estimates of the Tourism Authority of Thailand, for example, there were more than five million domestic tourists in 1996, and the number of Thai citizens travelling abroad was expected to reach almost two million in the same year, a growth of more than 500% since 1978. Television and the advertising industry have become powerful tools in expanding materialistic values, and there has been a remarkable increase of advertisements related to leisure and tourism activities in both the print and electronic media over recent years.

A flood of magazines, brochures, television documentaries and even soap operas, sponsored by tourism agencies, airlines and hotel companies, are targeted for potential tourists. For Watson and Kopachevski, this is a sign of societies approaching 'postmodernity':

'Tourism, like other commodities, is packaged for exchange by advertising, much of which appeals to people's deepest wants, desires and fantasies (often sexual), and is anchored in a dynamic of sign/image construction manipulation. As an integral part of modern culture, advertising's main function is twofold: one, to serve as a discourse about objects, symbols and ideas, and as a template for erecting monuments to consumption and self-indulgence; and, two, to persuade people that only in consumption can they find not only satisfaction, but also mental and physical health, social status, happiness, rest, regeneration and contentment'.

Such powerful symbolic messages spread through the mass media have certainly contributed to the change of attitudes towards work, leisure and tourism. A survey by the Far Eastern Economic Review showed that 60% of working men and women from Asian countries opted for more leisure - that is, spending less time at work - to improve their enjoyment of life. Significantly more of those with high incomes - Singaporeans and Hong Kong Chinese - were in favour of more free time than those from less developed countries such as the Philippines.

Car ownership is not only considered as a symbol of new wealth and prosperity in Asia, but has also brought a sense of individual mobility and facilitated the growth of leisure travel. But the explosion of car traffic has come with high costs, as it severely constrains already inadequate road infrastructure and causes a myriad of environmental problems.

In recent years, the massive advertising for all-terrain vehicles has also encouraged off-road driving as a fashionable leisure activity. To promote new tourist routes and destinations, for example, the Tourism Authority of Thailand, in concert with large automotive companies, has sponsored motor rallies and caravans in the country's nature reserves and off-road driving shows from Thailand to China, Burma and Laos, which has repeatedly provoked protests by environmentalists.

Another major reason for the domestic travel boom is the rampant pollution, congestion and the deterioration of quality of life in the large cities. On weekends and holidays, recreationists of all classes and ages are seeking to escape to beaches, nature reserves and rural areas, or visit religious and cultural sites in the provinces. It has also become common for government agencies, private companies, and even non-governmental organisations to combine work and leisure by holding staff meetings and seminars at upcountry hotels and resorts. Affluent city-dwellers are touring their countries by plane and car, stay at hotels of international standards and purchase expensive country homes.

GREATER PRIVATISATION

While the proliferation of hotels, secondary homes, golf resorts, theme parks and integrated holiday complexes is a visible sign of an increasingly leisure-oriented consumer culture, spiralling land, house and food prices have affected less privileged social groups and hundreds of thousands of low-cost houses are desperately needed. The development of commercial leisure and tourism facilities has also resulted in greater privatisation of natural areas, causing land use conflicts and environmental disruption. While recreational activities in natural settings were originally free for all, many of these have now become costly resort activities with limited social access.

Mega-shopping-centres which are proliferating in Asian cities are also spectacular monuments of consumer culture and have become an important part of social life for urban families. While greenery and open spaces for outdoor recreation are utterly lacking, developers in a continuing effort to attract customers have made shopping malls meccas for entertainment and dining with a wide range of restaurants, pubs, movie theatres, swimming pools and amusement parks. On weekends and holidays, malls are filled with young people and families who regard them as economical 'resort' destinations.

For the well-off consumers, shopping has become a major popular leisure activity not only at home, but also abroad. A TAT study of 1994 revealed an increase of 37.36% in the expenditure of Thais travelling abroad during the previous year. In 1995, the top two destinations for Thai outbound tourists were the regional shopping centres Hong Kong and Singapore, and about half of their expenditure was classified under souvenir purchases. The number of wealthy people joining organised shopping tours to Europe to buy fashionable designer goods has also increased. An article in a Thai-language newspaper commented:

'Going abroad may be beneficial in terms of education and foreign travel experience, but there are certain people who just throw their money around to buy things not to cover their bodies but just to satisfy their "desires". They desire to wear expensive brand-name clothes and they desire to flaunt it to others. They desire to be talked about in society, among their peers. In the final analysis, these very people are quietly creating an environment of competition for conspicuous consumption'.

Advanced technology, together with growing prosperity, has driven the proliferation of credit cards across the Asian region. The most lucrative targets are the middle classes and students whose professional skills ensure their future affluence and encourage them to spend more through 'plastic money'. A credit card offers financial flexibility and convenience, and many tourism advertisements have attempted to capitalise on this advantage by suggesting one does not need cash to go on vacation. Some card companies offer special services as incentives such as discounts on room rates at hotels, the option to become a member of an air travel mileage programme and international emergency assistance.

While there is the argument in Thailand that the shift from a society based on patron-client relationships to capitalism has its positive side as it fuels people's aspirations for individual liberty and, eventually, a more democratic and egalitarian society, social critics such as Sulak Sivaraksa regard the capitalist consumer culture - as revealed in the free-wheeling hedonism and overspending of many tourists - as a menace that affects the whole society. Sulak commented:

'Today's motto is "I buy therefore I am..." (Consumerism is) the promotion of greed for all... the social catastrophe of Thai society lies in the fact that consumerism has drugged people into climbing the social ladder. But all this is a deception, and whenever we fall into this trap, it's the end.'

TRAPPED

Large parts of society have grown accustomed to consuming on credit and less affluent people have been trapped in debts as a result of purchasing goods and services which are not necessary in everyday life. Many people are now seeking a short route to make money, often in inappropriate ways. Recently, it was found that a rising number of Thai teenagers enter prostitution, not because of poverty, but simply to indulge in a materialistic and a leisurely lifestyle. Neighbouring countries and even Japan are experiencing similar problems, with young people joining the sex trade just to be able to enjoy the fashionable crazes of the day.

How much consumption patterns - and thus the growth of regional tourism - depend on macro-economic developments shows the current recession in several countries. Economists have even predicted an end of the 'Asian economic miracle' in view of looming crises in the financial sector, the slowdown of investments, and feared mass layoffs of industrial workers and white-collar employees. Undoubtedly, a further free fall of Asian economies would have tremendous implications for the regional leisure and tourism industry. For instance, based on the forecasted growth of Thailand's gross domestic product (GDP), it was estimated that the number of Thai outbound travellers would rise around 14% annually in 1997 and 1998. But these optimistic forecasts are now unlikely to be realised.

Due to the increasing current account deficit in the country, the Thai government resorted to measures discouraging overseas travel. Apart from a public campaign to promote domestic tourism, it announced a limit on the value of products imported by Thai tourists of US$400 in order to reduce shopping expenditures abroad. As a result, the growth rate of travel abroad slowed down to 7% in 1996 compared to double-digit growth in previous years. The further deterioration of the Thai economy led to a 30% decline of outbound tourism during the first six months of 1997. But the depreciation of the local currency beginning in July 1997, has delivered the most serious blow: Not only is outbound travel expected to fall by more than 50% since the Thai baht lost over 20% of its value, but domestic tourism is also facing decline due to increased costs of travel, accommodation, food and beverages within the country.

Meanwhile, however, tourism officials have predicted higher inflows of foreign tourists because Thailand has become a much cheaper holiday destination in the wake of the baht devaluation. In South Korea, concerns have also grown that people spend far more on vacation overseas than the country receives from foreign visitors, which resulted in a US$2 billion loss in its tourism balance and contributed to its worsening current account deficit in 1996.

This prompted the government in May 1997 to impose a fee of US$11 on Koreans each time they book an overseas vacation. Even in Japan, normally associated with unbounded riches, average citizens have been called upon to curb non-essential consumer spending since the burst of the bubble economy in 1991. Although the continuing recession has so far not led to a decline in the number of Japanese outbound travellers, holiday-makers have tended to reduce their length of stay and to consume less inside and outside the country than during the economic boom times in the second half of the 1980s (The Nation,10 February 1997).

IMPACT OF THE ECONOMIC CRISIS

Intuitively, Singapore and its neighbours have always realised that Southeast Asia's security cannot be premised alone on military-political instruments such as alliances. The Association of South East Asian Nations (ASEAN) often spoke of the importance of economic growth in fostering national resilience, the possession of which in turn contributes to regional resilience. The financial crisis of last eighteen months has only reinforced the centrality of the economic element in the security equation. This chapter will attempt to assess the impact of the financial crisis on the Southeast Asian strategic environment. It suggests that the political repercussions of the crisis have not fully unfolded even though the economic crisis may be bottoming out in many of the affected countries.

Various views have been presented as to what caused the crisis. Easy money in the financial sector and over-capacity in production due largely to uncoordinated monetary and policies in the affected countries have been forwarded as explanations for the crisis. Euphoric foreign lending which collapsed into panic withdrawals, with the first signs of crisis, is another explanation. Whatever the real cause, the question for security studies analysts is what can we expect to happen in Southeast Asia in the near future. This is because the crisis, which was initially purely economic in nature, has adversely affected the political and social fabric of the countries of SEA, including Singapore, albeit in a less devastating manner.

In recent months, some analysts claim to have detected signs of favourable changes to warrant an optimistic outlook. These changes are:

- Declining global interest rates have eased domestic interest rates in the region without affecting exchange rates and look sustainable.
- Foreign reserves are showing marked improvements in the case of most countries.
- The new fiscal and banking packages introduced in Japan are more credible than earlier proposals, which will prevent the Japanese economy from slipping into deeper recession.
- A fundamental shift in the attitudes of leading industrialised nations in dealing with the financial crisis.
- Growing global concerns on the measures needed to address basic weaknesses in the global financial system.

Going by recent developments and compared with what happened in 1998, it would be fair to conclude that the region is showing signs that it is heading for recovery, although this is somewhat fragile and uneven among countries. Thailand and Korea are viewed as front runners and likely, if current trend continues, to achieve positive growth in the 2nd half of the year. Malaysia still has problems to sort out, but showing signs of improvement and economic recovery, albeit at a slower pace. Indonesia remains marred by serious political and social difficulties that she needs to overcome.

But it is also necessary to mention some domestic risks that might threaten this recovery. They are:

- Rising unemployment and poverty can unleash social and economic unrest, increase uncertainty and cripple any reform process. These are most apparent in Indonesia, where unemployment is expected to hit 15%.

- Financial paralysis could also be a great obstacle to a speedy recovery. High domestic debt leverage and an overhang of bad debts will prevent financial intermediaries from rescuing normal operations.
- External debt overhang - the unwinding of which is presently proceeding, but at a lower rate. The Domestic Debt overhang on the other hand has not been taking place as rapidly as for the external debt.

All these provide some indication of the winding-down process. In Thailand, aggressive liberalisation policies have speeded up the process, while in Malaysia economic analysts suggest that delays in restructuring and unwillingness to liberalise quickly can mean a slower and prolong adjustment period. In short, the jury is still out with regards to the question of how soon or fast the region can and will recover. It is therefore somewhat premature to conclude that Asia's crisis is over, because crisis-ridden Asian economies face much more danger from domestic economic, social and political concerns, than from external shocks. Like wise, it is feared that a moderate slowdown in the US economy while it would not spell disaster, could also hinder Southeast Asia's recovery.

POLITICAL AND SECURITY IMPACT OF THE ECONOMIC CRISIS

The next question is whether this crisis and its impact have fundamentally altered the political and security environment in South East Asia. A number of questions are being asked; amongst them are the following:

- What if the economic growth in Indonesia and to a much lesser extent, Malaysia continues to be negatively impacted because of political and social problems?
- How will South East Asia's inability to overcome the impact of the crisis in the next few years impact on Asean, AFTA, ARF and other multilateral structures in the region?

Answers to the above questions hinge in part on the largest state in Southeast Asia—Indonesia. The strategic importance of Indonesia both in Southeast Asia and within Asean is obvious. The emergence of over 100 political parties, the mushrooming of newspapers & magazines, the voices of NGOs and shrill calls by protesting students may all give the impression that responsible Democracy has at last come to Indonesia bringing to an end the kind of governance that marked the last 30 odd years.

Equally "reassuring" may be the developments in the political process with a time-table for the reform of the political process; with new laws on Elections; plans for 2 Houses and structures for Regional parliaments and, above all provisions for a Democratically-elected President. Past laws that limited contest to 3 political parties will also be discarded. Among the requirements that political parties will have to meet to contest the coming elections will be that they have branches in at least half of the 27 provinces and a presence in all districts. Also that they be accessible to all regardless of race, religion and ethnicity.

The suggestion that Pancasila be dropped as the sole ideological base may seem attractive, but it has already heightened Islamic fervour and some calls for the establishment of an Islamic State, which President Habibie has recently decried. But on the flipside, widespread unrest; tensions between the Rich & Poor; "pribumi & non-pribumi"; Religious-based differences between Muslims & Christians still dominate Indonesian politics. So has Centre (Java)-provincial relations. Against the emerging political background, the dual function of the Armed Forces and excesses by some elements within it in East Timor, West Irian & Aceh are now being questioned. This debate on the role of ABRI, will also have its repercussions in the overall political debate that is now taking place.

Efforts at reform have started and aimed at democratisation of Indonesia. But the question is how strong these reformist forces are. Have they the strength - moral and political - to bring about a change from the power-based political culture that has existed in Indonesia, this past 50 years, to a law-based political culture. What is lacking is the absence of a clear road map and the instruments to carry out what the reform groups are demanding. The priority is the need for economic reform to restore the economic & business Climate, but the reformist focus is entirely on political reforms. Added to these voices of discontent are the non-governmental organisations (NGOs) and proponents of civil society, who are predominantly urban, in a country where 80% are rural and strongly bound by tradition, especially in Java. Demands for strong leadership will be needed to help Indonesia get out of this crisis.

What will happen, once the electoral laws are passed & the process for electing the legislature and the President, is anybody's guess. Given the organisation and money that Golkar possesses, it should win a majority of seats in the June elections. This is because its organisational links extend throughout Indonesia, while the major contesting parties - Megawati's PDI; Amien Rais' National Awakening Party and Edi Sudarjati's Justice Party are reported to be focusing on Java. There are suggestions that these parties are perhaps paying less attention to provinces like Borneo, Sulawesi, West Irian or East Timor; because they do not have the means and the organisation to cover these areas. Will such a Golkar victory be widely accepted – given its past affiliation with Suharto? If not, will it heighten unrest and again threaten law and order and further bring down the economy? There are no clear answers to such questions.

The 2 dangers that Indonesia could face are:

- Peaceful co-existence among different groups being endangered due to austerity policy and reactions by some groups to acts of discrimination by the government.
- Disruptions of international co-operation towards assisting Indonesia.

Neither of these 2 dangers seem likely as of now - but either or both could arise depending on how the June Election results are received by the population and if serious disturbances to law and order are avoided until the President is elected in November 1999.

At a recent seminar in Singapore on the Regional Outlook for 1999 - Dr Hadi Soesastro, a respected Indonesia economist, argued that:

1. The economy is in disarray. While President Habibie's immediate task is to turn the economy around and revive economic activities, his more urgent task is to ensure a smooth and peaceful political transition. This is an enormous task that the President will find hard to achieve, because of his serious lack of legitimacy in the eyes of various groups in the country.
2. Students and other activists continue to demand total reform because of revelations that the government, including the military, is allegedly continuing to resort to political harassment and terrorising practices.
3. Economic policy making and implementations remain very confused, because the government has introduced new policies with a strong political agenda that interferes with the overall economic stabilisation and recovery programme.
4. Elements are demanding a review of the government's development strategy, which they feel should be re-oriented in the direction of exploiting Indonesia's own strength and become less dependent on External resources.
5. There is greater concern over the government's attention and efforts to move politically attractive measures such as empowering the co-operatives instead of making progress in implementing the more urgent social safety net programs.

With the President Habibie administration's record thus far being a mixed one, the question is how much longer before the Economy recovers. The estimates vary from the optimistic, that is, by mid-1999 it will begin to enter a recovery period that may take 3 years. The less optimistic cannot see how recovery is possible so long as the political situation remains fragile and unpredictable. They believe recovery could begin at the next century, while the more pessimistic think it may even take about a decade before it can return to the growth path.

In short, it is difficult to tell when the Indonesian economy will recover. Much will depend on the elections in June. The current unrest in Indonesia will hopefully pass because unlike the 50s, Indonesia now has a middle class, a consumer society which will want to get back as soon as possible to enjoying the good times, and the basic infrastructure is there for renewed progress.

THE FUTURE OF ASEAN

The countries outside the region have hitherto lauded Asean, as the success story among developing regions. They have now begun to ask a range of questions about Asean and its future. Primarily, they focus on what they see as Asean's inability to address and act together to prevent the spread or at least mitigate the worst effects of the financial crisis. In their eyes Asean has been found wanting. While Asean's increasing international profile could have contributed to such high expectations, the question is about Asean's inability to look forward, anticipate the crisis in Thailand and its subsequent spread to the rest of the region. Is this pessimism of the future of Asean justified?

Those who have followed Asean's 30 years history will recall that its strength always lay in the political diplomatic sphere and in staying together to help develop a climate of confidence. This enhanced prospects for peace and stability in South East Asia, without which, past efforts in the individual member countries to promote growth, with such admirable results, would not have been achievable. Admittedly, in this crisis, Asean has taken time to rally together and build consensus. The Asean Free Trade Area (AFTA) took 30 years to be launched. At a time of strategic uncertainty, Asean launched the ARF, which it continues to nurse to become a useful confidence building mechanism among major powers with an interest in peace and stability in the Asia Pacific.

Last but not least, Asean's commitment, even at a time of such serious economic crisis, to AFTA by advancing its implementation date from the year 2003 to 2002; the Asean

Investment Area by bringing it forward to the year 2003 from 2010, and its encouragement to members to relax their foreign investment regulations are all indications that Asean is not out. No doubt time will be needed to restore confidence in Asean and South East Asia as a region with strong economic prospects. With the economic downturn, Asean may have become more inward-looking temporarily. This is because Asean member countries' concerns are more with maintaining internal stability and maintaining national unity.

Nevertheless, the crisis also represents a security threat with strategic ramifications arising from the globalisation. The US resort to leverage in economic and political issues in times of domestic instability, US-Japan tensions over trade are all matters of South East Asian concern. The question that is asked is "Just how important is SEA to the United States and Europe"? From a South East Asian perspective "Asean Unity" remains intact, even though personal relations among Asean leaders which consolidated its Unity in the past, could be somewhat affected by leadership changes in member countries. Changes in a few governments of member states could have some effect in this respect. This is because they introduce generational and value changes that are liable to follow the changes of personalities. How Asean, as an institution will regulate relations between member states in the face of such changes, is a matter that only the coming months will reveal.

SOUTHEAST ASIAN SECURITY

On the surface, the external security situation for South East Asian States may appear to be non-threatening because of their preoccupation with the consequences of the economic crisis on their respective domestic situations. But the fact remains that there is strategic uncertainty. In that context, long standing causes of concern, include outstanding bilateral territorial disputes and that between some of the States and China over the Spratlys. These are the hot spots with potential for armed conflict.

Today, countries in the region are more concerned with issues of domestic stability. Indonesia has seen massive political turmoil, with no signs of the law and order situation returning to normal till at least the Presidential elections in November. Whether the riots and disturbances will immediately subside thereafter is doubtful. Social stability in most parts of the region is also being undermined by the rise of unemployment. Besides these the prospects of illegal immigration remains a potentially destabilising issue. While many commentators on the Asian economic crisis have viewed its political and security implications on South East Asia in starkly negative terms, the impact has in fact varied from country to country, with Indonesia the most seriously affected, while Malaysia and Thailand have been affected to a much lesser extent.

Given the nature and magnitude of the changes taking place in South East Asia it is difficult to attempt to isolate key determinants of external security that need addressing on a priority basis. During the Cold War it was possible to assess each potential actor among the Big Powers with security interest in South East Asia and calculate their potential course of action. Now it is more difficult to tell "ally from competitor" or "threat from opportunity". This is not to say that external threats are non-existent. The prospect of low-intensity conflict arising from the tensions over the Spratlys or navigation and over flight over the disputed areas is indeed there. If any of the countries involved choose to take advantage of the preoccupation of others with their domestic economic and social dangers, and resort to the use of force than armed conflict will follow. But there are no signs so far of such a development occurring in the immediate 2/3 years.

Given this evolving situation, it has also to be recognised that the countries of South East Asia being small and medium size states lack the strategic autonomy of larger powers. They also lack the commensurate strength to contend militarily with any larger power, should conflict arise with any of them. A Big Power can dictate the rules. We in South East Asia as

Target States, without the capability of deploying maximum power in response, can only respond proportionately, according to respective military capability. With the economic downturn, the concerns are more with monitoring internal stability and national unity. Nevertheless, the uncertain external security environment has strategic ramifications for the region. Thus, to keep as many options on the external situation while focusing on the domestic is what is pre-occupying those who have been badly affected by the Crisis.

SOUTHEAST ASIA AND THE MAJOR POWERS

As mentioned earlier, for the present the atmosphere beyond our immediate sub-region appears tranquil except for the Spratly Islands dispute. But things can and do change unexpectedly. While we will continue to face the consequences of the economic downtown in the region, the key to peace and stability still remains the triangular US, China and Japan relationship. For this to be sustained, a healthy balance between the three powers will be crucial. Compared to a few years ago, US-China relations, and with Japan have improved and we hope that relations between and amongst the three countries would continue to improve. For now, what we can say is that the situation is evolving and a new power balance will clearly emerge only after 10-15 years.

Looking at the positive side, if the Chinese economy takes off, China will see it in its interest not to destabilise the Asia-Pacific unless its vital interests are threatened. It is generally acknowledged that her economic progress is not stoppable in the long run with that it will grow in military strength, though not necessarily able to match the US anytime in the near future. With regards to US-China relations, it has been described as a phase where the 2 countries are suspended somewhere between friendship and rivalry. But a more sanguine view will be one of cautious optimism for the immediate future. The relations between China and the US and with Japan will be of critical importance to the security and stability of the Asia Pacific region, if not the entire world.

For a time, it did appear as though the US would view the rise of China as a threat to its global supremacy and pursue a policy similar to its "containment" strategy against the former Soviet Union. This would have ensured a new bipolar struggle to replace the US-Soviet rivalry of the Cold War period. But the Clinton administration has instead decided to pursue a strategy of "engagement". After some initial misgivings about this approach, the Chinese have come to accept it as positive and have responded with some restraints on their own strategic policies, to meet US concerns. China has also mounted a diplomatic offensive to regain the goodwill and cultivate countries of the region and expand economic ties.

With Malaysia it has even raised the prospect of greater trade and even supply of China-made weapons. It has similarly sought to reassure Indonesia that it does not lay claim to the Natunas, nor all the waters of the South China Sea. Despite recent developments with regards to Mischief Reef, China and the Philippines are unlikely to collide over the Mischief Reef. In 1995, China had already expressed its commitment to observing the UNCLOS. China has also signed the Asean Declaration on the South China Sea in 1992 and the China-Asean declaration of 1997, which commit her to settling the Spratlys issue in a peaceful manner. Recent statements from Malaysia suggest that Kuala Lumpur's view of China has also changed.

This is encouraging, given her differences with China over her territorial claims in the Spratlys. Dr Mahathir has even cast China as a non-threatening power that wants to focus on economic development. He has gone a step further to state that the region should not be taken up with assertions by some quarters in the US about China being potential military threat. But, Indonesia which has always viewed China as a threat, though preoccupied with her domestic concerns, has yet to announce any change in that perception. As to the minuses, Sheldon Simon has argued in a National Bureau of Asian Research Study, that the economic crisis has affected the balance of power in the Asia Pacific in that most of the countries in Southeast Asia have cut defence budgets and postponed arms modernisation programmes because of economic difficulties whereas China has continued to modernise its military capability.

While, (and as I have mentioned earlier), there is no imminent external security problems, in the longer term one cannot be so sanguine especially when the Spratlys issue remain unresolved. Simon concluded that more than ever, American presence as a stabilising force in the region is required. In the years since the end of the Cold War, we have seen US foreign and defence policy particularly towards East and Southeast Asia shift from one in which the containment of communism was the central pillar, to one that is more akin to what we understand as a balance of power. The United States describes its role in the region as a 'balance wheel of Asia', 'buffer force', 'ultimate security guarantor' and 'honest broker'. As the sole superpower today and with so many parts of the world requiring an American presence, the critical question for us is whether the US will remain in the region and what sort of staying power it possesses. We have established the makings of a multilateral security architecture for the Asia Pacific for the long term. I refer to the Asean Regional Forum (ARF). Unlike Europe, East and Southeast Asia neither have a history of a shared destiny nor experience in collective security as Europe had during the Cold War years. The security landscape is more ambiguous in Southeast Asia and different countries have different perceptions of threat.

The ARF is the only security forum in the world to include all the major powers but initiated and launched by a group of developing countries. Seen from this perspective, the establishment of the ARF is a significant milestone and achievement. The ARF process aims at building up trust and fostering greater confidence among its members so that differences can be resolved through peaceful means and without having to resort to the use of force. Since it was inaugurated in 1993, it has elicited a significant level of interest as a forum for both regional and extra-regional countries to discuss security issues of common concern and interest. At this stage of its evolution, it will be premature to prescribe immediate solutions to regional security problems. It is the hope that through the exchanges at the ARF, it would help the participating countries improve perceptions of each other.

A seminar organised by the Institute of Defence and Strategic Studies (IDSS) in 1998 which brought together all representatives, both academics and officials in their private capacity, to 'audit' the ARF concluded that the ARF, while it needs some fine-tuning is the only credible security forum in the region. In conclusion, in the near future, it is economic restoration (more than any conventional/traditional security threat) that is likely to take centre stage. All the countries in the region are focusing on their economy. Within Southeast Asia, much depends on developments in Indonesia, which is burdened with deep economic, social and political problems.

If its problems get more complicated, the region will take a much longer time to recover. Economists are of the view that the economies of South Korea, Thailand, Philippines, Malaysia and Singapore have more or less bottomed out. A clearer picture will hopefully emerge after the June 1999 Indonesian elections. Much will also depend on continued strong economic growth in the United States. If the American economy slows down too dramatically, it will affect our region negatively. An early Japanese economic recovery will give the region the much-needed lift. Finally, so long as China does not devalue the renminbi too soon, it will give the region a much-appreciated breather.

8

The Effect of Tourism on a Thai Seaside Town

Many developing countries perceive tourism as a fast track to economic growth. They assume that tourism development requires less investment than other industries; and they believe tourism to be an effective means of creating job opportunities and increasing local income. Thailand has long ascribed to this point of view; and it has devised a tourism marketing approach which encourages low-, medium-, and high-cost mass tourism to nearly all regions of the country. With the ubiquitous "Land of Smiles" advertising slogan promoted around the world, Thailand has become one of the best known, and most sought after, international tourist destinations.

Despite this success, however, the tourism industry in Thailand is not without problems and controversy. Critics charge that tourism promotion in Thailand has aimed at quantity rather than quality. The explosion of tourism has brought uneven distribution of financial benefits, in favor of large enterprises, while costs are shouldered by local people who have no direct gain from tourist promotion. Worse still are the environmental effects of unbridled tourism development. While the Thai tourism industry touts and actively markets the country's unique cultures, this commercialization of culture also causes its erosion or corruption.

Additionally, interaction between rural Thai dwellers and sophisticated urbanites from more developed countries introduces values, behavior and attitudes which may have corrosive or negative effects on local residents. Under these circumstances, then, it is worth examining the advantages and disadvantages of the tourism industry in Thailand-and what trends it might take in the future.

THE ROLE OF TOURISM IN THE THAI ECONOMY

The volume of tourists coming to Thailand may not compare to the 27 to 50 million people travelling to France, Italy or Spain every year. Yet, when compared to other high-volume tourist destinations around the world, the growth and development of the tourism industry in Thailand is impressive. Egypt receives approximately 2.6 million tourists per year, while India annually draws in approximately 1.8 million tourists. By comparision, Thailand now accommodates approximately 5 million tourists per year, one of the highest figures for Southeast Asia. The number of tourists coming to Thailand has steadily, and in some years, spectacularly grown-from 1.2 million in 1977 to 5.7 million in 1993. The income accrued from tourism contributes substantially to the Thai economy, now accounting for 5.4 percent of the country's GDP. This rate is higher than any other ASEAN country, except Singapore, whose tourism revenue accounts for 11.4 percent of its GDP.

The Thai Government's Sixth National Economic and Social Development Plan (1987-1991) gave particular focus and attention to the development of tourism; the result was a substantial boost to tourism revenue-from 50,000 million baht in 1987 to 123,135 million baht in 1992. This was partially caused by the government's promotion of "Visit Thailand Year" in 1987, a marketing exercise which increased national tourism income by 34 percent in 1987 and by 58 percent in 1988. By 1991, income from tourism was equivalent to two-thirds of the country's agricultural export earnings, and was nearly the same as the country's income from textile and garment exports.

The number of tourists coming to Thailand remained constant in 1991, despite the Persian Gulf Crisis and a military coup in Thailand. Although the industry initially suffered from the political turmoil in May, 1992, it soon recovered. It is important to note that the increase in tourism revenue since 1981 has mostly derived from greater numbers of tourists coming to Thailand, and tourists extending their stay, rather than from higher daily expenses.

POSITIVE AND NEGATIVE

Thailand is famous for its impressive historical sites, its rich and vibrant cultures, its beautiful beaches, its scenic countryside, and its gentle, polite and genuinely friendly people. A 1990-1991 study on tourism, in which 1,450 tourist agencies in 40 major cities in 26 countries were interviewed, ranked Thailand first in the categories of warmth and friendliness, moderate accommodation cost and interesting nightlife. The country ranked fourth in the category of excellent cuisine, after France, Italy and Hong Kong. Thailand does not appear on the list of the 14 Asian and Pacific countries with beautiful scenery, but it was ranked second after Australia in terms of its overall appeal. Sadly, however, Thailand was also rated the second most polluted and unsanitary nation after India.

Reviewing the attractions cited above, it becomes clear that other countries have similar attractions. What then accounts for Thailand's success in the tourism industry? The tourism industry came to the fore when Thailand was changing from a resource-based to a labor-based economy, an adjustment which was well suited for tourism development. This was coupled with the fact that the training and material input for tourist services were not as complex or extensive as those required for other kinds of industries. The high standard of service offered in Thai hotels and restaurants has remained consistently impressive. Thai hotels are known for their reasonable prices and top quality service. Thai staff are known for their pleasant, friendly and gentle character. Likewise Thai International Airways is world-renowned for its outstanding in-flight service. Good managerial skills have assisted in the maintenance of high quality service in nearly every realm of operation.

INFRASTRUCTURE MAINTENANCE AND DEVELOPMENT

The development of the tourism industry in Thailand-and the comparative advantages which have been created through it-are mostly a result of private sector investment and efforts. The public sector has not been active in upgrading infrastructure-e.g., roads, telecommunications, water facilities-to keep abreast with the industry's growth and to assure the industry's long-term stability. In certain areas, water allocation, waste disposal and the safety standards of public facilities are inadequate for the local population, let alone tourists visiting their villages or towns. Heavy traffic congestion in Bangkok is undoubtedly seen as a drawback by people contemplating a visit to Thailand.

Likewise inadequate waste and rubbish disposal in Bangkok and Chiang Mai may be seen as problematic by visitors to Thailand. In Bangkok, 500 tons of waste accumulates every day without being properly disposed of. In Phuket-one of Thailand's prime southern tourist destinations-water management is a serious problem. Water consumption has risen to 200 liters per person per day, while authorities have been able to supply only 27 liters per person per day. All such considerations make it imperative for the public sector to invest more in the country's infrastucture and to improve administrative policies on tourism. The important point here is that Thailand has long passed the first stage of tourism development which relied on nature. The second stage would require heavy capital investment in infrastructure.

THE AIDS FACTOR

The rapid spread of AIDS in Thailand has had a decided impact on the tourism industry in that the country's reputation for having a high incidence of AIDs discourages desirable tourists from visiting it. Likewise the tourism industry has had considerable impact on the spread of AIDS in Thailand.

Thailand has long been promoted as the "sex capital" of the world; encouraging tourists to come to Thailand specifically for this reason obviously brings a higher transmission of the disease from sources both inside and outside the country. (It should be noted that there are other important factors contributing to the high incidence of AIDS and HIV-positive cases in Thailand which have nothing to do with the tourism industry, one major one being Thai males' penchant for frequenting prostitutes both before and after marriage.)

Initially, the Thai government did not take prompt and appropriate action to deal with the AIDS crisis. It did not try to curtail the sex industry, believing that it would naturally fade as the economy prospered and job opportunities increased. Later, as the Government began to realize the severity of the situation, it tackled the problem only by promoting the use of condoms, rather than by using a multi-pronged approach, which would have included the attenuation of the sex industry.

TOURISM AND ENVIRONMENT

When tourists first started to come to Thailand, they were charmed by scenes of children playing in emerald green rice fields, monks walking tree-lined lanes accepting alms in the first morning's light, and exquisitely picturesque village vistas, picture-postcard perfect. Thailand's race to industrialize has eroded this image. Factories, traffic and clogged, polluted highways as well as a quickly vanishing rural way of life have removed some of the attractions which bring tourists to Thailand. Nature-based tourism is quickly disappearing, as once pristine beaches and forest areas become heavily polluted or destroyed. Pattaya beaches, for example, cannot be swum in anymore.

The famous Pa Tong Beach in Phuket has become so polluted so as to destroy fish and other marine life there. The Mae Kah canal running through the heart of Chiang Mai is now black with pollutants. Pattaya is a perfect example of how unmanaged, uncontrolled tourism destroys the environment and natural resources. Originally a small fishing village, Pattaya turned into an internationally known seaside resort in the short span of twenty years. At present Pattaya is second only to Bangkok in the number of tourists it receives. One in every three tourists visiting Thailand travels to Pattaya. The city's earnings from tourism in 1991 were 15,000 million baht, or 15 percent of the national tourist income. Environmental pollution and destruction, however, have brought about Pattaya's decline as a desirable tourist destination.

Research conducted by the National Environment Board shows that since 1986 the quality of marine water at Pattaya has dropped below the acceptable standard, due to poor rubbish and waste water management; and only 10 percent of the coral reef east of Lan Island (near Pattaya) remains. Uncontrolled construction along the beachfront has added a further negative factor.

All of the above resulted in a dramatic decrease in the numbers of tourists visiting Pattaya since 1987. What has happened in Pattaya perfectly illustrates the principle that tourist development goes hand in hand with responsible natural resource management. Investors must be made to understand that tourism relies on the conservation and sustainable utilization of natural resources, without which the industry cannot survive. They must be made to strictly comply with environmental regulations, and to contribute toward the environmental awareness of local residents and tourists alike.

QUALITY TOURISTS

Tourism in Thailand has often been criticized for aiming at expanding in quantity rather than quality. TAT has been pressured to search for an operational criterion targeted on "quality" tourists. Critics, however, often disagree in their opinions on what exactly a quality tourist is. Representatives from the Hotel Association often assert that quality tourists are the big spenders-those who stay in famous, international chain hotels, ride in chauffeur-driven limousines, and dine at expensive restaurants. Others argue that true quality tourists are those who most effect income distribution. A quality tourist, under this definition, stays in locally-owned hotels or guest houses, eats at local food stalls, and rides a tuk-tuk.

Income generated by these tourists is thought to penetrate more deeply and widely to the poorer segments of the industry. In contrast, money from big spenders tends to leak outside the country through franchise royalties and remitted dividends. More idealistic observers define quality tourists as those who venture to new places to broaden their knowledge of the world and its peoples by being directly exposed to local citizens and their culture. Cultural seekers buying packaged heritage tours are not considered full-fledged, quality tourists in the eyes of the idealist, because mass tourism does not allow person to person contact and cultural exchange.

The theory that big spenders bring more income to a country fails to be supported by empirical evidence. A recent TDRI study confirms that although the daily expenditure of typical guest house tourists may not be as high as that of hotel dwellers, they do, in fact, normally spend more because they usually stay in the country much longer. When the structure of tourist spending is examined, the highest proportion of the expenditure by "hotel tourists" is for accommodation. It is also claimed, however, that guest house dwellers have a close relation with the illegal drugs trade. A reply to this accusation is that the big spender criterion cannot guarantee that the source of the big money is clean. Proponents of both criteria, however, suffer from the identical mistake, i.e., applying economic yardsticks to an ethical attribute.

The cultural exchange argument is the most romantic, but the least operational. If this definition were taken seriously, Thailand would be left with only a few thousand "quality tourists." Most tourists simply want to escape from stress and strain, not to experiment with alternative ways of life and thought. As the trend-at least for Asia-Pacific travellers-is to take shorter and more frequent holidays each year, there is little time for personal and cultural exchange. If one was to define quality tourists as big spenders who are also culture seekers, what would be a likely group of such tourists?

According to TDRI's survey of over 1,200 local and foreign tourists, quality tourists tend to be female, aged over 40, who spend more money and are more interested in cultural attractions. It may be easier to identify "bad" tourists. If bad tourists are those who come to buy sex, or come to trade or consume illegal drugs, they should be banned. The relevant policies should not tolerate such practices. Drastic action should be taken to eliminate such services. The responsibility for ending "bad tourism" would thus be shifted from TAT to the Ministry of Interior.

CULTURAL CHANGE AS A FUNCTION OF TOURISM

Tourism is often attacked as one cause of cultural decline in Thailand. Some rituals, ceremonies and cultural events have become commercialized and have turned into a kind of show business where the focus is making money; this is perceived by some as being caused, or partially caused, by tourism. While it is undeniably true that the tastes of foreign tourists have an influence on the more tangible forms of culture, for example arts and crafts manufacture in Chiang Mai Province, and that some cultural events are organized with the express purpose of attracting foreign tourists, it is not correct to say that foreign tourists have a direct bearing on the evolution of Thai culture. This point is exemplified in a study done by Professor Nidhi Eoseewong on the Bang-Fai or Skyrocket Festival in Yasothorn Province.

This was initially a folk ceremony to bring rain and to assure agricultural people of fertility and a bountiful harvest. Over the years, the festival has been greatly modified in form and spirit. No longer a village spiritual ceremony, it now has become more of a performance which people attend for pleasure and fun. It has acquired new socio-political functions, creating important bonds between village and city residents as well as village residents and state authorities. Its changes are less a function of tourism (few tourists attend the festival) and more a function of societal changes. Whereas formerly the ceremony was performed locally in villages for religious reasons, it has now been transferred to the auspices of provincial authorities who have turned it into a show to be attended by provincial residents. Thus the character and "raison d'etre" of this ritual have been completely altered through changing societal structure and values.

FUTURE OPPORTUNITIES

Undoubtedly, there is fierce competition in the tourism industry among Southeast Asian countries. Following Thailand's 1987 "Visit Thailand Year," Malaysia followed suit with "Visit Malaysia Year" in 1990; Indonesia continued the trend with "Visit Indonesia Year" in 1991. Singapore has recently invested S$1 million for the improvement of infrastructure to cater to the tourism industry. At present Myanmar is planning its first "Visit Myanmar Year." Despite this competition, Thailand still holds comparative advantage in a number of realms. Malaysia has insufficient accommodation facilities, both in quantity and quality. Indonesia lacks experience in tourism management. And Singapore faces problems of high labor costs within the tourism industry. Our past advantage is due to sectoral efficiency. Our future advantage lies in our ability to manage our infrastructure both at a sectoral and macro level, especially to curb Bangkok's traffic problem.

Chonburi, Bangkoks nearest seaside town, is located on the eastern coast of the Gulf of Thailand, only 80 kilometers from Bangkok. The area boasts abundant natural resources, which are highlighted by delightful beaches, local colors, traditions, delicacies and fresh seafood. This is a popular resort among Bangkokians who seek the nearest escape from hectic weekly schedules as Chon Buri has something for everyone. In addition, Chon Buri is the center of the Eastern Seaboard Development Project, with its industrial parks and fishing villages.

PATTAYA A TRAVELERS PARADISE

Pattaya is nestled along a picturesque bay on the East Coast of the Gulf of Thailand, roughly 170 kilometers southeast of Bangkok. From a fishing village in the 1960's,

Pattaya has emerged as the favorite Southeast Asian vacation center. A fascinating escape where tourists, holiday makers and vacationers from around the world unfold an incomparable array of possibilities to unwind during an exotic holiday beach vacation. Unlike other beach resorts, where natural surroundings are used as magnets to attract tourists, Pattaya makes an all-out attempt to provide the best of everything.

Here, everything means everything a tourist can imagine while on holiday: recreation, entertainment, sports, sightseeing and fun. To put it simply, Pattaya is a paradise for everyone, as it has a variety of attractions suitable for all types of visitors. This is the place where you can fill your day, from dusk to dawn, with endless activities, or you may choose to do nothing at all and relax.

THE PAST

Pattaya's name was originated from the march of Phraya Tak (later known as King Taksin the Great) and his followers from Ayutthaya to Chanthaburi just before the fall of the Ayutthaya Kingdom to the Burmese invaders in 1767. When Phraya Tak's army arrived in the vicinity of what is Pattaya today, he encountered the troops of Nai Klom who tried to intercept him. When the two leaders met face to face, Nai Klom was awed by Phraya Tak's dignified manner and his army's strict discipline, thereby surrendering without a fight. The place where the two armies confronted each other was later called Thap Phraya, which means the Army of the Phraya.

This was later changed to Phatthaya, which happens to mean the wind blowing from the southwest to the northeast at the beginning of the rainy season. Today the spelling of the name has been simplified to Pattaya. For centuries, Pattaya was a small fishing village almost cut off from the outside world. But a big change occurred on 29 April 1961 when the first group of about 100 American servicemen who would join the Vietnam War arrived in Pattaya for relaxation.

Soon, sleepy Pattaya became Thailand's premier and most

successful beach resort, which annually attracts hundreds of thousands of pleasure-seeking visitors. A full range of accommodations from super deluxe hotels to bungalows and mini-pocket guesthouses replaced fishermens huts along the beach. Fishing vessels were adapted to become tourist boats and swimmers and sunbathers from various parts of the world frequented the quiet powdery golden beaches. Places of nighttime entertainment have also sprung up and are popular among international tourists.

THE PRESENT

Pattaya currently integrates the delights of a 1st class beach resort, city-like dining, shopping and night entertainment facilities with more than 300 assorted hotels, thousands of shops, restaurants and bars. In addition, there are an array of sports and recreational activities including beaches, golf courses, tennis courts, go-kart, gyms for working out, weight lifting and Thai-boxing gear. Pattaya offers a broad range of things to do.

During the day, one may enjoy riding elephants or driving humble automatic mini-bikes, monstrous motorcycles, or even monster multicolored convertible Jeeps. Others go for shooting firearms, scuba diving and surfing, deep-sea fishing, speed boats, scooters, water-skiing, parasailing, or aerial sports such as gliding ultra-lights and flying motor-propelled gliders. On the other hand, at night, there are restaurants, bars, theaters, cabaret shows, night clubs, bowling halls, billiard & snooker clubs, discos, sauna & massage parlors, not to cite its absolutely incredible shopping which is available non-stop both day-and-night.

PATTAYA FACTS

This exotic beach resort welcomes approximately 5 million visitors a year. The friendly and hospitable Thai nature boosts its promotion, frequently bringing back the repeat visitors and constantly increasing the number of newcomers. Pattaya city is located on the eastern coast of the country at latitude 13 N and longitude 101 E in the area of Chon Buri province.

It is 147 kilometers from Bangkok and lies parallel to Sukhumvit Road on its east and the coastline on its west. Pattaya occupies an area of 208.1 sq. km. that is divided into 53.44 sq. kilometers of land and 154.66 sq. kilometers of islands and sea. Its coastline is 15 kilometers long. Pattaya has a plain on the coast with some high mountains to the south. The area on the east slopes down towards the sea on the west.

9

Phuket

Urban Conservation versus Tourism

Phuket, 'pearl of the Andaman' is more than a beach resort. It has a rich history as tin-mining country peopled by Siamese, Chinese, Malays, Indians, Eurasians and sea gypsies. A unique community in Phuket is the 'Baba', with its own way of life, language, dress and food. The core of this community was formed by early unions between Hokkien tin-miners and Siamese women. This distinctive Baba heritage can be seen in old Phuket town. Since the 16th century, the Europeans have been interested in the tin trade of Phuket.

They called the island 'Junk Ceylon' (Ujong Thalang). The Burmese invasion of 1809 devastated the old settlement of Thalang, sparking an exodus of the original inhabitants. From the 1820s onwards, mining in Phuket was in the hands of Chinese adventurers from the British Straits Settlements, particularly Penang. During this period, fossicking spread from the interior at Kathu to the bay of Tongkah, and around 1850, the town of 'Tongkah' was formed. This settlement forms the historic core of Phuket town today.

Early Phuket town was linked by a few roads and a network of canals and waterways leading to Tongkah Bay. Coastal vessels transported tin from Phuket to Penang, and returned with foodstuffs and hardware. In the past, workers flocked to town to sell their ore, to stock up on provisions, and to remit money. In order to forget their hardship and homesickness, they indulged in the four pleasures - wine, women, opium and gambling. Thalang Road was the main street where the big traders had their shops. Soi Romanee was the red light district. In the early 20th century, a measure of civilization was brought by Phraya Rassada Nupradit (Khaw Sim Bee na Ranong) during his term as High Commissioner of greater Phuket (1900-1913).

He gave a large concession to an Australian-European mining company, Tongkah Harbour Dredging, in return for funds to develop the public infrastructure. Roads were built, canals were de-silted, and a number of public buildings were put up. With Phuket becoming safer, more traders and their families, especially those from Penang, settled down in Phuket. With greater prosperity, more schools and temples were endowed.

Tin from the frontier settlement of Phuket was smelted and exported at Penang, the nearest major seaport, Penang. Sea travel to Penang was faster and safer than land travel to Bangkok. Once communications were improved, Phuket gradaully changed its orientation towards Bangkok, especially after the Second World War. But by that time, Phuket had developed its distinctive local character.

With the inauguration of direct flights between Europe and Bangkok in the early 1970s, Phuket started to become a tourist destination. Ten years later, the tin market collapsed but fortunately the economy was rescued by the growth of tourism. Many former tin mines were converted into luxury resorts. The old town, on the other hand, has been largely bypassed by the tourism industry until recently.

ARCHITECTURAL HERITAGE

The cultural built heritage of Phuket is a reflection of the settlement's prosperity during the tin boom days. The townscape is unique in Thailand, but resembles that of the British Striats Settlements, which comprised, Penang, Malacca and Singapore. The architecture is usually called 'Sino-Portuguese' by the Bangkok architects today. However, any

Portuguese influence would have been rather indirect, via Malacca's historic influence on Straits Settlements architecture. Although Phuket had early contacts with the Portuguese, most evidence of European settlement was destroyed during the Burmese invasion.

Phuket town was really modelled after British colonial Penang, and that was the origin of any European influence on its architecture. Upon close examination, it is evident that Phuket's shophouses and villas resemble those in Penang in form, materials and design, although the occasional Thai motif reminds us that we are in Thailand. Phuket oral tradition in several cases claim that Penang architects, builders and materials were brought to Phuket for its best mansions. We are waiting for old building plans to be revealed to prove that this was indeed so. Thai architects entered the scene no later than 1930, and from then on, Phuket architecture began to diverge from Penang style.

In 1993, the Siamese Architects Association recognized this historic area with a conservation award given collectively to 'Shop and houses of Phuket city centre (Ancient Rowhouses)' on Thalang, Krabi, Dibuk, Phangnga, Rasada, Ranong, Yaowarat and Phuket Roads. These eight roads, plus two lanes, namely Soi Romanee and Soi Sun Uthit, form the pre-Second World War town. Phuket town has modernised with the rest of the island. In the historic centre, the narrow streets have to accommodate motorised traffic, while the five-footways are impenetrable in some parts. The streetscapes are largely intact, though broken up in some places by blockish modern infill and oversized plastic signage.

On the whole, the character of old Phuket town is distinctive and charming enough to attract both Thai and foreign visitors. Though the old town is no longer the commercial hub of Phuket, most of the shophouses are still functioning as shops and residences. Eating places abound in Phuket and the old town is no exception. The main street, Thalang Road is still known for certain trades, especially batik textiles. While the older businesses tend to be provisioners, wholesalers, tin dealers, hardware shops and machinery suppliers, today there is a slow but sure gentrification as antique shops, cafes and European restaurants are making their appearance.

THE PHUKET SHOPHOUSE

The dominant urban form in the old town is the 'shophouse', (from the Hokkien word tiam choo, literally, shop + house). Part of a row of houses, each unit has a narrow frontage on a long plot. The side elevation can be described as several pitched roof sections, alternating with internal courtyards (chhim chneh). These internal courtyards, which let air and light into the long, narrow houses, are the focus for lovely atrium spaces. Quite a few Phuket shophouses still have their original water wells.

If the front portion is used as a shop, the ground facade is usually open to the street, while the rest of the house could be used as a residence or storage area. The more affluent families use the whole 'shophouse' as a residence. In this case, the house would have an elegant facade concealing a private living space with ornate screens and indoor gardens. The upper part of the facade is often articulated with windows in three bays, surrounded by fancy stucco decoration. Fine examples of this can be seen along Dibuk Road. Whether residential or commercial, the shophouses are linked by a continuous front arcade known as a 'five-footway', which offer shade, shelter and safety to pedestrians.

The old town consists of a gridiron of streets, each flanked by double-storey shophouse rows, producing a dense living pattern. With criss-crossing lines of sight, this close-knit neighbourhood produced a high level of public safety and community networking. A dozen or so villas survive in the core area, a few with their gardens intact, others with compounds encroached by smaller buildings. Of these, the most attractive and accessible is the Pithak Chinpracha house, maintained by a sprightly 76 year old owner, Khun Pracha. The house is offered in the commercial cultural tours of Phuket.

Khun Pracha believes in the 'uniqueness of Phuket' and started showing 98 Krabi Road to visitors years ago, before most Phuket people had even heard of the word 'heritage'.

URBAN CONSERVATION

In the last two decades, development agencies, academia and City Hall have slowly but surely set the stage for the revitalization of the old town. The old town has been declared 'conservation of cultural heritage zone' by the Office of Environmental Policy and Planning (OEPP), of the National Environment Board. In the Development Plan of Muang Phuket Municipality Area published in 2004, the designated conservation area is 19 rai (about 0.5 square kilometres) with a built-up area of 31,069 sq metres.

Development guidelines specify a 12-metre height limit in order to maintain the 2-3 storey building scale of the shophouse neighbourhood. New infill buildings conforming to architectural prescriptions are no longer required to set back for road-widening. Guidelines are disseminated for appropriate signage. Traditional activities which reflect Phuket's identity are encouraged. Physical restoration is promoted, but as yet no financial incentives are available. From the 1980s, Phuket has been developing and modernising its local authority with the support of GTZ's 'Urban Environmental Management at Local Level Project'.

The Municipality has prepared a budget allocation for the conservation of the old town since 1994. Local authorities were strengthened when the government was restructured and decentralised following the financial crisis in Thailand in 1997. The conservation of old Phuket has been furthered through collaborations between the Municipality, the academia and local leaders. A special impetus has been provided since 1997 by the work of architecture lecturer Dr. Yongthanit Pimonsathean and his students from Bangkok.

With the full support of the City Hall, Dr. Yongthanit's university team has developed an architectural database, identifying heritage buildings, measuring and drawing them up. They have also assisted the municipality in conducting surveys, providing advice to house owners and sourcing appropriate materials and craftsmen. The Municipality and university team jointly organised exhibitions and facilitated community forums about the future of the old town. A few house owners volunteered or were persuaded to remove the obstructions to the five-footway sections in front of their houses. In celebration of this cooperation between the Municipality and residents, the first Old Phuket Town Festival was organised in 1998.

This event has been repeated annually since, with allocations from the Phuket government. The festival showcases the Baba lifestyle, food, costumes, performing arts and architectural heritage. During the Old Phuket Town Festival, Thalang Road has was closed off to cars and converted into a 'walking street', bringing back the ambience when the old town bustled with pedestrians instead of cars. An important exhibition and community meeting venue is the hall of Thai Wah School, the oldest Chinese school in Thailand, conveniently located at one end of the main street, on Krabi Road. As the school has moved out to new premises in the town outskirts, Thai Wah's Alumni Association now wants to convert their 1934 'Sino-Portuguese' building into a museum for Phuket Baba culture.

Between 1998 and 2002, the Municipality awarded more than 60 certificates of conservation effort to house owners who have restored or maintained their houses.

This scheme speeded up the process of building local awareness and pride. In addition, it helped ordinary people to differentiate between what was good conservation practice and what was not. New approaches to conservation have been explored. A motorcycle business had its new showroom, at the corner of Thalang and Phuket Roads, designed and built in sympathetic scale and design. Two very recent examples are worth mentioning. A 1950s shophouse has been adaptively reused with tasteful interior design employing traditional materials. A historic shophouse has been conserved and exquisitely interpreted as a cafe and gallery.

Phuket old town now faces the some of the same conservation issues as George Town as its unofficial 'sister city', Penang. However, there are important differences. The historic core of Phuket is perhaps one-fifth the size of that in Penang. Most of the old shophouses in Penang were mainly tenanted under the Rent Control Act, and the rift between the aspirations of owners and tenants worked against the objectives of conservation. In contrast, the majority of the old shophouses in Phuket owner-occupied, hence generally better cared for, even though the number which are sadly falling into decay is not negligible.

OLD PHUKET FOUNDATION

The special qualities of old Phuket town have created an extraordinary sense of belonging for those who grew up there. This is the impression I get from talking to a number of sons and daughters of Thalang Road-Krabi Road, who in mid-2005 are now leading members of the Phuket community. Collectively, they represent a phenomenon which could be called the 'old town movement'. This flame burns brightly during the annual Old Phuket Town Festival. The movement has several dimensions, including that of cultural identity, but for the purpose of this chapter, we will focus on the urban strategies pursued in the physical conservation and economic revitalization of the site.

After the tsunami of December 2004, many Phuket people had to rethink the way Phuket has developed. As the economy has temporarily slowed down, many busy local leaders finally have the time to turn their attention to something close to their heart - the revitalization of old Phuket. In 2003, the Old Phuket Foundation was established to spearhead initiatives that could be jointly supported by government, business sector and community. The City Hall appointed a committee of 15 civic leaders, each serving a four-year term. Its objectives are to revive, restore and conserve the Phuket way of life, arts, architecture and heritage; to raise awareness among Phuket people about the importance of the old town, and to promote Phuket's cultural life.

The Old Phuket Foundation chose the five-footway as its symbol. It represents the old town, safety, access, and the middle ground between the private and the public. For the same reasons, the recovery of the five-footway as public space has great symbolic value for all those involved in the old town revitalization.

Currently, the street is streamlined to one-way traffic and parking is allowed on right and left sides of the street on alternate days of the week, while pedestrians walk on a narrow but nicely made pavement covering the old drains. The City Hall, in collaboration with the Foundation, plans to turn Thalang Road, with its 141 units of shophouses, and the smaller Soi Romanee, into a permanent 'walking street' or pedestrianised zone, and to generally improve the street infrastructure.

The main objective is the revitalization of Thalang Road, and as such, the authorities and stakeholders alike recognize that pedestrianisation must work for and not against economic vitality. By starting with the Old Phuket Town Festival and graduating to the weekend bazaar, it is hoped that these experiments of closing of the street to traffic will prove economically and not just aesthetically successful. In preparation for this pedestrianisation scheme, the City has already converted an adjacent city block into a green city park and car park. A weekend bazaar is in the pipeline for the later part of 2005 as part of the 'Walking Street' project. The leaders of the Old Phuket Foundation have held public talks and also gone down to the ground, by conducting a house-to-house survey along Thalang Road.

The intention of the 'Walking Street' programme is to recreate a festive atmosphere in the street, showcasing traditional Baba lifestyle, dress, food as well as crafts and performing arts. The national government is also sponsoring cultural activities to coincide with the street bazaar, with funds specially allocated to boost to Phuket's recovering tourism sector. As part of the revitalization campaign, Thalang Road will be portrayed to tourists as the 'real Phuket'.

To the government, the old town is mainly another selling point for Phuket tourism, whereas the shopkeepers hope that the weekend bazaar will be good for business. But those who grew up on Thalang Road dream of bringing back the human bustle and the primacy of the main street. Whatever the individual motivations, community ownership of the 'Walking Street' project will be essential to its success, and the Old Phuket Town Foundation has a key role to play in making this a reality.

10

The Myanmar (Burma) Case on Tourism and Political Repercussions

Myanmar's military regime stood up to a wave of protest in September 2007. With social demands on the cost of living after new increases in petrol and gas prices, political demands were also put forward including compliance with the roadmap for democracy formally accepted by the junta, dialogue with the opposition whose leader Aung San Suu Kyi remains under house arrest, and respect for fundamental rights. Despite calls for negotiations, the State Peace and Development Council launched violent repressive measures that prompted the United States and Europe to impose tougher sanctions and Japan to suspend bilateral aid. China and Russia remained aloof, however, due to their close economic ties. The sanctions will thus have limited impact on the economy. The repercussions on the business climate will, however, be more severe with the political uncertainties compounding the concerns of foreign investors over the lack of transparency and frequent legislative changes.

In this context, statistical data is not very reliable. While the military junta announced double-digit growth, the IMF estimated it at 5.5 per cent in 2007 with 4.0 per cent expected in 2008. The gas and oil sectors should continue to drive the economy in view of the high demand from Myanmar's dynamic, energy-consuming neighbours: Thailand, India and China. Still dominated by commodities, the economy remains weak in this respect. Agriculture, which represents 40 per cent of GDP, has not performed up to its potential due to administrative controls limiting harvests.

Lacking competitiveness and hampered by import prohibitions in the United States, industry is underdeveloped. The extent of the informal economy and above all the unpredictability of the junta's economic policy have clouded the outlook. Myanmar thus remains the Asian economy most affected by poverty as evidenced by social indicators that rank it lower than Laos or Cambodia. While the consolidation of external accounts certainly paved the way for a substantial increase in foreign exchange reserves, the public sector nonetheless continues to run a deficit entirely financed by money creation. Inflation has thus been out of control and has eroded purchasing power. Despite the consolidation of the banking sector undertaken after the crisis in 2003-2004, intermediation remains very poor and prudential regulations underdeveloped. According to Myanmar government statistics, India is the largest market for Myanmar exports, buying about $220 million worth of goods in the 1999/2000 (April-March) fiscal year. India's exports to Myanmar were $75.36 million.

Most trade goes via Singapore because there are almost no shipping links between the countries. The road will make it easier for security forces to take on armed Indian insurgents who operate out of jungle bases in the northwest of Myanmar. Myanmar has problems with Kachins, and India has problems with Naga separatists, among others. As important, the road link is a major diplomatic gain for both nations. For isolated Myanmar it is being heralded as a coup for the military regime in challenging the international boycotts they face for the repression of democracy.

For its part, New Delhi gains much by deepening its engagement with Yangon to ward off what it perceives as a potential threat from China's growing influence in Myanmar.

The Indian foreign minister, making the first official trip to Myanmar since the military took power in 1988, said the road was proof of India's strong desire to develop and diversify its relations with Myanmar, and was the first of several cross-border cooperation projects. India and Myanmar also agreed to start border trade at four points and cooperate in battling Indian insurgents. Myanmar is likely to reopen the Indian consulate in Mandalay. Singh commented, "This is the first major project in the field of infrastructure cooperation between our two countries that has been completed. The significance of this road is its continuation of the great tradition of social and spiritual linkages between our two neighboring countries. Some 60 years ago, your country and mine faced the direct ravages of war led by others from afar, for the benefit of their empires. India and Myanmar were not yet free."

Before leaving Myanmar on his three-day visit Singh opened the Myanmar-India Friendship Center for Remote Sensing and Data Processing, set up with the help of the Indian Space Research Organization. It is the first of its kind in Myanmar and will have a vital role to play in the processing and dissemination of data from satellites. Its applications cover weather forecasting and disaster management capabilities, determination of forest cover and other land use delineations, cropping surveys, urban planning, environmental monitoring and ground water surveys. Ministers at the center's opening ceremony said it was the beginning of closer cooperation between our two countries in space and related technologies.

Following Singh's visit, India will also help in developing and exploration of Myanmar's oil and natural gas fields. Myanmar has significant gas reserves in the Arakan region which can be piped either to India or Southeast Asia. The gas could be sent to India along a corridor through Bangladesh, provided Dhaka did not object. India is also keen for Myanmese help in combatting drug smuggling from Southeast Asia into India, though the problem is not as serious as on the Thai border with Myanmar. India also sees scope in tie-ups in Myanmar in the railway sector. Trains in Myanmar run on meter gauge and its rolling stock is similar to that of India. Myanmar is also keen to sell its surplus power to India.

Myanmar's military regime has faced international condemnation for not respecting the verdict of a decade-old national election, which gave a landslide to Nobel Peace laureate Aung San Suu Kyi's National League for Democracy (NLD). However, the ruling State Peace and Development Council (SPDC) and Suu Kyi are holding talks for the first time in seven years. The UN-brokered dialogue is expected to lead to the first tentative steps towards restoring democracy. Beginning mid-January, the military regime has stopped harassing NLD members, several of whom have been freed.

"This new context diminishes the arguable diplomatic odium of a particularly warm handshake between India and Myanmar at this moment," commented the Indian national daily The Hindu in an editorial. New Delhi's policy is based on the reasoning that it is better to engage Myanmar than to ostracize it. The Association of Southeast Asian Nations (Asean) used the same argument when they admitted Yangon into the now 10-member regional grouping in 1997. During his visit Singh praised Yangon for the steps it was taking for the restoration of democracy, although he carefully did not mention Suu Kyi by name. Myanmar is India's gateway to Asean and the recent Ganga-Mekong initiative testifies to India's determined intent to engage the region.

CHINA'S INFLUENCE

China's increasing engagement with Myanmar's military junta since 1988 has made India uneasy. In particular, India believes its national interests demand the Bay of Bengal - which straddles Myanmar - does not become a hotbed of interference by foreign navies. New Delhi keeps a close watch on the Coco Islands in Myanmar, where China has upgraded its radar and naval auxiliary facilities. India monitors China as it supplies equipment and reportedly assists in constructing a naval base in Sittwe, a strategically important Myanmese sea port close to India's largest city, Kolkatta (formerly Calcutta). Beijing also funds road construction linking Yangon and Sittwe, providing the shortest route to the Indian Ocean from southern China.

China has helped in upgrading Myanmar's naval facilities and in setting up four electronic listening posts along the Bay of Bengal and Andaman Sea. One of these is very close to Indian defense facilities. The Chinese have built an all-weather road from Kunming in southern China to Mandalay in central Myanmar. There have also been reports of Myanmar providing some visiting and berthing facilities to the Chinese navy. Beijing also provides military support to the 350,000-strong Myanmar armed forces.

INDIA LOOKS EAST

In the early 1990s, former prime minister P V Narasimha Rao formulated the look-east policy as a fundamental shift in Indian policy. Since then, a special relationship with Myanmar has evolved as the centerpiece of the policy to establish close physical and economic links with its eastern neighbors. Sandwiched between South and Southeast Asia, Myanmar is a natural land bridge linking the two regions and India is keen to exploit this location by building cross-border roads into Myanmar. Geographically, the northern borders of Myanmar form a junction with Bangladesh, China and the sensitive eastern frontiers of India. Myanmar is an important country on the rim of the Bay of Bengal, lying astride India's southeastern trade routes.

The southeastern coast of Myanmar is close enough to the Andaman and Nicobar Islands of India, so developments in that area could affect India's security interests in the Bay of Bengal. For Myanmar's part, the government suffers economic and political sanctions imposed by the United States and the European Union, and its government does not entertain hopes for getting any aid from them. Despite being admitted to Asean, Myanmar's prospects for receiving major economic help are bleak. Only China undertakes some significant development projects, mostly in the field of infrastructure. But China alone is not in the position to satisfy Myanmar's needs in foreign aid and investment.

Hence Myanmar's government plans to receive such support from India's government and big business. Myanmar says its relationship with India is based on the Five Principles of Peaceful Coexistence, which are: mutual respect for each others' territorial integrity and sovereignty; non-aggression; non-interference in each other's internal affairs; equality and mutual benefit; and peaceful coexistence.

DEVELOPMENT OF TIES

Burma, as it was known then, was a major theater during World War II and the leadership of the period - headed by General Aung San (father of Suu Kyi) - has the unique distinction of shifting allegiance from Axis to Allied powers. On attaining independence in January 1948, Burma was held as a model for the developing nations in Asia and identified as a state with the highest potential and promise. Burma played a major role in emerging Asian solidarity and relations between Delhi and Rangoon (now Yangon) were strong. A large Indian population in Burma provided the substance to the relationship and considerable trade flourished by way of Burmese teak, rice and gems between the Indian east coast and Rangoon.

India provided considerable support to Burma in the early years when the state had to deal with insurgencies and sub-national militancy. However post-1962, Burma's fortunes underwent a radical change. Growing internal unrest abetted by external forces and the inability of the civilian leadership to deal with this turbulence saw the military in control. Then followed a period of intense xenophobia and insularity that pushed the country into near isolation with a resultant downturn in ties with India. Domestic policies including the expulsion of ethnic Indians and later a closer Sino-Burmese axis soured the relationship with Delhi and for a quarter of a century until 1988 there was virtually no contact. The ruthlessness of the army in the bloody repression of August 8, 1988, led to Delhi distancing itself further and the relationship was severely strained.

CHANGE IN TACK

In the early 1990s, New Delhi decided to engage Myanmar s' military regime, with both governments cooperat-ing in tackling cross-border terrorism, rebel activities and drug trafficking. This security component remains an important link in India-Myanmar ties. Preliminary discussions were held between India and the Myanmese foreign office between February and August of 1992, which led to the visit of the vice foreign minister of Myanmar, U Baswa, to India from August 11-13 of that year. The Myanmese delegation made three points during that visit. First, it said it respected India's commitment to democracy and hoped India would be patient about the revival of democracy in Myanmar.

Second, Myanmar acknowledged that security and political concerns existed which are shared by both countries. Myanmar was therefore willing to cooperate with India in taking joint action to meet the security and strategic interests of both countries. The third point Baswa made was that Myanmar would be willing to increase economic and technological cooperation. Subsequently, there were visits of the home secretaries, drug suppression officials and the ministers of commerce between the two countries.

BREAKTHROUGH

These contacts culminated in November 2000 with the visit of Maung Aye, Vice Chairman of the SPDC and the second most powerful leader in Yangon's military junta, to India, with a 16-member delegation. As leader of the armed forces he is the most likely candidate to become Myanmar's next supreme leader. This was the first exchange at the higher political level between the neighbors since the late Prime Minister Rajiv Gandhi travelled to Yangon in 1987.

During the visit the countries agreed to step up bilateral cooperation by establishing cross-border transport and communication infrastructure to improve trade and business ties and take advantage of the "many economic complementarities" between their countries. In a joint statement the countries also vowed to take steps to contain terrorist activities and enhance economic ties along their 1,600-kilometer border. The two sides described the visit of Aye as highly successful. The creation of transport and communication infrastructure would, the joint statement said, promote more frequent exchanges both at the government and people-to-people level, and actively encourage business ties.

The countries also discussed possible Indian participation in major developmental projects in Myanmar, such as the Tamanthi hydroelectric project and the Kaladan river navigation, road and gas pipeline project. The two sides felt the existing level of cooperation, especially in the economic and commercial fields, did not reflect its true potential. Bilateral trade between the two countries in 2000 was worth $295 million, with the majority of goods going from Myanmar to India. Besides economic ties, other issues that figured in Aye's discussions with Indian leaders was cooperation to curb the activities of extremist groups and drug traffickers along the Indo-Myanmar border and reports of China's growing influence in Myanmar.

Both sides expressed satisfaction at the level of cooperation in tackling terrorism and insurgency, with Union Home Minister Lal Krishna Advani highlighting the successes achieved by the Myanmar Army in operations against anti-Indian guerrillas. During the visitm New Delhi extended a $15 million credit line to Myanmar for the purchase of industrial and electrical equipment from India. This followed the full utilization of an earlier $10 million credit line for setting up industrial plants and purchasing railway rolling stock. Aye's visit, however, exposed some divisions within the Indian government over New Delhi's stance towards Yangon. Defense Minister George Fernandes, a staunch supporter of the pro-democracy movement in Myanmar, stayed away from all official functions organized for the Myanmar delegation. The visit also provoked criticism from Myanmese pro-democracy activists based in India who staged demonstrations in New Delhi and some of the northeastern states bordering Myanmar. The activists also expressed concern over the possible supply of Indian defense hardware to Myanmar.

In the spirit of improved relations, New Delhi was one of only four International Labor Organization (ILO) Governing Body members to oppose strict ILO action against Myanmar late last year for alleged forced labor practices. Critics of Indian foreign policy point to the apparent inconsistency of the Indian refusal to deal with the military government in Pakistan while courting the generals of Myanmar. However, India's reluctance to engage Pakistan is not based on the nature of the regime in Islamabad. It has to do with Pakistan's support for cross-border terrorism into India. While the military rulers in Islamabad are perceived as being relentless in their support to terrorism in India, Myanmar has been helpful in countering insurgency in the Northeast.

DRUG TRAFFICKING

In September of last year India and Myanmar agreed to control drug trafficking. At a meeting of senior officials of the home ministries of both countries, in Yangon, officials reviewed the implementation of programs to curb drug trafficking from Myanmar to northeastern Indian states. The meeting was also attended by Indian officials from the External Affairs Ministry and the Narcotics Control Bureau. The Indian team was headed by Home Secretary Kamal Pande, while the Myanmese delegation was led by Brigadier General Thura Myint Maung, the deputy minister of home affairs. Myanmar, Laos and Thailand form the Golden Triangle that produces the bulk of the world's illegal narcotics supplies. Large quantities of drugs, mostly opium, are smuggled into India from Myanmar, which has an extensive border with the northeastern states of Manipur, Nagaland and Arunachal Pradesh.

Since the two countries set in place a mechanism for national-level meetings between home ministry officials under a 1994 agreement, they have tackled the problem of drug trafficking, which has become serious due to the close links between insurgent groups in the northeastern Indian states and the Myanmese drug mafia. The Yangon meeting also discussed other cross-border issues, including training camps run in Myanmar by insurgent groups such the Khaplang faction of the National Socialist Council of Nagaland (NSCN-K), as well as the movement of people across the border and trade.

THE GANGA-MEKONG INITIATIVE

The Mekong-Ganga Cooperation (MGC) was launched in Vientiane, Laos on November 10 last year when officials from India, Myanmar, Thailand, Cambodia, Laos and Vietnam issued a "Vientiane Declaration" on the framework for cooperation. The declaration, which reflects an initial concept floated by India, said it had been "inspired by a common desire to develop closer relations and better understanding among the six countries to enhance friendship, solidarity and cooperation". The initiative has been criticized as being designed to counter-balance the influence of China in the region, specifically as China, which is a riparian Mekong River country, is not included. Supporters say this is not true as the grouping is not formal and is not military in nature.

Though similar in approach to the sub-regional grouping called the Bangladesh, India, Myanmar, Sri Lanka and Thailand Economic Cooperation (BIMSTEC), the areas of focus are different in the case of the MGC. In the tourism field, the MGC will conduct strategic studies for joint marketing, launch the Mekong-Ganga Tourism Investment Guide, facilitate the travel of people in the region, expand multi-modal communication and transportation links to enhance travel and tourism and promote cultural-religious package tours. The declaration committed the member countries the develop transport networks - in particular the East-West Corridor' and the trans-Asian Highway' - under the sector of transport and communication.

The promotion of air services and linkages in the MGC region and the strengthening of cooperation in the development of IT infrastructure and networks also formed part of the joint statement issued by the six Ministers. The grouping agreed to promote joint research in the fields of dance, music and theatrical forms and organize round-tables for journalists, writers and experts in literature, performing arts, women's empowerment, health and nutrition and the conservation, preservation and protection of heritage sites and artifacts.

The MGC consented to encourage the establishment of networking and twinning arrangements among universities in the region, translate classics of MGC countries into other MGC languages and assured the participation in book fairs in member countries on a commercial basis. A concept paper, approved by the six ministers at what was formally termed the inaugural ministerial meeting on the MGC, said the cooperation arrangement, primarily aimed at increasing tourism, will also serve as "building blocks" for other areas of mutual benefit. The MGC's objective was to announce to the international community its "political willingness and aspirations aimed at strengthening our traditional bonds of friendship".

It would also facilitate inter-state movement and transit transport of goods and people in the region. The concept paper made it clear that ministerial meetings would be led by Foreign Ministers and would take place back-to-back with the ASEAN Ministerial meeting (AMM)/Post Ministerial conference (PMC) held annually in July of each year.

11

Culture and Identity in Southeast Asia

The framework of the international security environment has always received much attention from all schools of thought. Each decade faces its own crises of confidence between various actors that make up the international system and no less is the Southeast Asian case.

With Southeast Asian domestic and international security challenges taking place in its many forms whether it be between sovereign states such as the Indonesia-Malaysia Konfrontasi (armed confrontation) between 1962 and 1966; within sovereign states such as the independence of Timor Leste (East Timor) from Indonesia in 2002 and sustainability concerns such as population renewal; regional challenges such as the discovery of avian 'flu in the 1990s and its subsequent (and continuing) spread or the mass internal displacement of people within Burma and its regional destabilising implications; the cross-level challenges of human rights, the Aceh peace process, the 2004 Indian Ocean tsunami with local and international non-governmental agency projects; the revival of some religious movements and their roles in national political processes, regional organisations and indeed international interactions.

All of these concerns have had a continuous affect on the regional makeup of Southeast Asia and have significant implications internationally and for greater understanding of Southeast Asian internal interactions. The new challenges that face Southeast Asia bring with them varied responses from different actors and create another forum of debate for scholars and practioners. In this book, many current challenges are discussed in detail to further the conversation initiated by the emergence of the various security challenges. These all arise as the world adapts to the globalisation processes in all their forms, whether it is the current neo-liberal economic globalisation agenda or the increased interaction of individuals, peoples, communities and other forms of identity. Whilst these two forms of globalisation frequently confront one another, their effects on the world have significant affects both locally, regionally and internationally.

The way in which states interact has grown more complex as these new challenges emerge. The significance of the ongoing avian 'flu epidemic is testament to that with the obvious need for greater attention to developing appropriate responses to a deadly virus. Tracey Churchill-Page tackles this issue and how the recent changes to the way in which world health is governed and what the interactions are between the mandated international body and the local responses to it. Churchill-Page argues that the recent avian 'flu epidemic and the 2003 emergence of Severe Acute Respiratory Syndrome (SARS) have challenged the way in which international health is governed.

The significance of Southeast Asia as the region under study lies in its place as a historically significant region of origin and subsequently predicted to reoccur. As the true spread of avian 'flu is realised there is a greater need to coordinate between different actors and stakeholders in the region of origin and ensure that future outbreaks are dealt with in the best possible way. Churchill-Page further analyses the role that the state plays in operationalising the Global Health Security Framework (GHSF) and the impact that identity, culture and human behaviour have on ensuring GHSF success.

Furthermore, Churchill-Page recognises the financial burden that the GHSF has and points to the international community as the source of help for a combination of self-interest and idealistic goals and aspirations. The ongoing development of the Association of Southeast Asian Nations (ASEAN) may well provide itself as a forum for greater interaction and better regional response mechanisms. Indeed, the future direction of ASEAN has many implications for regional security. Cook and Freise map out Southeast Asian forced migration and terrorist incidents and focus on how these human security challenges impact upon regional interactions. They approach both forced migration and terrorism in the region using an historical analysis.

It maps the development of Southeast Asia from a region dominated by European Colonial powers up to more recent attempts at shaping its own identity. They identify the fragility of the Westphalian state system and how it has brought together different peoples in a way that has led to forced migration and terrorism in the region. The authors suggest whilst the 1990s saw the prevalence of the self- determination norm, the twin challenges of forced migration and terrorism remain more likely to be intra-state than inter-state concerns; however, the increasingly transnational effects present considerable political and institutional challenges to ASEAN.

Whilst these twin challenges pose non- traditional security concerns for states and regional institutional development, there remains significant interaction which occurs outside of this realm. The non-governmental sector both within and across states are significant actors and how they perform equally affects people in the region. Zeccola focuses on the interactions between these two forms of non-governmental actors to evaluate how they influence one another. Zeccola demonstrates this interaction through focusing on post-tsunami Aceh and the sometimes irreconcilable differences between local and international nongovernmental organisations (NGOs).

On the one hand, local NGOs possess the necessary local understanding of a conflict scenario but are without the necessary funds. Whereas, on the other, international NGOs are restricted by governments and funding agencies on where they initiate projects. This scenario leaves a gap between what can be offered to an affected community and what is wanted and needed. Zeccola examines the development of the situation in Aceh looking at the historical, cultural and economic roots of the conflict alongside the development of human rights within humanitarianism. Whilst there are greater resources available for international NGOs, the smaller local NGOs outside of the international NGO and funding system are better equipt to respond to Acehnese issues as part of a broader social movement.

The development of grass-root social movements occur in various forms responding to issues of identity whether they take the form of human rights, religion or cultural movements to name but a few. Bustamam-Ahmad traces the development of both the Islamic revivalism and radicalism movements in Malaysia. This examination highlights the roots and responses of the movement to current phenomena in Malaysian domestic political arena and highlights its international connections.

The development of Islamic revivalism in Malaysia saw the establishment of greater faith based educational institutions and better provisions for those of the Islamic faith. However, this development did not stop the rise of Islamic radicalism in Malaysia but rather the indigenous development of Islam through Islamic revivalism ensures that there is less reliance of educating Islamic leaders in the Middle East where many become radicalised and bring these ideas back to Malaysia on their return. Bustamam-Ahmad differentiates between the two forms of Islamic teachings as ways to better understand these two divergent areas. Creating a regional identity in its various forms has undoubtedly been spurred on by but not limited to the impact of globalisation and regionalisation.

What emerges is a mixture of both global and local ideas being taken into account in the development of a regional identity. Hinton looks at the development of Singaporean welfare policies to combat its ongoing demographic challenges. In his analysis he compares the development of many theories of welfare identity and demonstrates how Singaporean welfare identity emerges. The delicate balance between the prevalent conservative authoritarianism and the neo- liberal market orientated economic policies constantly provide a tension in Singaporean policymaking. Hinton examines family payments in the welfare system and how they provide a new method of provision, which does not fit into the broader logic of the Singaporean welfare system.

Whilst the economic and political implications are played out through a response to demographic challenges in Singapore, other Southeast Asian states are susceptible to policy challenges and social developments that can alter the course of policymaking in any given state. In Indonesia the post New Order era has brought about many changes to the structure of the Indonesian state. Karim evaluates the changing nature of Pesantrens - Islamic residential schools - from a cultural to a more overt political actor. Karim evaluates the transition of their impact over the 2000 and 2005 elections in Sumenep, Sumatra.

During these elections, the Pesantren played a significant role in the recruitment of political candidates and the author demonstrates the significance of this development. The 2003 emergence of Severe Acute Respiratory Syndrome (SARS) and the ongoing avian Influenza (bird flu) epidemic highlight the dark-side of globalization, as these diseases spread rapidly to all four corners of the globe.

The spread of emerging and re-emerging infectious diseases however have also performed another function, as they have served to highlight the increasing significance of the role of international health governance in a rapidly globalizing world. Until the advent of these novel diseases the field of international health had been largely marginalized by academia, governments and the mass media, whose main interests were predominantly focused on the global political economy and the global war on terror.

However, as the 2003 SARS outbreak highlighted, international health governance is only as effective as its weakest link, thus the field of international health and international health governance has shifted from the periphery to a more central position within international relations. This has also resulted in a shift away from the Westphalian model of state-centrism with the World Health Organization (WHO) acting as the coordinating and collaborating agent in international health governance, to that of a model of pluralism and diversity involving non-state actors such as NGOs, private corporations, banks, philanthropic organizations, and inter-state initiatives.

Another example of this shifting attitude towards international health governance was the momentum gained in implementing revisions to the International Health Regulations after the outbreak of SARS, which places greater emphasis on national capabilities such as surveillance and response mechanisms, and reduces the risk of Member States hiding outbreaks within their borders. The frequent, and at times alarming, predictions of the emergence of a highly pathogenic influenza pandemic, as virulent as the 1918 Spanish flu, which was estimated to have killed as many as 50 million people globally, has firmly placed Southeast Asia and South China in the global spotlight, as it is from this region that previous outbreaks have occurred, and where the next highly pathogenic influenza pandemic is predicted to emerge.

This increased attention has highlighted the inequities between the developed and developing worlds, and most significantly for international health governance, the serious lack of capabilities within Southeast Asia. The realisation that infectious disease surveillance capabilities are essential to international health governance has seen the creation of public-private partnerships and funding frameworks, such as the International Partnership on Avian and Pandemic Influenza. Thus it would seem armed with the re-drafted International Health Regulations, and with multi-donor partnerships providing the funding essential for developing surveillance frameworks in Southeast Asia, when the predicted influenza pandemic hits, we will be ready for it...or will we?

This chapter analyses the changing nature of international

health governance, from its origins as a Westphalian strategy to prevent the spread of exotic or Asiatic diseases with the minimum disruption to trade, to the contemporary Global Health Security Framework established by WHO, the purpose of which is to contain infectious diseases, respond to unexpected events, such as bioterrorism, and improve the capability to detect, contain and manage infectious diseases at national levels. The Global Health Security Framework is only as strong as its weakest link, and one region that has been identified as a weak link is Southeast Asia. While much effort and funding has been focused on this region, there are determining factors which will, if left unaddressed, continue to undermine such efforts.

Through the analysis of the Malaria Eradication Programme, the 2003 SARS outbreak, and the current ongoing bird flu epidemic, this chapter seeks to explain how not only inadequate state capabilities undermine the Global Health Security Framework, but also how identity, culture and human behaviour can all act as impediments to establishing effective surveillance capabilities within States in Southeast Asia, and thereby undermining the Global Health Security Framework.

INTERNATIONAL HEALTH REGULATION HISTORY

The origins of international health regulation can be traced back to 14th century Europe with the introduction of quarantine practices. However the adoption of quarantine by many of the major European powers at that time was problematic, as the measures implemented were unregulated, arbitrary and corruptible, and often incurred serious losses for maritime trade. The practice of quarantine continued until the 19th century, by which time several developments converged and forced many European States to reconsider the unilateral and disorganized systems of quarantine.

These converging factors which culminated in the first attempts at international health regulation were the emergence of a bourgeois merchant class; European colonialism of the New World, and the resultant epidemics of novel, exotic diseases; the industrial revolution; and scientific/medical advances in the aetiology and transmission of infectious diseases. The emergence of the bourgeois merchant class was as a result of increased levels of trade and commerce. As this class gained more wealth, it also gained more political power, and was able to bring pressure to bear on governments to address the issue of irresponsible and unregulated quarantine practices in order "to relieve trade of these burdens or, if they could not altogether be abolished, to render them less irksome and particularly more stable and uniform". The major western European maritime powers began to travel great distances to undiscovered territories with the advent of technological developments such as improved navigational systems.

These voyages were devastating, both for the indigenous populations, as well as for the European explorers, as these different gene pools were each introduced to novel diseases for which there was no natural immunity. Thus many indigenous populations were decimated by influenza, smallpox, measles and typhus, whilst the European explorers also succumbed in large numbers to novel, endemic diseases such as cholera and yellow fever. However it was not until the advent of the industrial revolution that these diseases were able to reach the distant European shores. The industrial revolution gave rise to many important technological developments, however the most significant from a health perspective being that of transportation.

These advancements facilitated not only increases in travel and trade, but increased the distances covered and concurrently reduced the time required. This gave rise to a series of epidemics in Europe of non-endemic diseases such as yellow fever and cholera. A major cholera outbreak that spread from India, to Europe and the United States, from 1828 until 1832, and another major cholera pandemic in 1847, confronted States with the realization that the existing multilateral and unregulated quarantine measures were ineffective in containing and preventing epidemic outbreaks.

As a consequence, States had little alternative but to develop coordinated and collaborative strategies to combat infectious diseases whilst protecting their economic interests. Thus the major driving force for international health regulation at this time can be characterized as Westphalian, as European powers sought "the removal of hindrances to trade and transport, and … "the defence of Europe" against exotic pestilences". From as early as 1834, calls for an international conference for diseases and quarantine were made throughout Europe, although the first international sanitary conference was not held until 1851. The outcome of this intergovernmental International Sanitary Conference was the drafting of the International Sanitary Convention, which cited 137 regulations in the management and containment of infectious diseases.

Nevertheless the Convention was a dismal failure as, of the twelve signatory States only three ratified the Convention in 1852, and two of whom, Portugal and Sardinia subsequently withdrew in 1856. Notwithstanding, these Conferences and the International Sanitary Convention are extremely significant, as these attempts at regulation were the precursors of the International Health Regulations today. It was not until scientific and medical advancements, most significantly the discovery of the cholera vibrio, and intermediate vectors, such as mosquitoes, that any degree of international health regulation began to develop concretely. Earlier Conferences lacked medical technical expertise or scientific knowledge, as there was significant disagreement over the aetiology and transmission of exotic infectious diseases.

Without scientifically based knowledge or universal consensus, the establishment of coordinated and standardized practices of international health regulation was not possible. The 1903 Conference held in Paris was significant, as finally, scientific data about cholera, the plague and yellow fever, achieved consensus and became accepted facts. In understanding the aetiology and transmission of these diseases, the possibility of implementing the necessary measures became a reality. As a result of this scientific breakthrough, the establishment of an international public health office was proposed at the Paris Conference, although it took another four years before the Office International d'Hygiene Publique (OIHP) was established in 1907, under the auspices of the Treaty of Rome.

Attendance at the International Sanitary Conferences grew exponentially, and by the twelfth convocation in 1912, the Conference was attended by medical and diplomatic representatives of forty-one countries. By 1926, sixty-five States and territories were represented by Member State delegates, as well as representatives from the Health Organization of the League of Nations, the International Labour Office and the OIHP, culminating in the signing of an amended International Sanitary Convention. All signatory states agreed to comply with the codes of conduct and cooperate within the arena of international health through the collaborative management of quarantine measures and through the notification of infectious diseases, or conventional diseases, such as typhus, smallpox, cholera, yellow fever, plague and relapsing fever.

With the exception of the addition of regulations for aerial navigation in 1935, the International Sanitary Convention continued to provide the framework for international health regulatory practices until after the Second World War, when WHO adopted them in 1951, at which point they were redrafted and renamed the International Sanitary Regulations. They were renamed again - International Health Regulations - and further amendments were made in 1969, with the removal of typhus and relapsing fever, although cholera, yellow fever, plague and smallpox remained on the list of notifiable diseases.

In 1980, the Global Commission for the Certification of Smallpox Eradication presented its findings to the thirty-third World Health Assembly, namely that smallpox had been globally eradicated. As a result of these findings, smallpox was removed from the list of notifiable diseases (WHO 1983).

CONTEMPORARY INTERNATIONAL HEALTH REGULATION

The International Health Regulations (IHR 1969) have not

been amended or updated since this time. However, in response to the exponential growth of re-emerging communicable diseases, such as tuberculosis, and the emergence of new infectious diseases, such as Ebola haemorrhagic fever, WHO's 48th World Health Assembly (WHA) in 1995 raised concerns about new and re-emerging communicable diseases within the context of globalization. Furthermore it was agreed that the primary defence against rapid and international dissemination of infectious diseases was the "strengthening of epidemiological surveillance and disease control activities at [the] national level".

WHA Resolution 48.7 was passed, charging the Director-General with the task of drafting a report on the revision of the IHR (1969). Concurrently, the 48th WHA passed Resolution 48.13, which mandated the Director- General to provide the Assembly with proposed strategies for detection and response mechanisms for the emergence and re-emergence of communicable diseases (WHO 1995). As a result of these Resolutions, in 1997 WHO established an Outbreak Verification System (OVS) as a surveillance mechanism to globally monitor disease outbreaks. In collaboration with Health Canada, WHO now has access to over 600 sources of information through the Canadian electronic web-crawler - the Global Public Health Information Network (GPHIN).

WHO also accesses information through additional collaborations at the global and regional levels: ProMed-mail is "an Internet-based reporting system dedicated to rapid global dissemination of information on outbreaks of infectious diseases"; PACNET is a weekly e-newsletter "designed to facilitate communication on timely and fast breaking events in the region and to serve as a vehicle for sharing research results and analyses" is an electronic discussion board hosted by the International Society of Travel Medicine.

From the information received from these different sources, WHO's OVS team assesses data on previous outbreaks and endemic foci, as well as any other relevant background information, in order to assess the significance of an "event" (an outbreak of disease) and its potential to impact upon the welfare of international public health. The OVS team also assesses whether an event meets the criteria of an outbreak, for example whether the "observed number of cases exceeds expected number of cases in a given population for a given period". It then disseminates the data collated from the information provided through a variety of media: A subscriptions based e-mail Outbreak Verification List; WHO's Disease Outbreak news Website - which is accessible to the general public; and through the publication of its Weekly Epidemic Report. The OVS affords WHO the opportunity of a quicker response time to outbreaks and enabling it to provide technical and procedural assistance and WHO field personnel to the originating country of an event more effectively.

In 2000, the former Communicable Disease Surveillance and Response of WHO convened a meeting on "Global Outbreak Alert and Response", the outcome of which was the establishment of the Global Outbreak Alert and Response Network (GOARN), which represents a "major pillar of global health security aimed at the detection, verification and containment of epidemics". The Network "interlinks, in real time, 110 existing networks which together…keep the international community alert to outbreaks…[and] magnifies the resources of individual partners considerably".

The coordinated approach of OVS and GOARN in disease outbreak and surveillance also greatly reduces the risks of States not reporting an event within its borders, and to some extent gives WHO advance warning of unusual events prior to the uncontrolled spread of an infectious disease outbreak. WHO was further augmented in its global outbreak and alert programme by the passing of WHA51.14 Resolution during its 54th WHA, which, in addition to reiterating its commitment to the revision of the IHR, called for the "development of a global strategy" (WHO 2001c) in order to achieve an effective management system of potential and actual global epidemic outbreaks. Thus the CSR was restructured and mandated to meet the growing demands of re-emerging and newly emerging communicable disease and the result was WHO's

Global Health Security Epidemic Alert and Response.

The IHR are an integral and fundamental component of the Global Health Security Framework, as they provide the overall legal authority. Subsumed under the IHR is WHO's Global Health Security strategy which is a three-pronged approach to Epidemic and Pandemic Alert and Response (EPR). This triadic strategy iterates the following initiatives: To contain known communicable diseases, such as cholera, yellow fever and plague, which requires the development of surveillance and response mechanisms at the national level, as well as laboratory and diagnostic facilities.

The second initiative is to respond to unexpected events, such as newly emerging diseases, for example SARS, and the accidental and/or intentional release of biological agents and acts of bioterrorism. This is achieved through the collaboration of OVS, GOARN, WHO Collaborating Centres, other UN Agencies, and Member States through epidemic intelligence networks in order to contain epidemics. The third prong of the Global Health Security strategy is that of improving national preparedness.

For instance, in Southeast Asia for States to develop national preparedness plans for emerging infectious diseases outbreaks and implement national surveillance and verification systems will require medically and technically trained personnel, thus EPR "provides tools, expert assistance and carefully-tailored training to enhance multidisease skills in laboratory diagnosis, field epidemiology and public health mapping" (WHO 2001b). Another component to the establishment of WHO's Global Health Security Framework was the redrafting of the IHR, which at first glance seems to be a response to the changing nature of health within the context of globalization, such as the emergence of new infectious diseases such as HIV/AIDS, Ebola Haemorrhagic Fever, Severe Acute Respiratory Syndrome (SARS); the re-emergence of infectious diseases, such as tuberculosis (TB), cholera and plague.

However, the redrafting of the Regulations was not solely in response to these changes, the IHR (1969) contained serious inherent weaknesses, and without significant revision, would undermine WHO's new Global Health Security Epidemic Alert and Response framework. One major flaw of the IHR (1969) is the list of notifiable diseases, of which there are only three, cholera, yellow fever and plague, which Member States are legally obligated to report to WHO under the Regulations.

The IHR (1969) mandates that Member States notify WHO of "a disease subject to the Regulations" (WHO 1983), thus there is no obligation on the part of Member States to notify WHO of diseases that are not subject to the Regulations. It is hard to imagine that a Member State would not report or notify WHO of a disease which had the potential to become a global epidemic. However, the issue of notification highlights another inherent weakness of the IHR (1969), namely the negative effects of reporting a disease outbreak can have. Two diseases which exemplify these negative effects are plague and cholera. In 1994, Surat, India, experienced an outbreak of pneumonic plague. Media sensationalism caused panic, and in one night alone, 600,000 people fled Surat to escape the plague.

The high level of panic was exacerbated by the international community's response to the outbreak, as "countries throughout the world [responded:] airports were closed to aeroplanes arriving from India and imports of foodstuffs were blocked". These measures and irresponsible media coverage of the outbreak was estimated to result in economic losses of US $2 billion. However, the reality of the situation later became apparent, as the Head of the 1994 Technical Advisory Committee wrote: Between August 26 and October 5, 1994, 5,150 suspected cases of pneumonic or bubonic plague were reported from eight states of India, including 2,793 from Maharashta state, 1,391 from Gujarat state, 749 from Delhi, and 169 from five other states. A total of 167 cases were confirmed by serology by October 5, and there were 53 deaths, 49 from Surat.

Another example of the negative effects to Member States of reporting infectious diseases under the IHR (1969) is cholera.

From 1817 until today, there have been a total of seven pandemics. The current and ongoing seventh pandemic originated in Sulawesi, Indonesia, in 1961, gradually spreading to Bangladesh in 1963, India in 1964, and the Soviet Union, Iraq and Iran during 1965 to 1966. By 1970 it had spread to West Africa, and spread rapidly throughout most of the African continent (WHO 2000).

It reached Peru in 1991, and over the period of a year travelled to a further eleven Latin American countries, resulting in 400,000 cases and 4,000 deaths from cholera. By 2001, the same pandemic had appeared in 58 countries that saw a further 184,311 reported cases, and 2,728 deaths: "In Peru alone, the highly publicized arrival of cholera is estimated to have cost the country's economy up to US $ 770 million in lost trade, and tourism".

From such examples, it is possible to recognize that the international community's response, in the form of embargoes, affecting not only trade but international traffic; and the impact on tourism and related industries, act as serious disincentives for Member States to promptly and accurately report event outbreaks within their borders. Thus, the redrafted IHR (2005) has been revised to remove these weaknesses and introduce protocols which attempt to remove disincentives in notifying WHO of events which may develop into epidemic or pandemic outbreaks.

Moreover the emphasis of the purpose and scope of the Regulations has also changed significantly. IHR (1969) states that "[t]he purpose of the International Health Regulations is to ensure the maximum security against the international spread of diseases with a minimum interference with world traffic", which reflects the earlier Westphalian model of security of State's borders against infectious disease and the protection of trade. However, IHR (2005) emphasizes the importance of the purpose and scope of the Regulations through the inclusion of these issues as an Article, rather than in the previous Foreword of the IHR (1969).

Article 2 states that: "The purpose and scope ... are to

prevent, protect against, control and provide a public health response to the international spread of diseases in ways that are commensurate with and restricted to public health risks, and which avoid unnecessary interference with international traffic and trade". Whilst there are still echoes of its Westphalian heritage, the IHR (2005) clearly broaden the roles and responsibilities of the WHO.

To elaborate, the primary function of WHO at its inception was to "act as the directing and coordinating authority on international health work", whereas it now plays a leading role in Global Health Security, interacting and directing a multitude of State and non-state actors in detecting and verifying outbreaks, as well as providing guidelines, logistical technical support and recommendations to Member States in helping them to develop standardized national core capacities.

The IHR (2005) also places greater emphasis on national based surveillance and verification systems than its earlier counterpart. Article 5.1 (Surveillance) mandates that all Member States "shall develop, strengthen and maintain, as soon as possible but no later than five years from entry into force of these Regulations ... the capacity to detect, assess, notify and report events in accordance with these Regulations...".

Every Member State is also legally mandated to develop its core capacity requirements at the national, community and intermediate public health levels, with Annex 1 of the IHR (2005) iterating exactly what these capacities should be: The local community level should be able

a. To detect events involving disease or death above expected levels for the particular time and place...
b. To report all available essential information immediately to the appropriate level of health-care response...essential information includes the following: clinical descriptions, laboratory results, sources and type of risk, numbers of human cases and deaths, conditions affecting the spread of the disease and the health measures employed;
c. To implement preliminary control measures immediately.

The intermediate public health level should have the capacities:

a. To confirm the status of report events and to support or implement additional control measures; and
b. To assess reported events immediately and, if found urgent, to report all essential information to the national level ... urgent events include serious public health impact and/or unusual or unexpected nature with high potential for spread (WHO 2005a, Annex 1).

The national level should have the capacities:

a. To assess all reports of urgent events within 48 hours; and
b. To notify WHO immediately through the National IHR Focal Point when the assessment indicates the event is notifiable (WHO 2005a, Annex 1).

The public health response capacities are listed as able:

a. To determine rapidly the control measures required to prevent domestic and international spread;
b. To provide support through specialized staff, laboratory analysis of samples (domestically or through collaborating centres) and logistical assistance (e.g. equipment, supplies and transport);
c. To provide on-site assistance as required to supplement local investigations;
d. To provide a direct operational link with senior health and other officials to approve rapidly and implement containment and control measures;
e. To provide direct liaison with other relevant government ministries;
f. To provide, by the most efficient means of communications available, links with hospitals, clinics, airports, ports, ground crossing, laboratories and other key operational areas for the dissemination of information and recommendations received from WHO;
g. To establish, operate and maintain a public health emergency response plan, including the creation of multidisciplinary/multisectoral teams to respond to

events that may constitute a public health emergency of international concern; and

h. To provide the foregoing on a 24-hour basis.

Each Member State will also be responsible for designating or establishing a National IHR Focal Point (NFP). The NFP is to be accessible to WHO at any and all times. According to WHO's National Focal Point Guide: While the exact structure and organization of the NFP are left to the State, IHR (2005) define the role, functions and operation requirements for real- time management of information and for efficient communications ... NFPs will need clearly established links and coordination mechanisms with existing national health emergency committees and mechanisms, within or outside the health sector (WHO 2005b).

All signatory Member States to the IHR (2005) will be expected to establish or designate the NFP and ensure core capacities by a five year time limit from June 2007, when the IHR (2005) come into force. Article 11, Provision of information by WHO is also noteworthy. As the outbreaks in India and Latin America highlight, timely and accurate notification of disease outbreaks can be undermined by the potential disincentives of severe economic loss and social unrest and panic.

Article 11.2 ensures that if a Member State notifies WHO of an event that has the potential to develop into "a public health emergency of international concern" (PHEIC) (WHO 2005a), the notification will be treated in confidence. However, there are certain conditions attached to the confidentiality rule. Confidentiality will be broken if the event is deemed a PHEIC; if containment of the event is no tpossible due to the nature of the event; the Member State experiencing the event is unable to implement the necessary operational measures or contain the disease from spreading further. In addition, according to Article 10 Verification, if a Member State is invited to collaborate with WHO over an event that may constitute a PHEIC, and the Member State does not accede, WHO may share information with other Member States, if doing so is justified by the magnitude of the event (WHO 2005a).

In principle, close collaboration with WHO should minimize the negative impacts of reporting an outbreak, as WHO has access to technical resources, laboratory services and medical expertise and capabilities that many Member States lack. Despite the fact that the IHR (2005) does not come into force until June 2007, implementation of the Regulations has already begun. Resolution WHA59.2, which was passed in May 2006, calls for all Member States to implement, on a voluntary basis, aspects of the IHR (2005) which will help in combating avian influenza and developing preparedness for a human influenza pandemic (WHO 2006a).

The 2003 SARS outbreak played a major role in the redrafting process of the IHR (1969), in defining the parameters of WHO's power as the leading institution of international health governance, its roles and responsibilities, and that of its Member States. It achieved this in two ways, firstly SARS saw the application of the Global Health Security Framework in a real-life situation, and secondly this application drew a line in the sand of how far States were prepared to go in allowing WHO to halt the outbreak in its tracks.

In addition to "leading and coordinating the investigation and containment of an international epidemic", WHO implemented a virtual laboratory, by electronically connecting eleven laboratories from nine different countries, in an effort to "improve diagnostic precision and move forward on the development of a diagnostic test" (WHO 2003a) for SARS, and coordinated an electronic conference of "80 clinicians from 13 countries" (WHO 2003a) which was convened for the purpose of sharing clinical features and treatments of SARS. However, most significantly, WHO began to issue travel advisories, via its internet site and the mass media, directly to the general public instead of its Member States.

The issuance of a travel advisory was based on three criteria: the severity of the outbreak - the number of probable cases; transmission - whether the disease spread via the general population or was confined in transmission, for example, amongst health care workers, and thirdly, a Member-State's ability to contain the outbreak from spreading beyond its borders.

During the SARS outbreak there were three levels of travel advisories, the first alerted international travellers of the outbreak, and provided guidance on the early symptoms of the disease; the second travel alert made the "recommendation that people who have possibilities of postponing travel to these areas do so" (WHO 2004c), and the third level recommended postponing all but essential travel to the identified areas.

On April 23, 2003, WHO imposed level three travel advisories on Beijing, Shanxi Province and Toronto. In issuing these travel advisories WHO had acted beyond its mandate as the IHR (1969) makes no provision for such actions, and the health organization had not consulted with Member States prior to issuing these statements directly to the press. Perhaps most remarkable however was the absence of objection to the introduction of these travel advisories from Member States, whilst there were complaints, the most vociferous coming from Toronto, rather it was the level of travel advisory under which they were placed that caused complaint. However, analysis of the IHR redrafting process clearly highlights Member States' concern over WHO's ability to act independently of its Member States, and to implement policies, such as the travel advisories, that impacted deleteriously on State's economies.

One such example is the definition of "temporary recommendation", which in an earlier intergovernmental working group on the revision of IHR read: "means advice issued by WHO... for application on an ad hoc, time-limited, risk-specific basis, as a result of a public health emergency of international concern" (WHO 2004b); by the final draft of the IHR (2005) the definition of temporary recommendation now reads: "means non-binding advice issued by WHO ... for application on a time-limited, risk-specific basis..." (WHO 2005a); thus limiting WHO's ability to improvise, as it had during the SARS outbreak, and concurrently removing any authority to enforce temporary recommendations, which will not be legally binding under the IHR (2005).

WHO has always been constrained in any actions within

a Member State's borders, requiring a formal request of assistance before it can dispatch any representatives to any given country. In earlier drafts, Article 10.3 stated: "In the absence of such a request WHO may offer assistance to the health administration of a State ... and the health administration shall collaborate with WHO ... and, when necessary, in conducting on-the-spot studies by a team sent by WHO, with the purpose of ensuring that appropriate control measures are being employed". Interestingly in the finalized draft, the term "health administration" has been replaced with "State Party", and paragraph 10.3 has been completely removed.

This is particularly significant and potentially detrimental to future containment measures of infectious disease outbreaks, as the SARS epidemic highlights: Despite repeated offers of technical support (in the form of epidemiologists being dispatched), China did not request assistance from WHO until March 17, 2003, a full three months from the first recognised incidence of the disease in Guangdong Province, in November 2002, and over a month after WHO began to receive information through GOARN and GPHIN, and it was during this interim period that SARS began marching across the globe.

WHO's Global Health Security framework during the SARS outbreak was without doubt extremely successful, and it certainly gained a degree of power previously unavailable to it, through the incorporation of GOARN and GPHIN into its global surveillance strategies, as "[s]overeign states no longer monopolize information flows related to infectious disease events". However, it should be remembered that SARS was a newly emerging infectious disease, and as such Member States were galvanised into action by the unknown, and had little alternative but to follow WHO's leadership.

Nevertheless, as this chapter has shown, once that panic faded, notable changes were made during the revision process of the IHR to ensure that WHO could not circumvent or subordinate state sovereignty again. Fortunately SARS only killed 916 people globally during its 2002/3 emergence, the common garden variety of influenza on the other hand, accounts for between 250,000 and 500,000 deaths annually. There are three categories of influenza viruses, Influenza A, B and C. Of these, Influenza A is a particularly virulent pathogen, of which the Spanish Flu of 1918-19 (H1N1) is but one, another well known Influenza A strain is the bird flu, or avian flu (H5N1) and whilst it "is not easily spread from human to human... health specialists fear it could mutate into a virulent form like the Spanish flu".

Furthermore, there is a strong likelihood that avian influenza is now endemic to Asia. Moore identifies that from 1727 until 1968 there have been ten influenza pandemics, which "suggests that we are due a pandemic any time now". That a pandemic of a highly virulent strain of Influenza A could mutate at any time to become a global epidemic, raises major concerns about the state of readiness of States to respond to such an outbreak. For many States in the developing world, both in Africa and Asia, the legally mandated requirements of the IHR (2005) will place tremendous pressure on national governments, on fiscal and health policymaking, and national health systems, in order to meet these obligations.

In recognition of such pressures, WHO will extend an additional five year grace period to States who will need a longer time to restructure their national health systems, train public health and medical personnel and develop epidemiological surveillance, detection and verification systems. Yet this begs the question of what happens during the interim? It also raises the issue of what will happen to Member States who cannot meet their obligations, and are seen to be losing control or containment of an infectious disease outbreak will they be assisted or sanctioned by the international community?

International Health Regulations 2005 and Local Contexts WHO has established its Global Health Security Framework to prevent global pandemics, Member States have signed on to uphold these measures within the legal framework of the International Health Regulations (2005), and governments, corporations, non-governmental organisations and charitable organisations have all committed to funding these initiatives, but there is one dimension neglected in adopting a global approach: people.

The National Academy of Sciences Institute for Health (2005) identifies thirteen factors that can contribute to the emergence of infectious diseases, such as economic development and land use, human demographics and behaviour, and the breakdown of public health measures, of these, "human behaviour, both individual and collective, is perhaps the most complex factor in the emergence of disease". This is not to say that we should throw our arms up in despair, or resort to draconian measures to enforce compliance to adopted strategies, conversely it is possible to look at different programmes, events and behaviours and learn valuable lessons, which can then be adapted and applied to current and future strategies, for the benefit of all.

One such programme from which lessons can be learned was the Malaria Eradication Programme (MEP) established in 1955 and was a dismal failure. It was not solely as a result of human behaviour that the MEP failed, factors such as a lack of knowledge of the disease and programme design were also responsible. To elaborate, lack of knowledge regarding the mosquito-vectors significantly impeded progress in eradicating the mosquitoes, of which there are many different species, all of whom behave differently.

For example some species flourish during rainy season, "some breed in the shadows, some in sunlit pools, and some in tin cars and discarded automobile tires ... some feed at night; some during the day". Consequently the attitude towards malaria eradication resulted in a highly inflexible programme and one-size-fits-all strategy which Needham and Canning liken to a military exercise. With hindsight, it is clear that a more elastic approach to mosquito control was needed, which could be adapted to suit the diversity of local vectors. Human behaviour was another factor that at the time was not taken into consideration, but retrospectively can be seen to have had serious negative consequences for the programme, on both the part of the donor health workers and the recipient populations.

To elucidate, "Because the MEP treated malaria as a single problem with a single solution, it proceeded as if the people who had the disease did not exist". This contributed to the programme's failure, as the indigenous populations' attitudes towards malaria and beliefs were largely ignored. Malaria is a major killer, however, for those who do survive initial infection, and continue to live with malaria, as have their parents, and their parents' parents, "further back than anyone can remember - such a person may not view malaria as the greatest challenge in her life.

Other diseases, such as infectious diarrhoea and tuberculosis" were seen to be more serious. Malaria workers were ejected by villagers in Malaya, after DDT-immune caterpillars munched their way through the roofs of the villagers' homes. MEP lacked both cultural sensitivity and the necessary indigenous knowledge and experiences that would have assisted in the implementation of the programme and in gaining cooperation, instead of resistance, from the indigenous population.

A more contemporary example is that of Kampot province in Cambodia, which has one of the highest incidences of local transmission of malaria. After heavy landmining of the forests during the Khmer Rouge occupation, forests became no-go areas. Now that the forests have been cleared, "[m]any poor rural Cambodians, mostly men, have started venturing into forest areas to work as loggers, gem miners or to hunt".

Unfortunately for these workers, they have no natural immunity to the mosquitoes inhabiting the forests, and while many use the insecticide treated nets, this only protects them during the night while they are sleeping, whilst they are sat around camp fires during the evening, they have no protection whatsoever. Chatterjee posits that transmission rates could be higher than the Malaria Information Registers list, as people continue to elude malaria officials, either as a result of belief systems such as bad spirits causing malaria or that malaria and mosquitoes are unrelated, to continued fear of visiting government-run.

Bibliography

Adburgham, Alison. *Women in Print. Writing Women and Women's Magazines from Restoration to the Accession of Victoria.* London: Allen & Unwin, 1972.

Arnold, Ethel M. *Literature for Ladies, 1830-1930.* Manhattan: K.S.A.C. Press, 1930.

Barrell, Joan. *The Business of Women's Magazines.* 2nd ed. London: Kogan Page, 1988.

Beetham, Margaret. *Victorian Women's Magazines : An Anthology.* Manchester: Manchester University Press, 2001.

Boston Women's Health Book Collective. *Our Bodies Ourselves.* New York: Simon & Schuster, 1976.

Braithwaite, Brian. *The Business of Women's Magazines: The Agonies and the Ecstasies.* London: Associated Business Press, 1979.

Braithwaite, Brian. *Women's Magazines: The First 300 Years.* London: Peter Owen, 1995.

Brody, Michal, ed. *Are We There Yet? A Continuing History of Lavender Woman.* Iowa City; Aunt Lute Company, 1985.

Burman, Barbara, ed. *The Culture of Sewing: Gender, Consumption and Homedressmaking (Dress, Body, Culture).* Oxford: Berg, 1999.

Coakley, Mary Lewis. *1907-Sex, Sisterhood, and Self-Delusion: What Happened to Women's Magazines?* New Rochelle: Arlington House, c. 1979.

Dancyger, Irene. *A World of Women. An Illustrated History of Women's Magazines.* Dublin: Gill and Macmillian, 1978.

Danky, James P., ed. *Women's Periodicals and Newspapers from the 18th Century to 1981: A Union List of the Holdings of Madison, Wisconsin Libraries.* Boston: GK Hall, 1982.

Doughan, David, and Denise Sanchez. *Feminist Periodicals, 1855-1984: An Annotated Critical Bibliography of British, Irish, Commonwealth and International Titles.* Brighton: Harvester, 1987.

Eskridge, Melissa J. *How the Psychology of Women Is Presented in Women's Magazines,* 1986.

Ferguson, Marjorie. *Forever Feminine: Women's Magazines and the Cult of Femininity.* London: Heinemann, 1983.

Friedan, Betty. *The Feminine Mystique.* New York: Dell Publishing Co., Inc., 1963.

Gough-Yates, Ann. *Understanding Women's Magazines: Publishing, Markets and Readership.* London: Routledge, 2003.

Grimstad, Kirsten and Susan Rennie, eds. *The New Woman's Survival Catalog.* New York: Berkley Publishing Corporation, 1973.

Hermes, Joke. *Reading Women's Magazines: An Analysis of Everyday Media Use.* Cambridge: Polity Press, 1995.

Hoffmann, Phyllis P. *Women's Magazines.* 1983.

Incantalupo, Patricia. *The Portrayal of Women in Sport Advertising in Two Women's Fitness Magazines,* 1992.

Johnson, Judy M, ed. *Spot Illustrations from Women's Magazines of the Teens and Twenties: 828 Cuts of Women, Family, Home, Garden, Etc.* New York: Dover Publications, 1989.

Mann, Robert S. "Women and the Newspaper." *The University of Missouri Bulletin,* no. 2640.

Millum, Trevor. *Images of Woman: Advertising in Women's Magazines.* London: Chatto & Windus, 1975.

Ramet, Adèle. *Creating a Twist in the Tale: How to Write Winning Short Stories for Women's Magazines.* Plymouth: How To Books, 1996.

Shevelow, Kathryn. *Women and Print Culture: The Construction of Femininity in the Early Periodical.* London: Routledge, 1989.

Sievers, Sharon L. *Flowers in Salt: The Beginnings of Feminist Consciousness in Modern Japan.* Stanford: Stanford University Press, 1983.

Waller, Jane, and Michael Vaughan-Rees. *Women in Wartime; the Role of Women's Magazines 1939-1945.* London: Macdonald Optima, 1987.

White, Cynthia L. "Growth between the Wars: 1920-1938." In *Women's Magazines 1693-1968.* London: Michael Joseph Ltd, 1970.

White, Cynthia L. *Women's Magazines 1693-1968.* London: Michael Joseph Ltd, 1970.

Winship, Janice. *Advertising in Women's Magazines, 1956-74.* Birmingham: Centre for Contemporary Cultural Studies, University of Birmingham, 1980.

Winship, Janice. *Inside Women's Magazines.* New York: Pandora, 1987.

Yackey, Lena Millicent. *Contributions of Women's Magazines to Homemaking Problems on Food.* New York, 1930.

Index